CW01582821

THE DIVE SITES OF KENYA AND TANZANIA

INCLUDING PEMBA, ZANZIBAR AND MAFIA

ANTON KOORNHOF

PASSPORT BOOKS
a division of *NTC/Contemporary Publishing Company*
Lincolnwood, Illinois USA

This edition first published
in 1997 by Passport Books,
a division of NTC/Contemporary Publishing Company
4255 West Touhy Avenue,
Lincolnwood (Chicago), Illinois 60646-1975
U.S.A.

Copyright © 1997 New Holland Publishers
Copyright © 1997 in text: Anton Koornhof
Copyright © 1997 in maps: Globetrotter Travel Maps
Copyright © 1997 in photographs the individual photographers and/or their agents as listed: **D & S Balfour** 9, 22, 50 (top), 56, 59; **Andrew Bannister/Struik Image Library** 12, 15 (top), 27, 34, 40, 66; **P Blackwell/Struik Image Library** 17, 25, 50 (bottom), 51, 84-85, 93, 122, 127; **Colour Library/Struik Image Library** 76-77; **C Hansen** 10, 15 (bottom), 77 (bottom), 87, 94-95, 96, 97, 118-119; **D King** 4, 20-21, 35, 41, 47, 49, 91, 100, 101, 104, 109, 110 (top and bottom), 113, 116, 117, 126, 129, 140; A Koornhof 48, 133, 143; **P & S Lamberti** back cover inset, 131; **S Lamberti** front cover, front cover inset, spine, title page, 13, 16, 38 (bottom), 67, 69, 89, 108, 112, 118 (bottom), 119 (bottom), 120, 148; **J Mackinnon** 11, 14, 23, 26, 37, 38 (top), 44, 45, 46, 52, 53, 57, 60, 61, 62, 63, 64, 70, 71, 73, 74, 78, 79, 80, 81, 107, 115, 123, 125, 132, 134, 136, 137; **P Ribton/Struik Image Library** 86, 88, 128; **D Steele (Photo Access)** 105; **P Wagner (Photo Access)** 19, 90.

Editor: Brenda Brickman
In-house editor: Alfred LeMaitre
Consultant: Jeannie Mackinnon
Concept design: Philip Mann
Design manager: Odette Marais
Design and DTP: Damian Gibbs
Cover design: Damian Gibbs
Map DTP: Bill Smuts

Reproduction by Unifoto (Pty) Ltd, Cape Town
Printed and bound by Tien Wah Press (Pte) Ltd, Singapore

All rights reserved. No part of this publication may be reproduced, stored in a retrieval system or transmitted in any form or by any means, electronic, mechanical, photocopying, recording or otherwise, without the prior written permission of the copyright owners.

ISBN 0 8442 4861 4

Library of Congress Catalog Card Number: on file
Published in conjunction with New Holland (Publishers) Ltd

Although the author and publisher have made every effort to ensure that the information in this book was correct at the time of going to press, they accept no responsibility for any loss, injury or inconvenience sustained by any person using this book.

Author's Acknowledgements

My sincere thanks to the following people who assisted in making this book possible, as well as to those people whom I may have inadvertently omitted: **July Sandies-Lumsdaine** for letting me use her computer at a critical stage; **Duncan Willetts** for the use of his underwater photographic equipment; **Jennie Willott** for typing much of the manuscript; the Wasini Island Restaurant for their assistance; **Jurgen Visser, Peter Wagdi, Luc Mella** and **Michaele Cervasazio** for life's small luxuries from Europe; **Mike Sismey** for equipment and information; **Adrian Mumby** and **Colin Fitzpatrick** for help with compressors and equipment; and the management and staff of the Bahari Beach Hotel, Dar es Salaam.

Special thanks also to the following divers and friends who assisted generously with information on dive sites: **Van and Shelagh Ballard** of Pemba Channel Diving, Shimoni; **John Edmondson** of Dive Safari Kenya, Kilifi; One Earth Safaris and the owner and crew of *Poseidon's Quest;* **Bruce Phillips** of Buccaneer Diving, Mombasa; the staff of Indian Ocean Divers, Zanzibar; **Lorenz Riedl** of Scuba Diving Kenya, Watamu; **Susie Weekes** of Mombasa; and all the dive buddies and diving students from KLM, Swissair and Gulf Air, as well as the expats and tourists who dived with me in Dar es Salaam, Diani Beach and Shimoni.

CONTENTS

HOW TO USE THIS BOOK

The Subregions

The East African dive sites described in this book are divided between Kenya and Tanzania, and subdivided into seven main geographical areas. An introduction to each of the eight subregions describes the key characteristics and features, as well as the diving conditions. The topographical features of these areas vary considerably, which influences the diving conditions. Distance, accessibility and infrastructure also have a bearing on the division into subregions. Background information on climate, environment, points of interest and advantages or disadvantages to diving in the subregions are also provided.

The Maps

A main map featuring both countries illustrates the whole East African region. Individual country maps then denote the diving subregions. Each subregion features an enlarged, detailed map to easily identify the approximate location of the dive sites described: this is achieved by repeating the number in the dive sites section, and on the map. For example:

1 will cross-reference to both the map and the dive site.

As most of the diving in Kenya and Tanzania is organized through centres operating from hotels, the maps indicate the hotels from which divers can access the sites. The marine national parks and reserves are indicated, as are reefs, lighthouses, wrecks, major towns and places of interest. The map legend illustrated below pertains to all maps used in this book.

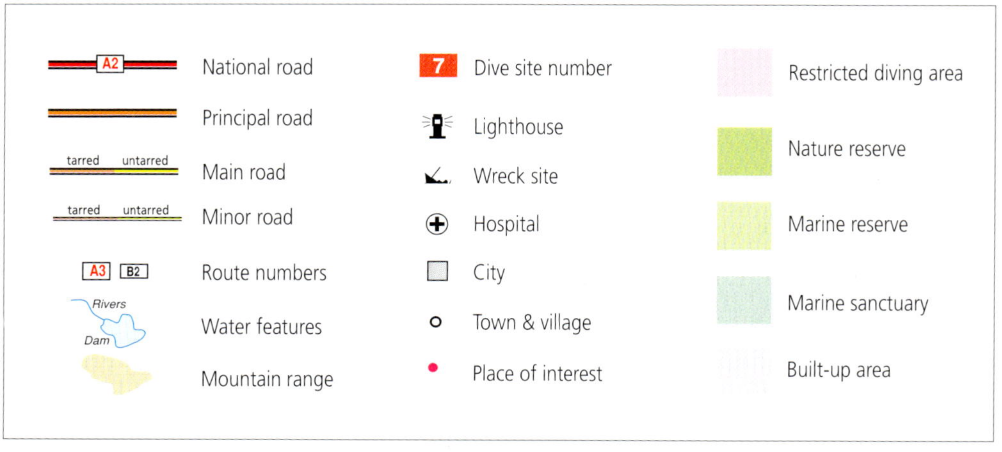

THE DIVE SITE DESCRIPTIONS

Each region's premier dive sites are listed and begin with a number corresponding to the relevant map, a star rating, and symbols indicating key information (*see* below) pertaining to that site. Critical practical details (i.e. location, access, conditions and average and maximum depths) precede the description of the site, its marine life and special points of interest.

Suitable for diving	Can be reached by live-aboard boat
Particularly suitable for snorkelling	Can be reached by swimming from shore
Normally reached by local boat	Suitable for night diving
Suitable for all levels of diver	Wreck dive

THE STAR-RATING SYSTEM

Each site has been awarded a rating, with a maximum of five and a minimum of one star.

★ pertains to scuba diving, and

★ to snorkelling, as follows:

★★★★★	first class
★★★★	highly recommended
★★★	good
★★	average
★	poor

THE REGIONAL DIRECTORIES

At the end of each subregion in the dive sites section is a regional directory with helpful telephone numbers and addresses, largely relating to diving centres which operate in East Africa, but also containing other interesting snippets of information.

OTHER FEATURES OF THIS BOOK

- Each section of the book is colour coded for ease of reference, as per the contents page.
- A general introduction to Kenya and Tanzania respectively will fill you in on historical details of East Africa, and tell you a bit about the people and the economy. This is followed by travelling tips – how to get there and how to get around once you are there. There is a wealth of information on diving and snorkelling in each region.
- Boxes containing interesting tips and concise information on certain species of marine life exist throughout the text.
- Feature spreads on special items of interest, such as the ubiquitous and versatile coconut palm tree and a history of the Arab sailing vessels known as dhows, make this a wholly informative and interesting book which no diver should be without.

SUDAN
ETHIOPIA
SOMALIA
UGANDA
K E N Y A
RWANDA
BURUNDI
T A N Z A N I A
ZAMBIA
MALAWI
MOZAMBIQUE
INDIAN OCEAN
Wendo
Arba Minch
Moyale
Mandera
Numule
Kitgum
Arua
Aru
Gulu
Soroti
Bunia
Masindi
Mbale
Tororo
Fort Portal
KAMPALA
Kitale
Eldoret
Bungoma
Kisumu
Homa Bay
Kericho
Nyahururu
Nakuru
Naivasha
Nyeri
Meru
Embu
Isiolo
Maralal
Marsabit
Wajir
Thika
NAIROBI
Machakos
Kitui
Lamu
Malindi
Kilifi
Mombasa
Voi
Moshi
Arusha
Lake Victoria
Bukoba
Musoma
Tarime
Goma
KIGALI
Butare
BUJUMBURA
Mwanza
Shinyanga
Kigoma
Ujiji
Tabora
Singida
Dodoma
TANGA
Pemba Island
Zanzibar Island
ZANZIBAR
DAR ES SALAAM
Morogoro
Iringa
Mafia Island
Moba
Sumbawanga
Ngomba
Mbeya
Mpulungu
Tukuyu
Itungi Port
Chisenga
Lake Tanganyika
Lake Malawi
Songea
Masaguru
Lindi
Mtwara
Mocimboa de Praia
Sibiloi National Park
Malka Mari N.P.
South Turkana N.R.
Nasolot N.R.
Marsabit N.R.
Losai National Reserve
Shaba National Reserve
Meru N.P.
Kora National Reserve
Mt.Kenya N.P.
Masai Mara National Reserve
Arawale National Reserve
Boni National Reserve
Dodori National Reserve
South Kitui National Reserve
Tsavo National Park
Burigi Game Reserve
Biharamulo Game Reserve
Serengeti National Park
Ngorongoro Conservation Area
Mt Kilimanjaro N.P.
Tarangire National Park
Mkomazi Game Reserve
Moyowosi Game Reserve
Kigosi Game Reserve
Ugalla River Game Reserve
Mahale Mountains National Park
Katavi Plains National Park
Kisigo Game Reserve
Rungwa Game Reserve
Uwanda Game Reserve
Ruaha National Park
Mikumi National Park
Udzungwa National Park
Selous Game Reserve
N
0
5
10km

INTRODUCING EAST AFRICA

The place where man was born

Torn apart during the creation of the Great Rift Valley millions of years ago, East Africa is today widely accepted as the birthplace of modern humankind. Both Kenya and Tanzania have contributed richly to the archaeological proof of human origins. The discoveries made by the Leakey family around Lake Turkana in Kenya and in the Olduvai Gorge in Tanzania have provided us with strong evidence suggesting that *Homo sapiens* did not originate from the apelike creatures formerly believed to be our ancestors, but from a third contemporary species named *Homo habilis*. After this rather impressive start this region has continued to provide us with a treasure trove of scenic, historical and cultural splendour which is perhaps unparalleled elsewhere in the world.

The People

The first humans to follow in the footsteps of *Homo habilis*, around 2000 B.C., were pastoral, Cushitic-speaking nomads who migrated from Ethiopia, moving as far south as central Tanzania. After them, nearly a thousand years later, followed the Eastern Cushitics, who settled in central Kenya. Between 500 B.C. and A.D. 500, East Africa absorbed different tribes from all over Africa, including the Bantu-speaking Kikuyu, Akamba, Meru, and Gusii from West Africa, and the Nilotic-speaking Maasai, Luo, Samburu and Turkana from the Nile Valley in the north. This melting pot of races and cultures inevitably resulted in clashes between rival groups. Some of these rivalries have continued until the present, although to a much lesser extent than in some other regions of the continent.

The hospitable coastline offered safe harbours and these, coupled with the alluring riches to be gained from trading in exotic wares – which included slaves – soon brought foreigners to the shores of East Africa. The first of these to arrive, around the 8th century, were Muslim sailors from Arabia and, later, Shirazis from Persia. These seafaring traders plied

Above: *Red robes and beaded jewellery – often of very large dimensions – are typically worn by Maasai women.*

Mock battles take place at Makunduchi on Zanzibar, during Nairuzi, a festival held to welcome the new year.

the Indian Ocean aboard their sturdy dhows, which sailed with the prevailing monsoons, or, more aptly-named trade winds. At a later stage trade extended as far as India and even China. The influence of the Arabian traders was richly woven into the historical background, culture and architecture of the East African region, and the effects of this cultural mingling can still be experienced today. The language is liberally influenced by Arabic words and the name Swahili – referring to both the language and the people – has its origins in the Arabic plural of the word *Sahel*, which means coast. Many towns were named in the Arab tongue with descriptive and poetic-sounding names such as Dar es Salaam (haven of peace) and Zanzibar (the black coast).

The Islamic religion accounts for the largest minority faith (6%) after Christianity (Protestant 38%, Roman Catholic 28%), with the remainder of the population being Sikhs, Hindus, or followers of traditional animist religions.

THE HISTORY

The Swahili community, which today exerts the greatest influence on language, culture and politics, emerged as a distinctive group by the 14th century. The opportunities and pleasant living conditions of the region enticed many traders to settle permanently. By the beginning of the 16th century, a number of prosperous coastal towns had become firmly established – from Somalia in the north to Mozambique in the south. These included Pate, Lamu, Malindi, and Mombasa in Kenya, towns on Zanzibar and Mafia islands, and Kilwa on the mainland in Tanzania. Trade and life continued without incident until the arrival of the Portuguese at the end of the 15th century.

Under the command of Vasco da Gama, Portuguese seafarers rounded the Cape of Good Hope in 1498, and sailed up the east coast of Africa on their way to India. They reported Kilwa to be a 'large city' and, determined to break the Arab monopoly, tried to land in Mombasa, where they were repulsed. The Portuguese did, however, receive a royal welcome from the sultan in Malindi to the north. They took their revenge on Mombasa a few years later when Cabral followed Da Gama and sacked the town. After burning the city to the ground again in 1505 and 1528, they occupied Mombasa in 1593 and began construction of the massive Fort Jesus, which was completed five years later and is today one of the city's most famous attractions. A century later, beginning in 1696, the 33-month siege of Fort Jesus (which earned Mombasa the name of 'Island of War') lasted until 1698. The end of Portuguese occupation came in 1729, when the last garrison departed. The Portuguese left remarkably little behind other than sport bullfighting on Pemba Island, the remains of the forts, a few additions to the Swahili language and maize, cassava and tobacco, which were introduced from the Americas.

By the beginning of the 19th century, the Sultan of Oman had dispatched forces to seize power on the islands of Pate, Pemba and Mombasa from the Mazruis. In 1824 the embattled Mazruis begged Captain William Owen, the commander of the British warship HMS *Leven*, for protection. On condition that slavery be abolished at Mombasa, Owen agreed to proclaim the city a British protectorate. This lasted for a very short three years and two months, when Owen's protectorate was repudiated. The half century that followed was a time of unequalled prosperity for the Sultan of Oman, who moved his capital from Muscat to Zanzibar. The trade in ivory was revived, and the lucrative trade in human slaves continued.

The slave routes crossed far into the interior of the continent and during this period some 1.2 million slaves reached the coast, with an estimated one in every ten dying on the way. During the 1860s and 1870s, European missionaries increasingly took up the cause of the abolition of slavery. In 1873 a decree passed by the British prohibited the export of slaves. Zanzibar's slave market collapsed, but it took another 25 years before the slaves were freed; in 1897 on Zanzibar and Pemba, and in 1919 on the mainland. Today the sad remnants of this miserable trade can best be seen in the Cathedral Church of Christ, built on the site of the old slave market in Zanzibar, and at the museum in the centre of mainland Bagamoyo.

While British influence paved the way for 19th-century colonialism, important developments were taking place in African society. Much of East Africa was devastated by the slave trade and tribal warfare, but from the battles emerged strong and settled communities. The Swahili language, which incorporated many foreign words, became the lingua franca of the region, and a basic knowledge of the language is most useful today. During the second half of the 19th century, Europeans arrived in significant numbers and this accelerated the pace of change. British curiosity was fuelled by the discovery of snowcapped Mount Kilimanjaro, situated almost on the equator, as well as the snow-covered peaks of Mount Kenya, which straddles the equator. Explorers such as Burton and Speke, Livingstone and Stanley in Tanganyika, and Thomson and von Szek in Kenya, began to open up the interior.

In 1896, the British began building a 1 000-km-long (620 miles) railway line from Mombasa to Uganda. Despite attacks by lions on the predominantly Indian labour force, the route was completed in 1901 – a stupendous achievement – and today the line carries thousands of travellers from Nairobi to the coast.

Under the Anglo-German agreement of 1886, Tanganyika became a German colony. The Germans set up enterprises based on plantation agriculture, establishing large sisal, cotton, coffee and rubber estates. These schemes met with resistance from the local population, and in 1905

The Cathedral Church of Christ, Zanzibar.

A Lamu craftsman carves a doorpost.

triggered the greatest rebellion in Tanzanian history – a war against foreign rule. An estimated 75 000 Africans were thought to have died in the subsequent depression and famine.

By the outbreak of the First World War, the Germans had contributed greatly to the economic development of the country. The new capital, Dar es Salaam, boasted churches and stately government buildings in tree-lined avenues. During the war, German East Africa – as it was then called – suffered a second devastating guerrilla conflict (which left more than 100,000 dead) between German troops under the wily General Paul von Lettow-Vorbeck and superior British and colonial forces. After the war, the League of Nations mandated the territory – which was renamed Tanganyika – to Britain.

Tanganyika emerged relatively unscathed from the Second World War and was soon ready for self-government. As it was not a fully-fledged colony, the transition to independence was smooth. Tanganyika's new green, black and gold flag was raised on 9 December 1961, and Julius Nyerere became the republic's first prime minister.

THE POLITICS

In December 1963 Zanzibar, until then a British protectorate, gained its independence. This was followed by a fierce revolution which led to the expulsion of most Arabs. The People's Republic of Zanzibar and Pemba and the Republic of Tanganyika merged three months later to become the United Republic of Tanzania, turning the country into a one-party constitutional democracy. A blue band representing the sea was added to the flag.

The Arusha Declaration on Socialism in 1967 set the guidelines for the country to be governed under a socialist system. To this end, key industries, banks, estates and trading houses were nationalized. The *Ujamaa* (familyhood) system was introduced by Nyerere, and communal villages where the people shared all were actively encouraged.

Over 11 million people were moved from rural areas and resettled into 'villages of development'. This led to a huge concentration of people in towns and cities, with an inevitable increase in poverty and unemployment. Shortages of household necessities made life uncomfortable for visitors and tourism consequently suffered a serious setback – from which the country is still struggling to recover.

The early 1990s brought acceptance of multiparty politics in Tanzania. In 1991, Ali Hassan Mwinyi was elected as president and leader of the CCM, or Party of the Revolution. The new ruler contributed greatly to fostering free enterprise and encouraging economic growth, but was ousted by Benjamin Mkapwa, who was elected as the country's new president during the somewhat controversial elections held in October 1995. Mkapwa has vowed to stamp out corruption in the Tanzanian government and civil service.

In neighbouring Kenya the transition from colonialism to independence did not proceed as smoothly. Kenya was a British colony in the true sense of the word and the acquisition of land by settlers was deeply resented by the tribal inhabitants. The lifestyles of the early colonialists are well known through books set in this era, such as *Out of Africa* (Isak Dinesen, or Karen Blixen) and *White Mischief* (James Wood), both of which have been made into films. The works of Elspeth Huxley, especially *The Flame Trees of Thika* and *Whiteman's Country,* are notable evocations of the flavour and atmosphere of the colonial period.

Kenya's struggle for *uhuru* (freedom) was more violent than that of Tanganyika. The winds of violence that raged through the country left a sad trail of death and distrust. Robert Ruark's bestselling novel *Uhuru* describes the tribulations of the Mau Mau Rebellion of the early 1950s, and provides some insight into these turbulent years. The rebellion began in 1953, and led to a state of emergency that came to an end in 1956.

Jomo Kenyatta, who led the major political party, the Kenya African National Union (KANU), had been imprisoned for complicity in the Mau Mau uprising, and KANU refused to cooperate with the colonial authorities until Kenyatta's release in 1961. Kenya gained its independence in 1963, and was proclaimed a republic in 1964, with Jomo Kenyatta as its first president. With the achievement of freedom, in the form of independence from Britain, Kenya discarded any traces of bitterness and resentment, and the country's people united in the spirit of *harambee* (pulling together) to make Kenya into a model of co-operation and prosperity.

After the death of Jomo Kenyatta in 1978, Daniel arap Moi was sworn in as president. Under his leadership, Kenya has grown to be a major tourist destination in Africa, with tourism the main foreign-exchange earner, and a leading exporter of top-quality tea and coffee. As a sporting nation, Kenya is one of the stars among developing countries, and

CARVED DOORS

One of the most exquisite legacies of Arab influence in East Africa, particularly on Zanzibar and Lamu islands, are ornate and intricately carved wooden doors. These still adorn many buildings in the old towns on the islands and along the coast. The wood used in the crafting of these extraordinary doors is obtained either from the breadfruit tree, or from the hard and durable *mvule,* or African teak, which is imported from the mainland. The beautifully carved symbols depicted on the doors are further enhanced by the large yellow copper nails hammered into the leaves and central jamb. The most common symbols represent the different wishes of the inhabitants: a border of chains means security and protection against intruders; date trees symbolize abundance; and fish are the harbingers of fertility. The monogram of the owner, which is often accompanied by an excerpt from the Koran, is carved into the lintel above the transom. Elaborate motifs on Arabian and Indian doors vary in appearance and symbolism. The old custom of Zanzibar was to carve and erect the door first and then to build the house around it. Many of these doors have been magnificently restored, and the export of these exquisite furnishings has been prohibited in many places.

Printed textiles for sale at a market on Zanzibar.

where social welfare, health and education is concerned, the country is amongst the leaders in Africa. The one-party rule that lasted for ten years was rescinded in 1992, but did not affect the stability that has secured Kenya its firm footing in the international arena.

As a result of differing political developments, there is a vast gap in tourism development and infrastructure between Kenya and Tanzania, with Kenya decades ahead in both respects. Tanzania has only recently realized the importance of tourism, although it has as much to offer as its neighbour to the north. The Tanzanian government now actively promotes tourism and, in many ways, has been successful in attracting foreign visitors.

The Culture

Both Kenya and Tanzania are rich in architectural history, which was dominated by Arabic influence. The best examples of this style, although somewhat dilapidated in many cases, can be seen in coastal towns such as Lamu, the Old Town of Mombasa, Kilwa and, of course, on the islands of Pemba and Zanzibar. On Zanzibar, a project is underway to restore the old Stone Town. Some of the majestic old buildings have successfully been turned into hotels and guest houses featuring exquisite Arabic furnishings. A marvellous feature of many of the old buildings and even small houses in the villages are the intricately carved and lovingly restored Arabic doors, most of which tell a story about the inhabitants of the building. (*See* box on page 13.)

In the villages on the mainland, as well as on the islands, the buildings consist mainly of wooden structures with walls of wooden posts clad with mud and covered by *makuti* (thatched palm leaf) roofs. At the coast and on the islands the walls are built of quarried coral stone, sometimes plastered with lime and whitewashed. The buildings are mostly rectangular, with steep, pitched thatched roofs and wide awnings that provide shelter from the sun. Glass is not commonly used and the windows are covered by woven mats when it rains.

In the newer sections of Nairobi, Mombasa, Dar es Salaam and Arusha, unattractive modern architecture predominates. Some architectural treasures can still be found in the old colonial-style hotels and homesteads, as well as in German-influenced churches and Catholic cathedrals. There are unfortunately also some eyesores, such as the blocklike hostels erected by the East German government on Zanzibar and Pemba, but architectural gems such as the Muslim mosques and minarets still grace the skylines of the old towns.

The East African tribal culture is a rich stew concocted from a myriad of influences, both ancient and modern. Authentic tribal rites and dances can today only be found in remote areas, but diluted examples of these are often dished up for tourists in hotels and resorts.

A Mombasa trader offers a rich harvest of local fruit.

The visitor often has the feeling that the Muslim culture predominates in East Africa, but this is perhaps because of the distinctive style of dress which was also adopted by many Swahili women in the form of the long black *bui bui*. Many of the tribal communities have fortunately retained their individual style of colourful dress, particularly in the case of the handsome Samburu and Maasai tribes. In the cities and the larger towns descendants from the early European immigrants and settlers and the large expatriate communities have all added their particular contribution in the form of clubs, theatres and schools. Cities such as Nairobi and Dar es Salaam are true cosmopolitan centres, with their inhabitants drawn from almost all regions of the globe. This creates a kaleidoscopic mixture of race, religion and culture which lends a unique atmosphere to a visit to East Africa.

The Cuisine

The staple diet of the local inhabitants is not unlike that of many other African countries and consists mainly of a stiff maize porridge (*ugali*), accompanied by beans, meat, or vegetables, while the coastal inhabitants favour a variety of fish dishes – employing both fresh and dried fish – often with rice as a base. International cuisine can, however, be enjoyed in restaurants in the cities and at the coastal resorts.

The Heritage

The individual splendour of the two East African countries in their scenic beauty, bountiful wildlife, and underwater wonders, which, together with a fascinating historical and cultural heritage, is perhaps unequalled anywhere else on such a scale, making Kenya and Tanzania a combined travel destination that is incomparable.

The lavish interior of a hotel at Tembo on Zanzibar suggests the lifestyle of the island's former Arab rulers.

DIVING AND SNORKELLING IN EAST AFRICA

East Africa has always been the epitome of the African safari and must be one of, if not the most popular holiday destinations on the African continent. Fast becoming as popular as game-viewing is the great tropical diving to be enjoyed on the splendid coral reefs off the East African coastline and the main islands in the warm waters of the Indian Ocean.

Diving Facilities

Scuba diving gained popularity in Kenya in the late 1970s and today there are numerous diving facilities along the coast, most of which have their own dedicated dive boats, while some offer dive packages including accommodation. Most of the bigger hotels contract out to a dive operator who provides all diving facilities.

The main training agency on the coast is PADI (Professional Association of Diving Instructors). Some schools also offer NAUI (National Association of Underwater Instructors), CMAS (World Underwater Federation) and BSAC (British Sub Aqua Club) certification. All recognized qualifications are accepted by the dive centres, but the completion of a medical questionnaire is mandatory. In some cases a valid medical certificate must be produced. Courses cater for novices and experienced divers. Excursions to the islands and marine parks sometimes include dhow trips and lunches as part of the package.

In Tanzania, scuba diving is best enjoyed around the main islands of Pemba, Zanzibar and Mafia, which offer arguably the best diving in East Africa, and provide good diving facilities. Most of them are operated from the Kenyan coast on live-aboard diving excursions. There are now fairly recently established but excellent NAUI and PADI land-based training facilities on Zanzibar Island, and there is one diving base on Mafia Island. Diving courses cater for divers on all levels, and boat trips to the many excellent dive sites are organized on

Left: *Gorgonian coral has a semi-rigid internal skeleton that produces spectacular fan shapes.*

Above: *A day trip aboard a dhow adds spice to any diving holiday.*

a daily basis. On the mainland all diving activities centre around and to the north of Dar es Salaam. Independent diving may be done with your own equipment by renting a local boat from one of the hotels on the north coast.

The Kenyan authorities have commendably woken up to the important issue of reef conservation and have established a number of marine parks and reserves to protect the sensitive reef environments. The destructive evil of dynamite fishing was, unlike in neighbouring countries, hardly ever committed in Kenya, and the reefs are generally in good condition except for some past anchor damage in places. For this reason, the more popular dive sites have all been buoyed by the local dive school operators, a factor which contributes immensely to the prevention of damage to reefs.

In Tanzania, however, dynamite fishing was rife, and although strictly illegal, is still carried out because of a deplorable lack of enforcement by the authorities. The bitter fruits of this wasteful and devastating method of killing fish (and almost everything else in the vicinity), which has destroyed extensive sections of the fringing reefs, are now being realized in the form of severe beach erosion, which has brought some hotels on the north coast to the verge of flooding and collapse. It has also led to overfishing, and this can clearly be seen when comparing the marine life of the two countries. Fortunately, little damage has been done in Pemba and none in Zanzibar, but unless the authorities on the mainland take firm action to halt this practise a total collapse of the Tanzanian fishing industry is imminent.

The reefs along the Kenyan coast are of the fringing type and are intact and generally quite close to shore. In many places, they can be reached by a 20-minute snorkel swim. The water on the inside of the reef is shallow, clear, shark-free and very safe to snorkel (beware of passing boat traffic, though), but due to the extreme height difference in tides the coral growth is sparse. In some areas, excellent snorkelling may be done from shore. All organized scuba dives are done from boats as an experienced skipper is needed to manoeuvre through the *mlangos* (Swahili for 'doors'), or natural breaks in the reef. During rough conditions these rides through the surf can be quite exhilarating. Shore dives can be done from some of the islands and these are mentioned under individual dive sites where applicable. The reefs around many of the islands also offer excellent snorkelling in clear, shallow waters, especially in the unspoilt marine parks and reserves where wardens keep a close watch to ensure that snorkellers do not stand on or damage the coral.

The best diving in Tanzanian waters is done farther out to sea, where the depths of the reefs have precluded dynamite fishing, and excellent snorkelling can be done off the small islands close to the mainland. The reefs around the main islands are superb and, on the whole, undamaged. They range from immense drop-offs to flat offshore, or fringing, reefs.

The average temperature of the surface waters of the north-flowing East African Coastal Current varies from 25°C (77°F) in September to 29°C (84°F) in March, which makes diving a real pleasure. Average visibility during the best diving season (from October to April) is 10–30m (33–100ft), and around the islands may increase to an average of 30–50m (100–165ft). There are fortunately few rivers emptying into the sea, but a plankton build-up (East African waters are notorious for this phenomenon) can reduce visibility considerably. In the case of dive sites situated near a river, however, visibility can drop to almost zero during the rainy season due to the copious inflow of mud and silt. The most dependable diving conditions are generally found in the waters immediately surrounding the islands.

An interesting phenomenon is the effect that the trade winds have on the water conditions and even the marine life: during the southeast monsoon (the *Kusi*), which blows from April to October, the South Equatorial Current brings water from Indonesia. During the northeast monsoon (the *Kaskazi*), which blows hard from November to March, water is drawn in from the Indonesian region on the South Equatorial and Counter Equatorial currents, which in turn affect the East African Coastal Current. These inflowing waters bring with them a great variety of marine fauna which, having survived the long journey across the Indian Ocean, settle down to live and breed in the coral reefs of the East African coast.

RECOMMENDED EQUIPMENT

The average water temperatures along the East African coast are on the top end of the scale in seas where tropical reefs grow. Temperatures stay constant to depths of up to 70m (230ft). A 3mm (⅛in) wetsuit with short sleeves or a diving skin will suffice. It is not uncommon to dive without insulation during the warm-water months. Open-heeled or closed-heel fins may be used, but open-heeled are easier to remove, especially before climbing up a boat ladder. Gloves are not needed, but can be worn for protection, although bare hands discourage divers from grasping and breaking delicate coral growths. All equipment is available from the dive centres for organized dives, but there are very few dive 'shops' where equipment can be bought or even rented. Even when one is fortunate enough to find a shop that sells equipment in Nairobi, Mombasa or Dar es Salaam, prices are extremely high. It is suggested that divers bring their own snorkelling equipment. In most cases a discount of approximately 10 per cent is given on dives when divers bring their own mask, fins, regulator and buoyancy jacket. Tank valves in Kenya are mainly of the DIN type and adaptors have to be fitted to accommodate the international A-clamp-type regulator. It may be a good idea to bring an adaptor if you have this regulator, just to be on the safe side.

HUNTING AND COLLECTING

No hunting or collecting of any marine fauna or even dead shells is allowed inside the parks and reserves. Spearfishing on the reefs is not illegal but is severely frowned upon. Marine rules and regulations are strictly enforced in Kenyan waters and it is hoped that Tanzania will follow this highly successful example.

Divers disembark from a dive boat into the shallow lagoon that is typical within Watamu's fringing coral reef.

INTRODUCING KENYA

The name Kenya invokes visions of rolling savanna grasslands, snowcapped mountains, great lakes and white beaches set against towering palms and gigantic baobab trees. This part of Africa has been eloquently portrayed in well-known films such as *Out of Africa*, as well as in countless coffee table books and travel magazines. Firmly established as the epitome of the 'Great African safari', Kenya is rich in historical and scenic splendour.

The Natural Environment

The coastline of Kenya stretches some 480km (290 miles) from Somalia in the north to Tanzania in the south, and is washed by the warm waters of the Indian Ocean and the north-flowing East African Coastal Current. Tropical climatic conditions prevail along the entire coast, including the Lamu Archipelago, the estuary of the Tana River (Kenya's principal river) and a narrow, low-lying and fertile coastal strip. The coast is hot and humid throughout the year, but is cooled by welcome sea breezes. The rainfall averages between 1 000 and 1 250mm (40 and 50in) per year and falls mainly during the short or 'mango' rains from the end of October to early December, and the long rains from mid-March to the end of May.

Beyond the coast the land rises fairly steeply towards the central plateau, which forms the greater part of Kenya and includes the Rift Valley, the Central Highlands and part of Lake Victoria – the biggest lake in Africa. The central plateau straddles the equator and covers an area of some 583 000km^2 (225 000 sq miles).

The placid face of this spectacular part of Kenya was transformed millions of years ago when earthquakes tore Africa apart from the Red Sea to Zimbabwe to form the Y-shaped Great Rift Valley. With its lakes, craters and mountains, this part of Kenya offers some of the most dramatic and stupendous scenery in all of Africa, and probably the world.

Previous pages: *Yellowtail goldies swirl around contour coral formations.*

Left: *A family of elephants in Kenya's Amboseli National Park, with Mount Kilimanjaro in the background.*

Above: *In Tsavo National Park, a desert rose reveals its colourful heart.*

Kenya's capital city, Nairobi, is situated at the eastern end of the highlands, which also include the massif of Mount Kenya – Africa's second highest mountain after Kilimanjaro.

The climate of the Rift Valley and the Central Highlands is very agreeable, with average temperatures ranging from a maximum of 22–26°C (72–80°F) and a minimum of 10–14°C (50–57°F). The main water catchment area consists of the Aberdare Mountains and Mount Kenya, and rainfall measuring up to 3 000mm (120in) per year is often recorded.

WHAT TO SEE AND DO

As a diving destination alone, Kenya cannot be classed in the same bracket as the Red Sea, the Maldives or the Caribbean, for instance, but the combination of underwater beauty coupled with the scenic splendour of the land will be hard to beat anywhere else in the world. This is one destination where divers can safely bring their non-diving companions and rest assured that they will enjoy the holiday equally.

A safari to one of the world-famous game parks of Kenya is an absolute must and there are many to choose from. The most popular ones are generally arranged by travel agents on behalf of their clients and form part of an all-inclusive package. Some of the agencies and hotels include dive packages in all-in-one excursions, and these generally represent excellent value for money. For the traveller seeking a measure of solitude, there are self-drive options, or a vehicle can be hired with a driver. Catering can be arranged. At the top end of the range, and for the more discerning visitor, there are ultra-luxurious safaris in private camps, where every need is catered for.

The distances from the coast vary greatly, from the Shimba Hills National Reserve close to Mombasa and Diani Beach, to Masai Mara National Reserve and Samburu National Park. A wealth of information is available to the first-time visitor from most established travel agents, in the form of books, brochures and video presentations, and prospective visitors would be well advised to shop around to find the excursion most suited to their needs. One of the most spectacular ways to view game must surely be in the form of hot-air ballooning over the Masai Mara wildlife wonderland. This experience, which has become one of the most sought-after adventures in the world, lasts for approximately one hour.

As far as watersports are concerned, deep-sea fishing probably rivals scuba diving for the number one place. These fishing waters were immortalized by Ernest Hemingway in his novel *The Old Man and the Sea*. There is ample reason for this high reputation, as game fishing in Kenyan waters is a tremendously exciting sport, and the country is widely recognized for its record-breaking catches. These include black, blue and striped marlin, sailfish, barracuda, wahoo, kingfish, tuna and dorado, to name but a few. The main fishing season lasts from November through to the end of March, when most of the big catches are made, and it is very seldom that a boat returns without at least something for the table. The main fishing bases are situated at Lamu, Malindi, Watamu, Kilifi, Mombasa, Diani and Shimoni.

Mount Kenya, the second highest mountain in Africa, is only one of the country's many mountains, and climbing and trekking are

MOUNT KILIMANJARO

When measured from its base to its snowcapped peak, Kilimanjaro is not only the highest mountain in Africa, but also the tallest free-standing mountain in the world. At a height of 5 896m (19 340ft) this great mountain – which lies only 3° south of the equator – mystified local inhabitants for almost 2 000 years. Early European explorers who mentioned the existence of a snow-covered mountain on the equator were ridiculed, until its existence was confirmed in 1861. Kilimanjaro, which may mean 'Mountain of Water' in Swahili, falls within the boundaries of Tanzania, but is equally popular with visitors from neighbouring Kenya, and each year hundreds of people make the journey to the top.

favourite pastimes which are well catered for. The dry seasons, from January through March and July to October, are for obvious reasons the best times to plan climbs and treks in the mountains.

Apart from comfortable climbing and walking shoes, a well-equipped pack should include the appropriate clothing for all temperatures, a medical kit, sufficient water containers, sunglasses, a thin mattress, padded anorak or parka, sun block, lip salve, torches, matches, eating utensils and emergency food rations.

Ballooning over Masai Mara National Reserve.

When planning high-altitude climbs, or even travelling inland by vehicle, always keep the 24-hour 'no flying after diving' rule in mind, which also applies here. A special consideration for altitude climbs is the risk of mountain sickness, a condition which, if ignored and left untreated, can be fatal. Always climb in the company of others, and preferably with an experienced guide.

While divers are enjoying themselves underwater, there is no need for friends or family to feel neglected. Almost all of the hotels offer recreational facilities such as windsurfing tuition and rentals, tennis, aerobics, glass-bottom boat trips, waterskiing and para-sailing. There are also fabulous day outings where scuba diving can be combined with a dhow trip to snorkelling reefs, island tours and great cuisine.

For night-time revellers there are a number of good restaurants available which offer a variety of dishes, from traditional Swahili to Chinese cuisine. Expect to pay European prices at most of the resort restaurants, though, as dining out on the coast is an expensive luxury. Excellent wines from around the world are available if one is willing to shell out the rather high asking prices. There are casinos on the north and south coasts and a variety of discotheques to choose from, depending on the visitor's taste. Most of the hotels also offer in-house entertainment during the peak seasons.

There is, of course, the tempting alternative to take everything *pole pole* (slowly, slowly), and to simply relax and enjoy the splendid beaches and scenery.

HIGHLIGHTS OF NEIGHBOURING COUNTRIES

Kenya borders on five countries: Ethiopia and Sudan to the north, Uganda to the west, Somalia to the northeast, and Tanzania to the south. Unfortunately, because of the political instability prevailing in Ethiopia, Sudan and Somalia, it is not recommended to visit these countries at the present time. One of the most favoured destinations for visitors to East Africa is Mount Kilimanjaro – the highest mountain in Africa – located in neighbouring Tanzania (*see* box on opposite page). For divers, there are also live-aboard charters to the magnificent dive sites around Pemba and Zanzibar islands, which fall within Tanzanian waters. For the more adventurous travellers with enough time to spare, the unforgettable gorilla encounters of Uganda and Rwanda are well worth the expense and effort. A great number of visitors to Kenya return again and again, as the country has so much to offer in the way of wildlife, scenic splendour and underwater experiences that it is impossible to see and do everything in a single visit.

TRAVELLING TO AND IN KENYA

Kenya is renowned as a top travel destination, especially with visitors from Europe, so tourism is not new to the country. Unlike many other African destinations, Kenya is safe and easy to get around. Most of the harrowing red tape that one may encounter in the rest of Africa has been done away with. As long as the visitor makes advance arrangements and takes common-sense precautions, no serious problems should be encountered.

Entry Requirements

Passport-holders of Denmark, Eire, Ethiopia, Finland, Germany, Holland, Italy, Norway, South Africa, Spain, Sweden, Turkey and Uruguay do not need entry visas. Neither do Commonwealth citizens unless they are Australian, Nigerian or Sri Lankan passport-holders. Visitors who do not require visas and are in possession of an onward or return ticket can obtain a visitor's pass (valid for three months) free of charge upon arrival. Proof of sufficient funds to stay in the country may be required. It is advisable to double-check visa requirements prior to departure. A valid yellow fever vaccination certificate is obligatory and visitors arriving from cholera-affected areas should bring proof of inoculation.

When to Visit

Kenya straddles the equator, and so enjoys a true tropical climate. The tourist season extends throughout the year. There are two rainy seasons, with the short (or mango) rains falling from the end of October to early December and the long rains from mid-March to the end of May. The high season stretches from early December to the end of March and from mid-September to the end of October. Bookings during these seasons should be done well in advance to secure travel arrangements and accommodation. Game reserves are very popular from the end of June to mid-September.

Left: *An* ngalawa *(outrigger canoe) drawn up on Diani Beach, with waves breaking over the offshore coral reef.*

Above: *The colourful prow of a small dhow, Malindi.*

The tropical climate ensures hot and humid conditions throughout the year. Welcome sea breezes cool the temperature along the coastal belt down to pleasant levels most of the time. The average temperatures on the coast are pretty constant and range from a maximum of 30°C (86°F) to a minimum of 22°C (72°F). In upcountry areas slightly lower temperatures can be expected, with an average maximum of 22–26°C (72–80°F) and a minimum of 10–14°C (50–64°F).

LANGUAGE AND CUSTOMS

The official language of Kenya is English and the national language Swahili. There are more than 80 vernacular languages. In the tourist industry English, German, French and Italian are widely spoken and understood. Most dive schools offer courses in English and German and some in Italian and French.

All the major faiths are represented, with the majority of the population being Christian and the minority Muslim. Topless bathing is frowned upon in most public places.

THE BAOBAB TREE

In African folklore, the baobab *(Adansonia digitata)* was among the first trees God created. Next came the tall, slender palm tree. When the baobab saw the palm, it cried out wanting to be taller. Then God made the flame tree with its beautiful flowers, and the baobab was envious and asked God to give it flowers. The baobab then saw the magnificent fig tree, with its foliage and fruit, and cried out to God demanding fruit as well. God was very angry and pulled the baobab tree up by its roots and turned it upside down to keep it quiet. That is why the baobab tree today looks the way it does. Baobabs are widespread in East Africa, especially in the coastal areas where they are found in great numbers, and on most of the islands. These grotesque giants are among the oldest living organisms found on earth, and may reach an age of up to 2 500 years when fully grown. A tree with a diameter of 5m (17ft) may be as much as a thousand years old. Portuguese cannonballs that are more than 400 years old have been found embedded in the baobab trees lining the entrance to Mombasa harbour. Baobabs provide a home for many nocturnal creatures, such as owls, bats and bushbabies, and are still regarded by many tribes as a house of spirits. The trunk reaches girths of up to 25m (82ft), and is appropriately bottle-shaped; during dry periods, the baobab stores water in its trunk, as well as calcium in its bark. It is for these reasons favoured by elephants and often subjected to great hammerings by them. The tree's large brown seeds contain tartaric acid, and the pulp may be used for flavouring, or soaked in water to make a refreshing drink. The fibrous bark is used for the weaving of ropes. The leaves may be cooked as a vegetable.

PUBLIC HOLIDAYS

January 1	New Year's Day
March/April	Good Friday/Easter Monday
May 1	Labour Day
June 1	Madaraka Day (anniversary of self-government)
October 10	Nyayo Day (anniversary of President Moi's inauguration)
October 20	Kenyatta Day (anniversary of Jomo Kenyatta's release from prison)
December 12	Jamhuri/Uhuru Day (anniversary of independence and formation of republic)
December 25	Christmas Day
December 26	Boxing Day
Variable	Idd-ul-Fitr (Muslim holiday celebrating the end of Ramadan)

TIME ZONE

Kenya time corresponds with East African Standard Time, which is three hours ahead of Greenwich Mean Time.

HEALTH AND SAFETY

When compared to some other African countries Kenya is a fairly healthy place to visit. Should one be unfortunate enough to fall ill, there are generally good but expensive medical services within easy reach. It is suggested that medical insurance coverage be obtained prior to arrival in Kenya. Good dentists and opticians can be found in Mombasa and Nairobi. Chemists and drugstores can be found in and around the resorts and in all the big towns and cities. They are generally closed on public holidays, Saturday afternoons and Sundays. Most prescription drugs are readily available or can be ordered without too long a wait. Tap water is safe to drink but can cause upset to unaccustomed stomachs. It is therefore advised that you boil and filter tap water, or drink bottled water if you are uncertain. Tap water at the coast is brackish (salty) and drinking water is distributed by means of hand carts or water tankers.

Malaria is endemic throughout the country and the prescribed prophylactic should be taken for two weeks prior to arrival in the country and for at least six weeks after departure. Should any flu-like symptoms develop within this period, it is advised that a blood test for malaria be done as soon as possible as early treatment will prevent most of the more serious symptoms and lead to an early recovery. Remember, too, that the incidence of HIV infection is high in Kenya and throughout East Africa.

The tropical sun is extremely powerful due to the proximity to the equator, so use strong sun filters and even stronger common sense. It is possible to burn even in the shade, and keep in mind that the rays extend down to at least 1m (3ft) below the water's surface, so remember to cover up when snorkelling. On boat trips it is advisable to take a hat or peaked cap as well as sunglasses. Drink lots of water throughout the day, as dehydration may occur rapidly through loss of moisture through the skin.

Kenya is not unsafe for tourists, but again common sense must prevail. It is unwise to make a show of wealth in any country where the per capita income is fairly low. Avoid lonely places at night unless in a large group, as muggings have occurred along some of the roads and in the cities. The beaches are safe, with the main hassle being the persistent attention of the ubiquitous 'beach boys', who solicit any form of business imaginable.

Currency and Insurance

The monetary unit is the Kenya shilling, which is divided into 100 cents. Notes are printed in denominations of 1000, 500, 200, 100, 50, 20 and 10 shillings. There are five different one-shilling coins, and 50, 10 and 5 cent coins. It is advisable to bring a good supply of traveller's cheques in hard currency. These can be exchanged at banks during normal banking hours or at one of the many bureaux de change, which usually offer better exchange rates and stay open longer hours. Beware of roadside money-changers on the black market, who are generally out to relieve travellers of their money through various ingenious means. All major credit cards are widely accepted and cash can be withdrawn at the banks once confirmation of the credit balance has been made. Exchange control regulations have been extensively relaxed, and it is not much of a problem to receive or effect bank-to-bank transfers. Banking hours are from 09:00 to 15:00 on weekdays, and on the last Saturday of the month from 08:00 to 11:00.

Before leaving your home country check with your insurers that you are covered against theft and loss of personal property.

Communications

Opening hours for post offices are from 08:00 to 13:00 and from 14:00 to 17:00 on Monday to Friday, and from 08:00 to 12:00 on Saturdays at main post offices. The telephone system is good but very expensive for international calls. Public telephones that take coins are not reliable but there are telecom bureaus at most resorts and in the cities, where telephone cards may be purchased.

ELECTRICITY AND FUEL

The electricity supply is 240 volts (50 cycles AC). Wall sockets in most hotels are for 110-volt appliances. The power often peaks, which can damage sensitive appliances, and power cuts are frequent. The power points are mainly for square, three-pin 15-ampere plugs.

Petrol, diesel and kerosene (paraffin) fuel is readily available. Gas refills can be obtained in most places, though critical shortages sometimes occur. Most batteries are available in the cities, but it is advisable to bring spares as they may be expensive to replace.

CUSTOMS AND IMMIGRATION

Customs and immigration posts are found at harbours and international airports. The import of firearms, agricultural and horticultural produce and domestic animals is strictly forbidden, but regulations allow for the temporary import of personal possessions and vehicles. In some cases refundable deposits are required, mainly for electronic gear. Duty-free imports of 200 cigarettes, 50 cigars, one litre of alcohol and a quarter-litre of perfume are allowed.

MAJOR ENTRY POINTS

International flights

Airlines from around the world operate regular scheduled flights from most major cities to Kenya, with more than 30 international air carriers competing for business. The two main entry points by air are the Jomo Kenyatta International Airport in Nairobi and the Moi International Airport in Mombasa. Modern facilities are available at these airports, but visitors should not rely too heavily on them being open at all times.

By road

Surrounding countries are served by the following main customs and immigration checkpoints: Somalia and Kenya – Mandera; Ethiopia and Kenya – Moyale, Fort Banya (Ileret), and Todeyang; Sudan and Kenya – Lokichoggio; Uganda and Kenya – Oropol, Katikekile, Bukwa, Malaba, and Busia; and Tanzania and Kenya – Sirari (Migori), Namanga and Olotokitok, and Taveta and Lunga Lunga. It is advisable to check opening and closing times prior to departure to avoid spending the night at the border post.

By sea

Mombasa is the largest port on East African coast. Cruise liners make short stopovers but regular passenger services were suspended in the early 1970s. For budget travellers or adventurers, large dhows depart for Pemba or Zanzibar from here, and enquiries should be made in the port area. There is also a regular ferry service from Dar es Salaam to Mombasa via Zanzibar. Customs and immigration formalities are minimal, unlike many other African countries where visitors often feel that they are being discouraged from visiting the country.

By rail

After an interval of 18 years, Kenya and Tanzania have resumed railway links. A train departs from Voi in Kenya at 05:00 on Saturday mornings and arrives at Moshi in Tanzania at 11:00 the same morning.

GETTING AROUND BY AIR

The national carrier, Kenya Air, connects the cities of Nairobi, Mombasa, Kisumu and Malindi. Book in advance and confirm departure times before departure to the airport if possible. The smaller towns are efficiently served by private airlines which can be found in the main cities. Most of these also have regular scheduled flights to the game parks and from Mombasa to Malindi and Lamu.

NAIROBI

Mile 327 of the East African Railway line marks the spot where the capital city of Kenya had its humble beginnings in 1899. Nairobi was named for the steep valley, *Ewaso Nairobi*, which in Swahili means 'Stream of Cold Water', in which it is located. Today Nairobi is one of Africa's largest and most modern cities, with a growing, cosmopolitan population of more than a million people.

The mixture of ethnic groups and foreign races creates a colourful but somewhat ambiguous atmosphere and the true identity of Kenya's capital is hard to pinpoint, though commerce rather than community plays a major role. As can well be expected from such a young city, Nairobi is thoroughly westernized and most modern comforts may be found here in the form of excellent accommodation, restaurants, bars and a night life that should satisfy almost all tastes. Many visitors to the coast have to get connecting flights from Nairobi to Mombasa. There are many excellent guide books to the city available for sightseers and fun-seekers. Visitors should, however, be aware that security, as in many other large cities, presents a problem and some sections of the city are notorious for muggings and robberies. Take special care and heed the advice of local inhabitants. Reliable information is always available at the better hotels and guest houses. Getting around this vibrant city should not present a problem as long as common sense prevails.

GETTING AROUND BY RAIL

A popular, affordable and comfortable way to get around is by train. Kenya Railways operates a network that totals more than 2 700km (1 600 miles) of track. The main lines run from Mombasa to Kisumu and from Nakuru to Malaba, with branch lines from Nairobi-Thika-Kiganjo-Nanyuki, Voi-Taveta, Konza-Kajiado-Magadi, Gilgil-Ol Kalau-Nyahururu, Rongai-Solai, Leseru-Kitale and Kisumu-Butere. The services are mostly punctual and the train is generally a far safer mode of travel than either bus or *matatu* (minibus).

GETTING AROUND BY ROAD

Cars are available for hire at the airports and many of the hotels provide minibus services for residents. Driving is done on the left-hand side of the road (as in Britain and in most southern African countries), and a valid International Driving License is required. Personal vehicles require a *Carnet de Passage* and *Triptique* and International Certificate of Insurance. The main roads are tarred and mostly in good condition, but visitors should check road conditions before setting off. Some destinations can be reached only by four-wheel-drive vehicles, which are available from most car hire companies, of which there are many. Rates can be negotiated on a weekly or daily basis, plus mileage and insurance. A driver can be supplied at additional charge. Regular bus services run between all major towns and to some neighbouring countries. *Matatus* dominate the roads, but are generally overloaded, driven at breakneck speed with no regard for other road-users, and cannot be recommended as a safe and comfortable way of travel. Take extra care with money and personal possessions when travelling by *matatu,* as pickpockets are rife. Taxis are abundant and generally in fair to good condition. These are not metered, so agree upon a fee before setting off. One of the delights are the comfortable, London-style Austin 'cabs', which look antiquated but are, in fact, fairly new.

HOTELS, GUEST HOUSES AND RESORTS

Kenya offers some of the best accommodation on the African continent. Travellers can pick and choose to suit the budget. The luxury camps in the game parks are very pricey but offer excellent value for money. Competition is keen in the tourist industry as a whole and this keeps standards high. Guest houses offer clean and comfortable accommodation, and are much less expensive than resorts aimed at tourists. Many budget tour packages, which include bed and board as well as air fares, are available at very affordable prices.

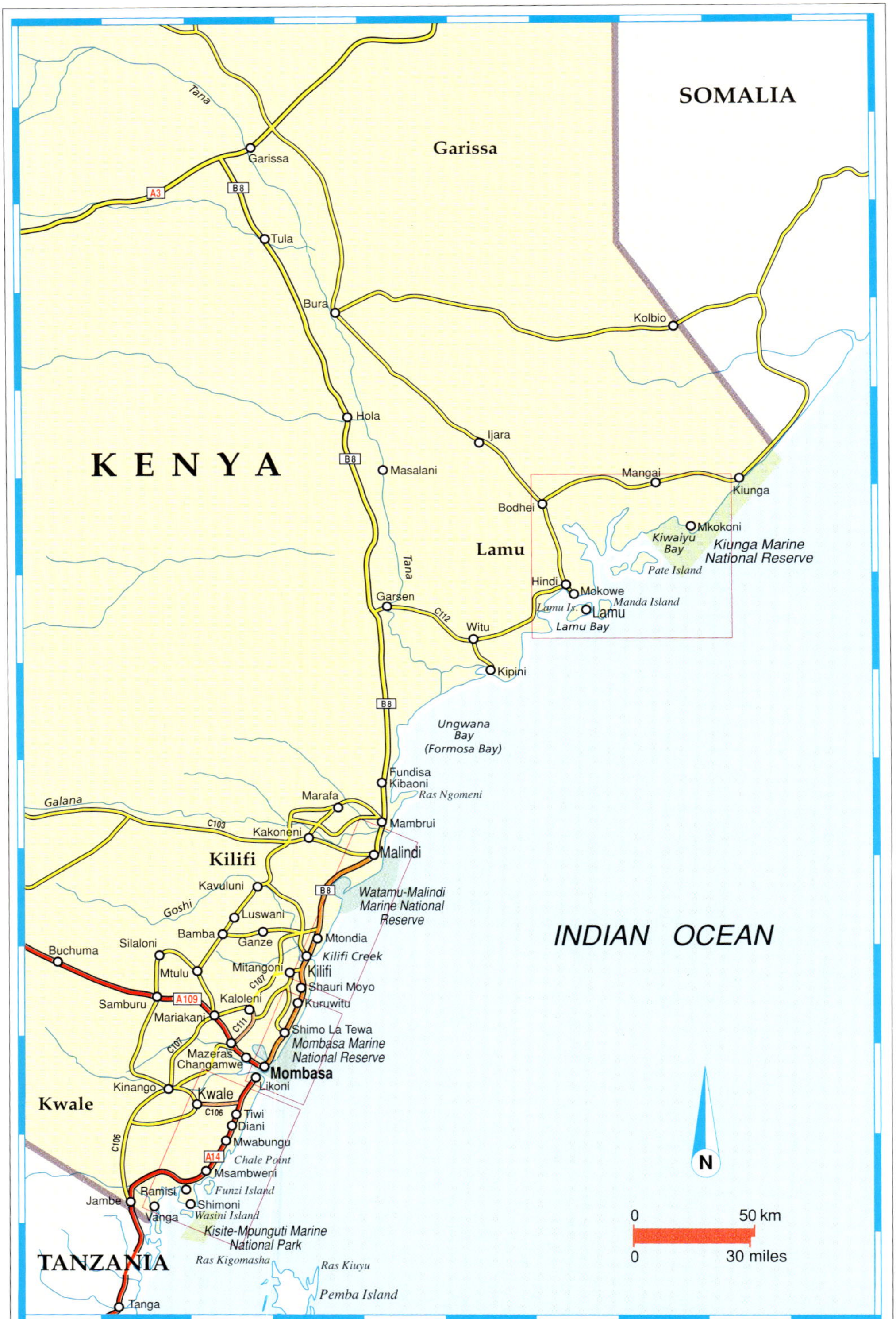
SOMALIA
Garissa
Tana
Garissa
A3
B8
Tula
Bura
Kolbio
Hola
Ijara
KENYA
B8
Masalani
Mangai
Kiunga
Bodhei
Mkokoni
Kiwaiyu Bay
Kiunga Marine National Reserve
Lamu
Tana
Pate Island
Hindi
Mokowe
Garsen
C112
Manda Island
Lamu Is.
Lamu
Witu
Lamu Bay
Kipini
B8
Ungwana Bay (Formosa Bay)
Fundisa
Kibaoni
Ras Ngomeni
Galana
Marafa
Mambrui
C103
Kakoneni
Malindi
Kilifi
Kavuluni
B8
Watamu-Malindi Marine National Reserve
Goshi
Luswani
Bamba
Ganze
Mtondia
INDIAN OCEAN
Buchuma
Silaloni
Kilifi Creek
Mitangoni
Kilifi
Mtulu
C107
Shauri Moyo
Samburu
A109
Kaloleni
Kuruwitu
Mariakani
C111
Shimo La Tewa
C107
Mombasa Marine National Reserve
Mazeras
Changamwe
Mombasa
Kinango
Likoni
Kwale
Kwale
C106
Tiwi
Diani
C106
Mwabungu
A14
Chale Point
Msambweni
N
Ramisi
Funzi Island
Jambe
Shimoni
Vanga
Wasini Island
0
50 km
Kisite-Mpunguti Marine National Park
0
30 miles
TANZANIA
Ras Kigomasha
Ras Kiuyu
Pemba Island
Tanga

INTRODUCING THE DIVING REGIONS OF KENYA

The Kenyan coastline commences not far south of the equator, at the country's border with Somalia, and winds its way down to Tanzania in the south for a total distance of approximately 480km (290 miles). This relatively short stretch of coast falls entirely within tropical climes, and so is governed by the expected typical tropical water conditions and aquatic life. The warm and generally clear water is inhabited by an array of extremely colourful and diverse marine fauna.

The Kenyan coastline stretches in a generally southeasterly direction and is often interrupted by the mouths of ancient rivers. These now form tidal creeks and river deltas, and include the mouths of the country's two largest rivers, the Tana and the Sabaki. The Lamu archipelago in the north embraces most of the islands on the coast, with other islands farther to the south at Watamu, Mombasa and south of Diani to Shimoni.

For diving purposes the coastline of Kenya can be subdivided into the following four diving regions:

Islands of the North Coast:
The Lamu Archipelago

The North Coast:
Malindi, Watamu and Kilifi

Mombasa and Environs

The South Coast:
Tiwi Beach, Diani Beach, Shimoni, Mpunguti Islands and Kisite Island

Diving Conditions

The Kenyan coast is best dived from the beginning of October through to the beginning of April, when the water is warm and normally clear. The best visibility normally occurs during the months of November and February/March when an average visibility of 15–20m (50–65ft) is not uncommon. In areas where major rivers empty into the Indian Ocean, bringing large amounts of silt, visibility is drastically reduced during the rainy season.

The rainy season exerts an adverse effect on diving conditions during the month of May, and rougher conditions are experienced during the months of June, July and August, when windy conditions prevail. These conditions make diving impossible in many places, as crossings of the reef become treacherous. Many of the dive bases along the coast close their doors for business during these winter months, but there remain some diveable sites around the islands to the south of Mombasa. Further details on specific diving conditions can be found in the individual chapters on dive sites.

JAMBO

ISLANDS OF THE NORTH COAST

Seven islands make up the archipelago of Lamu. The shores of Manda, Pate, Kiwayuu, Tukutu, Kisigati and Ndau islands are fringed with mangrove forests (Lamu's top export commodity), and the islands are surrounded by snow-white dunes and colourful coral reefs.

Lamu Island is wonderfully rich in history, culture and architecture, but because of unsafe road conditions, the dive sites of these northern islands are not nearly as popular as those found further south. For the same reason there are few organized diving facilities, but, for the keen and adventurous diver the atmosphere of Lamu, coupled with unspoilt diving conditions and uncrowded reefs and dive boats, will be ample reward.

The town of Lamu, situated on the main island, was established in the 14th century. It faces away from the sea and has likewise turned its back on Western civilization. Donkeys represent the main mode of transport, and dhows carry visitors from here to the nearby islands. The 12km-long (7.5-mile) beach is deserted and good for snorkelling.

Much remains to be explored and discovered in these northernmost waters of the Kenyan coast, which are situated a mere 100km (60 miles) south of the Somalian border.

Diving Conditions

The Tana River empties into the Indian Ocean in this area. During the rainy season (from May to July) the inflow of silt-laden river water diminishes the visibility to such an extent that diving is not feasible. The muddy water also has a retarding effect on coral growth and the reefs are, in general, not as massive and colourful as those found farther to the south.

During the best diving season, which lasts from October to April, the diving conditions are generally good and the fish life is quite spectacular. The average water temperature varies between 25 and 29°C (77 and 84°F). Currents are mostly tidal, normally slight and do not present a problem for divers. During the diving season the visibility in this region averages around 8–10m (27–33 ft).

Left: *The Dhow Palace Hotel at Lamu evokes East Africa's Arab seafaring heritage.*
Above: *Blue-banded snappers are often seen shoaling on tropical reefs.*

ISLANDS OF THE NORTH COAST
KENYA
SOMALIA
INDIAN OCEAN
Dar es Salaam
Kiunga
Kiunga Marine National Reserve
Boni National Reserve
Dodori National Reserve
Mkokoni
Kiwayuu Island
Boteler Islands
Kiwayuu Beach
Kiwayuu Bay
Mangai
Ndau Island
Faza
Siyu Channel
Siyu
Pate
Pate Island
Dodori Creek
Mtangawanda
Manda Bay
1 Jiwe La Mpupu
Manda Toto Island
2 Jamba La Simba
Manda Island
Manda
Takwa Milinga
Ras Mwana
3 Kinyika Island
Manungwi Islands
Lamu
Ras Kitau
Lamu Bay
Mokowe
Ferry
Matondoni
Lamu Island
Hindi
C112
Bodhei
N
0 10 20 km
0 10 miles

Manda Island

This island is within easy access (only 1.5hr across the channel) from Lamu. Manda is the site of the famed Takwa ruins, which date back to the 15th century. Some of the best diving and snorkelling in the area can be done off the northeast coast of Manda Island and around Manda Toto Island, where there are good reefs. Farther to the south are some other worthwhile sites, such as Tenewe and Kipini, but these involve a two-hour trip by boat and there are no organized diving facilities.The only access is by dhow, and there are lovely beaches to while away the surface time between dives.

Pate Island

The large, low-lying island of Pate (as in *de foie gras*) houses the old towns of Faza, Siyu, Mtangawanda and Pate, which are best known for their historical sites and ruins. Pate's history dates back to the 13th century, and tells a chequered tale of frequent wars with Lamu (which the town of Pate resembles, though it is more run down). The island can be reached by motor launch from Lamu, a journey of about 2hr. Pate is not known for its diving, but may be worth a visit for topside divers.

Kiwayuu Island

Long, narrow Kiwayuu Island lies at the northeastern-most point of the archipelago, not far south of the border with Somalia. This island is incorporated into the Kiunga Marine National Reserve, which was established in 1979 and covers an area of 250km^2 (37 sq miles). More than 50 small islands are enclosed by the reserve, and there are coral reefs to the east of Kiwayuu Island which may offer great diving opportunities during the diving season. The park is also a breeding ground for the endangered dugong and green turtle. The island can be reached by speedboat for guests of the upmarket lodge, or by dhow – a highly recommended experience.

DUGONGS

In days gone by, the siren song of the mermaid led many a ship to falter on rocky shores. In real life, the romantic myth of the mermaid may have had its origin in the low whistle that the dugong *(Dugong dugon)* makes when it inhales air on the surface. These homely creatures are sadly on the brink of extinction, and are among Africa's most endangered large mammals. Dugongs bear live young that are suckled on teats situated high on the chest of females, and are believed to be the origin of many a sailor's mermaid fantasies. Resembling a large sea lion or walrus, dugongs were once plentiful off the East African coast but have almost certainly been hunted to extinction in Tanzania and the Comoros for their succulent flesh. During a recent aerial survey by the Centre for Dolphin Studies in Port Elizabeth, South Africa, in conjunction with the Kenya Wildlife Service, researchers expected to see hundreds of dugongs, but only seven were counted during 254 hours of flying. Their natural habitat is the seagrass beds in lagoons, where coral reefs afford protection. Dugongs hardly ever venture below 30m (100ft) and are mostly seen close to the surface. Their mode of propulsion is the same vertical tailfin strokes as that of dolphins and they often rest on the bottom. They occur as far south as northern KwaZulu-Natal, in South Africa, and are still quite plentiful around the Bazaruto Archipelago off the coast of Mozambique.

The coral rockcod preys on fish and crustaceans.

Lamu

This area is still relatively unexplored and only the more well-known sites are described in some detail here.

1 JIWE LA MPUPU

★★★★★

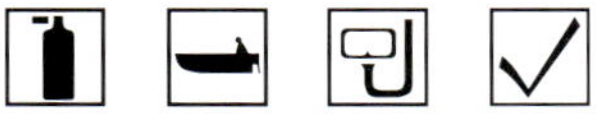

Location: Opposite the Barracuda Channel where a large mushroom-shaped rock is exposed above the water line.
Access: Only accessible on high tide by boat from Lamu. The duration of a motorized dhow trip from Lamu is around 45 minutes.
Conditions: Best dived on low tide.
Maximum depth: 8m (27ft).
Average depth: 6–8m (20–27ft).
Average visibility: 8m (27ft) in the diving season.

Crescent-tail wrasse feeding on the eggs of zebrafish.

Average water temperature: 25–29°C (77–84°F).
The reef here is in the form of a channel about 300m (1 000 ft) long which cuts into the exposed banks. The colour of the unspoilt coral formations is predominantly brown and there are a number of large coral heads.

The fish life here consists of most of the tropical varieties typical to the Kenyan coast. Many pelagic fish, which include many caranx, known locally as jacks (or kole-kole), also frequent this site. It is also the territory of many large rockcod and potato groupers.

2 JAMBA LA SIMBA

★★★

Location: Marked on the charts as Manda Toto. The site itself is not easy to find and a local guide with knowledge of the site is needed to accompany divers.
Access: A trip by motorized dhow takes around 20 minutes from Lamu.
Conditions: Only diveable during the dry season.
Maximum depth: 25m (80ft).
Average depth: 12–18m (40–60ft).
Average visibility: 8m (27ft) in the diving season.
Average water temperature: 25–29°C (77–84°F).
The pinnacle at this dive site juts to within 12m (40ft) of the surface and falls away to a maximum depth of 25m (80ft). There is little live coral because of the dirty water and silt settlement during the rainy season, but there are many colourful sponges and whip coral growths which adorn the pinnacle. The main attraction for divers, however, are the many caves and holes which are homes to really big potato groupers, or giant rockcod.

A further attraction that makes the site worth visiting during the diving season is the great number of pelagic fish, which include barracuda and giant trevally (caranx), that may be seen here.

3 KINYIKA ISLAND

★★★★★★★★

Location: The dive site is on the southwestern side of Kinyika Island, which is located to the south of Lamu Bay.
Access: Approximately 1hr by motorized dhow from Lamu. There is a good anchorage on the south side of the island.
Conditions: Best dived on a high neap tide.
Maximum depth: 20m (65ft).
Average depth: 12–15m (40–50ft).
Average visibility: 15m (50ft) in the diving season and often up to 20m (65ft).
Average water temperature: 25–29°C (77–84°F).
The dive site is in the form of a number of exposed rocks jutting out high above the sea, and there are good unspoilt coral formations on the southwestern side. These reefs are decorated with dense clouds of yellow snappers and an array of other colourful tropical marine fish species. There are also many shy groupers, some large Napoleon wrasse in the deeper sections, and jacks and barracuda to be seen during a dive. The shallow waters around the island offer excellent snorkelling opportunities during the diving season when the water is clear. The dhow trip should in itself be an enjoyable experience and visiting divers should make the effort to dive on this excellent site.

A close-up of a sea fan shows its delicate 'leaves'.

How to Get There

Lamu

By air: The airport for the islands is on Manda Island. From there, take the ferry across the channel to Lamu. There are two flights a day between Mombasa and the islands; air charter companies include: Eagle Aviation, tel. Mombasa (011) 434480/316055, Malindi (0123) 21099, Lamu (0121) 33119; Prestige Air Services, tel. Mombasa (011) 221443/ 223073, Malindi (0123) 20860/1; and Skyways Airline, tel. Mombasa (011) 221964, Malindi (0123) 21260 or Lamu (0121) 33226.

By road: There are daily bus services between Mombasa, Malindi and Lamu. The journey (340km; 210 miles) from Mombasa to Lamu takes 8-10hr. The road is notorious for bandits from Somalia, but bus journeys are quite safe. The buses are often packed, and it is worth arriving early to ensure a seat. The buses stop at the ferry jetty on the mainland and from there one takes a motorized ferry to Lamu.

By sea: Passage on a dhow that sails from Mombasa to Lamu is the easiest option. Be sure to bring sleeping gear and enough food and water for two days' travel. Permission from the district commissioner is needed for the journey, but the captain may be able to take care of this. A ferry service operates between the bus terminus on the mainland and Lamu, and between Lamu and Manda Island, and Lamu and Pate Island.

Kiwayuu Island

The only way to get to Kiwayuu Island is by dhow from Lamu; the trip may take as long as three days and two nights.

Pate Island

A motor launch leaves three times a week from Lamu to Mtangwanda (about 2hr) and Faza (4hr). From Mtangwanda it is about an hour's walk to Pate town.

Manda Island

There is an airport on Manda Island that can be reached from Mombasa or Malindi. Other options include a ferry ride from Lamu to Manda Island (about 1.5hr), or by dhow, where the cost is shared by the passengers.

Dive Facilities

Lamu

At time of writing, the only reliable organized diving facilities in the Lamu archipelago are operated from the **Peponi Hotel,** tel. (0121) 3029. Martin Schutz operates **Dhow Diving Tours,** tel. (0121) 33154, fax. 33029. Good gear is available for rental, and Martin knows the best reefs. A dhow excursion, including two dives and lunch, offers good value. Closed during May and June, but it is advisable to check on this.

Where to Stay

Lamu

The best accommodation is at the **Peponi Hotel,** P O Box 24, Lamu, tel. (0121) 3029/33423. The hotel offers self-contained cottages and is classed among the world's best. The other top-range hotel is **Petley's Inn,** P O Box 4, Lamu, tel. (0121) 33107, fax. 33378, which is the only hotel with a bar in Lamu. The best cheap lodgings are the **Full Moon Guest House** and the **Kenya Lodging.**

Kiwayuu

The luxury **Kiwaiyu Mlango Wa Chanu Lodge,** P O Box 55343, Nairobi, tel. (02) 503030. Opposite it on the mainland is the **Kiwaiyu Safari Village,** P O Box 48287, Nairobi, tel. (02) 331231. Also on Kiwayuu is the much less expensive or exclusive **Kiwaiyu Camping Site,** with beautiful bandas.

Pate Island

Visitors are invariably invited to stay with villagers, but it is a good idea to take a tent as there are no formal lodgings. Take ample water and insect repellent.

Manda Island

There are two rather exclusive hotels on Manda Island and bookings are essential. They are: **Manda Island Village,** P O Box 99, Lamu, tel. (0121) 3206; and the **Blue Safari Camp,** P O Box 3205, Lamu, tel. (0121) 3205.

Where to Eat

Lamu

The Peponi Hotel's **Barbecue Grill** is open to non-residents and offers excellent food. The **Equator Restaurant** is popular but pricey. Also recommended is the **Barracuda Rooftop Restaurant,** tel. (0121) 33290, at the Island Hotel in Shela village. Less expensive places to eat are the **Bush Gardens** and the **Hapa Hapa;** and for a good breakfast, the **Coral Reef** (formerly the Yoghurt Inn). One of the cheapest places is the **New Star Restaurant** (opens at 05:30 in the morning).

Kiwayuu

At the camping site, there is a covered dining and cooking area. Stock up on basic provisions before travelling here.

Pate

Simple eating places offer stews and tea. Stock up on necessities; meals can be arranged with local families, who will provide accommodation for a fee.

Manda Island

A dhow trip from Lamu harbour may be followed by a barbecued fish lunch; check that this is included in the price. Stock up with provisions if planning to camp. There is a bar and restaurant at the **Blue Safari Club,** tel. (0121) 33025.

Regional Highlights

Visitors to Lamu should not miss the **Lamu Museum** (open daily 08:30-12:00; 14:00-17:00), which has superb exhibitions on Swahili and mainland culture. Dhow trips are a good bet. There are excellent guide books to this region which are well worth the money.

Emergency Measures

There is one **hospital:** the Lamu District Hospital, tel. (0121) 3012.

Recompression facilities are available at the Kenya Navy's base in Mombasa. Contact the Staff Officer or Duty Officer at tel. (011) 45 1201 ext. 3308 (24-hour standby availability).

The international **emergency radio channel** is **#16**.

THE NORTH COAST

The fringing coral reef that protects most of the Kenyan coast starts at Malindi and stretches for 230km (150 miles) to Vanga (near the Tanzanian border) in the south. The Malindi Marine National Reserve, the famous Watamu Marine National Park and Marine Reserve, Mida Creek and Kilifi, all of which fall into the north coast region, are situated in and just beyond this pristine reef, making the entire Kenyan north coast a popular venue for divers from all over the world, as well as for locals.

Malindi, Watamu and Kilifi all offer well-organized diving opportunities and superb diving and snorkelling conditions on exquisite hard and soft coral reefs teeming with pelagic (open ocean) and tropical marine life.

Diving Conditions: Malindi

The town of Malindi borders on the Malindi Marine National Reserve to the south, which was established in 1968 and covers an area of 213km^2 (82 sq miles). Within the reserve is the 6km^2 (2.3 sq miles) Malindi Marine National Park, which offers fabulous diving and snorkelling conditions on the coral reefs off Casuarina Point. The area within the marine national park and reserve is well known for its variety of habituated fish on the reefs. Unfortunately the corals have suffered some damage.

During the rainy season this area is not diveable as large amounts of silt flow down with the Galana River (called the Sabaki at its mouth) to the north, disturbing the generally good visibility quite severely. The water is also murky from November through to March, and at this time most of the divers are taken to the Watamu Reefs further to the south.

From July to November the maximum visibility is in the region of 25m (80ft), and from December to April a maximum of 10m (33ft). Most dives in the Malindi area are carried out as drift dives as there is often a fairly strong current present. Night dives are, for safety reasons, only carried out in the Watamu area.

Left: *Sailing craft, dhows and ferryboats moored in Kilifi Creek.*
Above: *The band-dot goatfish, largest of the bottom-dwelling goatfish family, forages along the base of a reef.*

NORTH COAST
Garashi
Kakoneni
Galana
Dagamra
Sabaki
C103
Pishi Mwenga
Lake Jilore Bird Sanctuary
Mango Inn
Lady Cheetah
La Malindina
Eden Rock
Sinbad
Blue Marlin
Ganda
Malindi
1 Stork Passage and Barracuda Channel
Arabuko
Arabuko Sokoke Forest
Msabaha
Malindi Marine N.P.
2-5
Malindi Point
Gedi
Gedi National Monument
6 Manta Place
Kililepwa Island
Watamu
E899
Watamu
7-10
Old Mosque
Blue Bay
Ocean Sports
Turtle Bay
Hemingways
Watamu-Malindi Marine National Reserve
Watamu Marine Nat. Res.
Sudi Is.
Penda Kula
11 Moray Eel Reef
Malindi Marine National Reserve
Dida
B8
Old Mosque
Watamu Marine N.P.
12 Wreck of the Shakwe
Mida Creek
Old Mosque
Roka
Kilifi
2-5
2. Tewa Reef
3. Ed's Caves
4. Shark Point
5. Snorkelling Reefs
7-10
7. Deep Place
8. Black Coral Reef
9. The Canyon and Canyon North
10. Dolphin Corner
Reef
Sokoke
Tezo
C115
Rare
E921
Mtondia
Kilifi Bay
Sea Horse
Bofa Reef
Bandari Ya Wah
Kilifi
13 14 Barracuda Reef
15 Kilifi Creek
16 Southern Reef
Mnarani
Pinnacle Point
C107
Sinawe
Takaunga
17 Vuma Caves
Mitangoni
Kibaoni
B8
Dindiri
Shauri Moyo
INDIAN OCEAN
Wimbi Mtoni
Junju
Tropicana
Kurwitu
N
Vipingo
0
10 km
0
5 miles

DIVING CONDITIONS: WATAMU

Watamu is well known for its excellent scuba diving and snorkelling during the dry season and offers some of the best reefs and marine life on the East African coast. The fringing coral reefs, of which there are three, are distanced approximately 1.2–2km (0.8–1.2 miles) offshore. Beyond these are some isolated underwater coral 'islands' which afford spectacular dives. The Watamu Marine National Park area ends on the first reef, and the marine reserve area covers the other reefs. Only traditional subsistence fishing by local fishermen is allowed in the reserve, and the long-time establishment of the reserve has caused the marine life to flourish and to become habituated. The reefs are in excellent condition and there are large shallow caves in the mouth of Mida Creek where giant groupers hide, though it seems that many have unfortunately been caught by bottom fishers. There are very good snorkelling sites on the shallower reefs inside the marine park which may be enjoyed by all. An entrance fee must be paid, and there are many facilities available which make the fee worthwhile, including glass-bottom boat trips.

This beautiful section of the coast boasts the largest number of whale shark sightings on the East African coast, and probably the entire east coast of Africa. As many as 60 have been sighted on one occasion! This huge congregation of whale sharks was joined by large numbers of manta rays – a spectacular sight indeed. The reason for the frequent presence of the numerous large filter feeders such as whale sharks, manta and eagle rays and dolphins, may lie in the flow of the currents in Watamu Bay. The Malindi headland juts far out into the ocean and causes the north-flowing current to turn south and follow a circular pattern. This brings in large concentrations of plankton and krill, which are of course the staple diet of the filter feeders, at the same time giving the coral spores time to settle and grow on the bottom. The currents are also, for this reason, quite mild and therefore attractive to divers during most of the diving season.

Typical marine life on most of the reefs includes Napoleon wrasse, groupers, jacks, barracuda in small schools, and turtles (found mainly on top of the reef – as many as 15 may be seen during a single dive). Night dives are regularly organized for more experienced divers on the sites which are within easy reach of the dive bases. During the months of May to September the *Kusi* (the southeastern monsoon wind) blows directly onto the reefs and this makes any crossing through the *mlango* (Swahili for 'door') hazardous. As all dives in this area are done by boat, many of the dive bases close their doors during May and June, or even in July, when maintenance is carried out. It is therefore best to check in advance before undertaking a trip to this spectacular diving haven. The scuba diving facilities are of high standard, and diving expeditions are well organized by long-established operators who know every nook and cranny of the reefs.

DIVING CONDITIONS: KILIFI

The fringing coral reefs around the Kilifi area are completely unspoilt and stretch for long distances. For this reason the descriptions of the dive sites are separated by area rather than by individual site. All dives are done by boat and the best areas are on the outside of the fringing reefs. Exits are through the *mlango* in front of the creek and shore dives are only possible for persons who have access to the beach through residential properties. The creek often offers diving possibilities when conditions in other areas do not allow, and spectacular night dives are often done in the sheltered waters. There are also some good snorkelling sites alongside the banks of the creek. There are a few organized diving facilities, which include training facilities and live-aboard excursions along the Kenyan coast and to Pemba, Zanzibar and Mafia islands aboard a luxury sailing yacht.

Malindi

The town of Malindi has a history that dates back to the 13th century. Today it is Kenya's most famous water-sports resort, and has excellent facilities for diving, fishing, water-skiing, sail-boarding and surfing. It has been renowned for its excellent big-game fishing ever since author Ernest Hemingway first fished here in the 1930s. Even today many record-breaking catches are made, with six world records and 79 all-Africa records already in the bag. As recently as 26 March 1995, the second largest black marlin ever caught in African waters, and the biggest in Kenyan waters – a giant of 568kg (1 250 pounds) – was brought ashore by Angus Paul off the Malindi coast. (The record is held by a Mauritian catch.) The north coast is also one of the few places on the Kenyan seaboard where real surfing can be enjoyed, as the big breakers roll in through the break in the fringing reef into the wide bay from late June to early September. Another advantage of this is that the beaches are free of the unsightly seaweed that is common on many of the popular beaches to the south. The town and resort are home to a cosmopolitan mixture of Swahili, Italian, English and German residents, who add to the colourful culture of this historic Swahili settlement on the north coast of Kenya. Malindi has grown into a tremendously popular tourist resort and there are many excellent hotels strung along the pristine beaches. Unfortunately, muggings occur on this section of the coast and care should be taken not to walk along uninhabited roads or on deserted beaches at night.

WHALE SHARKS

The whale shark *(Rhincodon typus)* is the world's largest fish, and, fortunately for divers, also one of the ocean's most harmless creatures, allowing divers to come into close contact with it.

These cold-blooded fish should not be confused with whales, which are warm-blooded mammals. The smallest free-living newly born whale shark is only 55cm (22in) long, and the biggest may grow to an enormous 12m (40ft), although maximum sizes are uncertain. They are highly migratory filter feeders but prefer temperate and warm tropical seas. The animal's head is broad and flat and its wide mouth, filled with numerous minute teeth, is situated just in front of the eyes. The whale shark's diet includes small crustacea, squid and fish – especially sardines, mackerel and tuna. The colour is almost black and patterned with white spots whilst the ventral parts are whitish.

The whale shark's only natural enemies are fishermen, and the animals are sometimes found drowned or entangled in nets. They are most often seen individually, but are sometimes found in aggregations. Whale sharks often pass close to reefs on the seaward side and are frequently seen off the East African coast. The site of one of these gigantic fish is guaranteed to turn any dive into an experience that will never be forgotten.

An inquisitive moray eel greets a diver. These fearsome-looking creatures are dangerous only when provoked.

1 STORK PASSAGE and BARRACUDA CHANNEL

★★★★

Location: There are two buoys on this reef. See map.
Access: Approximately 30 minutes by boat from Malindi.
Conditions: Generally a fairly strong current is present and so Stork Passage should be treated as a drift dive from the southern to the northern mooring. This dive is not for beginners.
Average depth: 10–20m (33–65ft).
Maximum depth: 20m (65ft).
Average visibility: 10–20m (33–65ft); can be very variable.
Average water temperature: 24–28°C (75–82°F).

This dive site is in the form of an approximately 1km-long (0.6 mile) channel. The dive takes place on the outer wall of the coral garden lagoon, with a steep wall on one side and the open sea on the other. There are magnificent rose corals, and on the bottom at 20m (65ft) many isolated coral outcrops can be seen.

An outstanding and exciting feature of this reef are the thousands of barracuda which congregate in the channel. The size of these fish vary considerably, with the smaller kind found generally closer to the bottom and the larger individuals above.

Sightings of black-, white-tipped and grey reef sharks can almost be guaranteed here. The sight of one of these always adds great excitement to the dive. Big groupers, stingrays, jacks (caranx) and turtles are also present in good numbers, and the combination of this wide variety of marine life makes this a spectacular dive when conditions are perfect.

2 TEWA REEF

★★★

Location: In the Malindi Marine National Park off Casuarina Point. To the south of the dive bases at the hotels. The reef is buoyed. See map.
Access: Approximately 45 minutes by boat from Malindi.
Conditions: Generally a fair current present and should be treated as a drift dive.
Average depth: 10m (33ft).
Maximum depth: 12m (40ft).
Average visibility: 10–20m (33–65ft).
Average water temperature: 24–28°C (75–82°F).

The reef is in the form of a small underwater island, with large round coral heads hosting schools of snappers, beautiful fusiliers and surgeonfish.

There is a lot of rose coral on this site, and several other varieties of soft coral are present. The hard corals are generally large in size, and are mostly of the brain and potato type.

At night, the tree coral extends its polyps to feed.

3 ED'S CAVES

★★★

Location: In the Malindi Marine National Park. To the south of the dive bases at the hotels. The reef is buoyed. See map.
Access: Approximately 1.5hr by boat from Malindi.
Conditions: Generally a fair current present; should be treated as a drift dive.
Average depth: 10m (33ft).
Maximum depth: 12m (40ft).
Average visibility: 10–20m (33–65ft).
Average water temperature: 24–28°C (75–82°F).

The dive takes place on the edge of a fringing reef, where a few small caves may be explored. Typical marine life consists mainly of schooling fish, stingrays and a colourful array of smaller marine tropicals.

4 SHARK POINT

★★★

Location: In the Malindi Marine National Park off Casuarina Point. To the south of the dive bases at the hotels. The reef is buoyed. See map.
Access: Approximately 45 minutes by boat from Malindi.
Conditions: There is generally a fair current present, but divers should be able to circumnavigate the reef in about 45 minutes.
Average depth: 10m (33ft).

Maximum depth: 12m (40ft).
Average visibility: 10–20m (33–65ft).
Average water temperature: 24–28°C (75–82°F).
As the name denotes, this site is often visited by small reef sharks, particularly the white-tipped ones. It is also a small underwater island, with large coral heads and a good variety of soft and hard coral. There is an incredible variety of fish, as well as large turtles. Octopus and the rare flying gurnard may also be seen.

5 SNORKELLING REEFS

★★★★★★★

Location: In the Malindi National Marine Park, south of Malindi town at the park headquarters. See map.
Access: An entry fee is charged at the park entrance gate. Small boats may be rented at the park headquarters, and glass-bottom boat trips are available for non-snorkellers.
Conditions: Calm but not always clear.
Average depth: 3m (10ft).
Maximum depth: 5m (16ft).
Average visibility: 10m (33ft).
Average water temperature: 24–29°C (75–84°F).
The fish life is varied and colourful and consists mainly of small tropical reef fish. The fish have become quite used to the presence of visitors. The reefs are unfortunately somewhat damaged by the impact of people, silt and wave action, but the coral variety is great.

Watamu

Watamu, which is situated only 24km (15 miles) south of Malindi and on Turtle Bay, is renowned for its breathtaking coral reefs. The marine life is just as spectacular, with large numbers of whale sharks and manta rays, and eagle rays and dolphins at certain times of the year.

The reefs fall within the Watamu Marine Reserve and the Watamu Marine National Park. Both the reserve and the park were established in 1968 and cover areas of 32km^2 (12 sq miles) and 10km^2 (4 sq miles), respectively. The once serene fishing village of Watamu has turned into a bustling resort, and there are a number of first-class hotels along the snow-white beaches. The coast is divided into three coves with lovely sandy beaches separated by jutting headlands. Mida Creek and Whale Island are the nesting grounds of thousands of birds, and Mida Creek's caves house giant groupers of astonishing size.

There are a total of 18 dive sites in the Watamu area. These are all buoyed by Scuba Diving Kenya to protect the reefs against anchor damage and to facilitate diving. Only the most popular of these dive sites are mentioned here, but the variety will be enough to satisfy even the choosiest of divers.

A school of silvery fish fry presents a dazzling sight as it passes a bank of hard coral.

6 MANTA PLACE

★★★★

Location: On the northern section of the third fringing reef. The reef is buoyed. See map.
Access: Approximately 25 minutes by boat from Watamu Bay.
Conditions: Generally calm; mild or no current present.
Average depth: 10–15m (33–50ft).
Maximum depth: 15m (50ft).
Average visibility: 15–20m (50–65ft).
Average water temperature: 24–28°C (75–82°F).

The name of this site already gives divers a good idea of the type of marine life that may be expected here, and graceful manta rays are often sighted. The reef also attracts large numbers of juvenile pelagic fish, and fish life is generally abundant.

The exquisitely coloured blue-and-yellow ribbon eel (*Rhinomuraena quaesita*), which can change its sex from male to female, may be found on this site. The eel protrudes from the sandy bottom and feeds on small fish passing by. The entire reef area, which is in the shape of a small, flat underwater hill, is unspoilt, with an excellent variety of coral.

7 DEEP PLACE

★★★★

Location: Opposite the southern end of the northern bay, on the third fringing reef. The reef is buoyed. See map.
Access: Approximately 15 minutes by boat from Watamu Bay.
Conditions: Generally calm with mild or no current present. The reef may be dived upon at any time during the diving season.
Average depth: 10–25m (33–80ft).
Maximum depth: 25m (80ft).
Average visibility: 15–20m (50–65ft).
Average water temperature: 24–28°C (75–82°F).

Before the dive sites on the fourth and deepest reef were discovered, this was the deepest reef that could be dived on around Watamu, hence the name. One of Deep Place's major attractions is that there is a good possibility of spotting dolphins, manta rays and whale sharks. When this happens, this site can definitely be classed as a five-star dive.

The reef forms a wall that reaches down to a sandy bottom at 25m (80ft) and is totally unspoilt. There is an excellent variety of soft and hard coral. The latter forms overhangs and small caves in which small and large marine life are present in copious numbers. There are lots of small brown moray eels that poke their heads out of the reef in many places from time to time.

False brain coral is usually green or brown in colour.

8 BLACK CORAL REEF

★★★★★

Location: Approximately 300m (0.6 miles) further out from Deep Place (No. 7) on the fourth fringing reef. The reef is buoyed. See map.
Access: Approximately 25 minutes by boat from Watamu Bay.
Conditions: Generally calm but not dived upon when a strong current is present due to the size and delicate nature of this reef. For experienced divers only, due to the depth at which the top of the reef starts.
Average depth: 32–40m (105–132ft).
Maximum depth: Beyond maximum sport-diving depths: 45m (150ft).
Average visibility: 15–20m (50–65ft).
Average water temperature: 24–28°C (75–82°F).

The top of this special and spectacular reef starts deep at 32m (105ft) and is in the shape of an underwater hill with the sides angling down to the sandy bottom some 45m (150ft) below the surface. There are several overhangs in the coral formations, which present a superb variety of hard and soft coral. The outstanding coral features on this five-star location are the big bushes of black coral (*Antipathes*) which grow to more than 1.8m (6ft) in height in some places, as well as the tall ropes of sea whips (*Juncella*) and gorgonian (*Eunicella*) coral, which are all covered in feather stars. There are also some large basket or vase corals (*Tubinaria frondens*) on the shallower parts of the reef, which often host an array of cleaner shrimps. This reef is also the only place in the area where the extremely attractive blue sea cucumber (known locally as *Kukumaya*) is found in considerable numbers. The dive operators at Watamu take care in preserving the pristine state of the reef by limiting the number of dives and by only allowing experienced divers on the reef.

Coconut palm trees fringe an alluring stretch of beach south of Mombasa.

Picture a tropical paradise and the mind readily conjures images of long white beaches fringed with swaying coconut palms. The people of the East African coast, however, do not see the tall trees as a mere adornment to the landscape. The daily activities and even the livelihood of many people revolve around the ubiquitous coconut palm *(Cocos nucifera)*. Apart from the famous nut, the coconut palm yields an impressive variety of products, among them materials for weaving, building and cooking. Its many uses make the coconut palm one of the most versatile of all plants.

The coconut palm is widespread along tropical coasts. The coconut – the seed of the tree – floats easily and so can be carried great distances by ocean currents. The husk surrounding the kernel is tough and highly resistant to salt water, enabling the nut to survive the long ocean journeys. The seeds sprout in sandy soil close to the shore, and after five to six years, the tree bears fruit. It reaches maturity after 15 years.

Coconuts take about a year to ripen. The unripe, green nuts contain a large amount of juice *(madafu),* one of nature's most invigorating drinks. The green coconuts are sold at markets, where vendors slice off the top of the nut to offer an inexpensive and healthy alternative to bottled drinks or tap

Discarded coconut husks at a coastal processing plant.

water. The meat of the green coconut may be eaten fresh, but is much thinner than in the ripe nut, which attains a dark yellow, orange or brown colour.

To harvest the prized mature coconuts (*nasi* in Swahili), which cluster as high as 25m (60ft) above the ground, a bargain is struck with a roving coconut harvester. In return for a fee or a share of the crop, he scales the slim, ringed tree trunk and chops down the ripe nuts with swift strokes of a sharp *panga* (machete).

The pure white meat or kernel of the ripe nut is hidden beneath the fibrous husk. After this has been removed, the meat is scraped from the shell, and the grated coconut meat wrung through a fine conical sieve woven from mature coconut leaves. The creamy milk so obtained may be thinned with water or used in its pure form for cooking. Coconut milk imparts a deliciously rich flavour to rice, shellfish, fish and meat. When mixed with fresh pineapple juice and white rum, you have the authentic equivalent of the piña colada cocktail.

Dessicated or dried coconut meat is mainly used in confectionery and baking. Vegetable oil is extracted from the dried kernel of the coconut, called copra. In many tropical countries, copra is one of the most important export products.

A strong fibre called coir is woven from the nut's outer husk. Coir is still often used as a stuffing for mattresses, and is indispensable in the weaving of ropes for ships' rigging. Attractive and durable mats, often brilliantly dyed, are woven from coir, and industrially woven coir carpeting is a sought-after item in many modern homes. Long-wearing baskets, brushes and brooms are also made from coir.

The mature leaves of the coconut palm tree are an important building material, and are used as thatching *(makuti)* for houses; even large buildings and resorts are roofed with this material. Palm leaves are woven into baskets, hats, hammocks, mats, containers, fish traps and the spray shields on dhows known as *talbisi*. The leaf stalks are also stripped into thin raffia-like strips to bind anything from chicken legs to dhow sails. Many women and elders make woven goods, and weaving is an important source of income for coastal communities.

The sheaths that enclose the palm leaves may be used for wrapping objects, and food can even be cooked in a green sheath. When dry, the felt-like fibres provide tinder, caulking and filling for pillows.

Palm wine is obtained by extracting the sweetish sap from a cut in the young flower stalks of the tree. When fermented, it becomes a potent drink called *toddy* or *kongo,* which is outlawed on certain islands such as Zanzibar.

Crab traps woven from palm fibres on Zanzibar.

Palm cabbage, or heart-of-palm as it is known in restaurants, comes from a delicate young bud cut from the top of immature trees. In most cases, the trees have been specially planted for this purpose.

The trunk of the tree is fibrous and tough, quickly blunting the tools of workmen. Palm trunks are nevertheless used in house construction, boat-building, cabinet-making and to produce axe handles. Trunks are sometimes split and hollowed out for guttering, drainpipes, troughs and drums.

Several other palm species grow in East Africa. These include the oil palm *(Elaeis guineensis)*, raffia palm *(Raphia farinifera)* and betel pepper *(Piper betle)*.

9 THE CANYON and CANYON NORTH

★★★★★

Location: To the south of Deep Place (No. 7) on the third fringing reef. The reef is buoyed. See map.
Access: Approximately 20 minutes by boat from Watamu Bay.
Conditions: Generally calm and may be dived upon at any time during the diving season.
Average depth: 10–25m (33–80ft).
Maximum depth: 25m (80ft).
Average visibility: 20–30m (65–100ft).
Average water temperature: 24–28°C (75–82°F).

This reef, as its name indicates, takes the shape of a canyon. Its sandy bottom, at a depth of 25m (80ft), is lined by coral walls which taper to 30m (100ft) at the narrowest end. The walls have numerous overhangs and swim-throughs, and the great variety of hard and soft coral which is found here is completely unspoilt. Adding further to the dramatic seascape are the large number of stingrays, moray eels and garden eels that are found on the sandy bottom. Black- and white-tipped reef sharks are often encountered in varying sizes during a dive.

10 DOLPHIN CORNER

★★★★

Location: Opposite the northern end of the middle bay, on the third fringing reef. The reef is buoyed. See map.
Access: Approximately 20 minutes by boat from Watamu Bay.
Conditions: Generally calm with mild or no current present. The reef may be dived upon at any time during the diving season.
Average depth: 10–25m (33–80ft).
Maximum depth: 25m (80ft).
Average visibility: 20m (65ft).
Average water temperature: 25–29°C (77–84°F).

Dolphins seem to prefer coming through the small gap or *mlango* in the reef, and when they are encountered by lucky divers, they often oblige and stay around for some time – to the delight of the underwater visitors to

The distinctive honeycomb moray eel, shown below displaying its teeth, attains a length of up to 200cm (80in).

The African dwarf is the smallest angelfish.

this reef. Reef sharks are also frequently seen, and numerous stingrays and dense shoals of sweetlips and bigeyes form part of the typical marine life to be found here. The reef itself is in the form of a flattish underwater hill, with overhangs and a sandy bottom at 25m (80ft). There is a great variety of coral and this is densely inhabited by thousands of small and colourful reef fish.

11 MORAY EEL REEF

★★★★★

Location: Opposite the northern end of the middle bay, on the third fringing reef. The reef is buoyed. See map.
Access: Approximately 10–15 minutes by boat from Watamu Bay.
Conditions: Generally calm with no current. The reef may be dived upon at any time during the diving season.
Average depth: 10–25m (33–80ft).
Maximum depth: 25m (80ft).
Average visibility: 20–25m (65–80ft).
Average water temperature: 24–28°C (75–82°F).

As the name implies, this reef is the refuge for numerous large moray eels, including the giant (*Gymnothorax javanicus*) and honeycomb (*G. favagineus*) morays, as well as many spotted varieties. Ribbon eels and garden eels abound on the sandy bottom. There are also a few tame morays which appear to enjoy being touched and hugged by the long-time divers of the area. There are many leaf fish, of various colours, which may be spotted by attentive divers interested in the superb variety of small marine life to be found on this excellent site.

Like Dolphin Corner (No. 10), this reef is in the form of a small, flat hill, with overhangs and a sandy bottom at a depth of 25m (80ft). The coral formations are varied, and abound with copious numbers of both small and large marine life typical to the reefs of this area.

12 WRECK OF THE *SHAKWE*

★★★

Location: Opposite the northern end of the middle bay, on the third fringing reef. The reef is buoyed. See map.
Access: Approximately 30 minutes by dive boat from Watamu Bay.
Conditions: Generally calm with little current in shallow waters. The wreck may be dived upon at any time during the diving season and is suitable to most levels of divers.
Average depth: 8–12m (25–40ft).
Maximum depth: 12m (40ft).
Average visibility: 20m (65ft).
Average water temperature: 24–28°C (75–82°F).

The *Shakwe* is a small prawn trawler which sank in January 1989. The wreck now rests on its side on the sandy bottom. The marine life that has made the trawler their home includes some big groupers, stingrays and crocodile fish (*Pappiloculiceps longiceps*). In its very short life as a wreck, the *Shakwe* has been luxuriantly covered in colourful soft corals, and many ropes of whip coral or sea whips extend horizontally from her keel. The wreck is also used as a training site for advanced diving courses.

Kilifi

The deep Kilifi Creek reaches inland for a distance of 15km (9 miles) and separates Kilifi from Mnarani to the south. The creek is a popular natural venue for water-sports enthusiasts, and windsurfing, sailing, power-boat racing, water-skiing, and diving facilities are all available here. In 1991 a suspension bridge was built across the creek, considerably reducing the crossing time. The beachfront area is almost entirely occupied by private residences, for the most part the homes of white Kenyans – many of them artists, adventurers and writers. Kilifi is also the home of a large cashew nut factory, where these delicious nuts are processed and available at the cheapest prices in Kenya. The atmosphere is refreshingly untouristy, unlike the towns further north and to the south, and the views along the creek and overlooking the ocean are the best along the entire Kenyan coast.

13 BOFA REEF

★★★★

Location: To the north of Kilifi Creek, approximately 600m (0.25 miles) out. See map.
Access: Approximately 15 minutes by dive boat from Kilifi Creek.
Conditions: Best dived on an incoming tide during the diving season. A mild current may be present at times.
Average depth: 15–25m (50–80ft).
Maximum depth: 25m (80ft).

Zebra humbugs will colonize a coral head, and use it for protection when threatened by a predator.

Average visibility: 15m (50ft).
Average water temperature: 25–28°C (80–84°F).
The reef inclines at a fairly steep angle to the sandy bottom on the seaward side, and features small overhangs and an excellent variety of unspoilt coral in a pristine state. There are a good number of large vase corals (*Turbinaria frondens*) growing on some sections of the reef. It is always interesting to peer into these to see what small forms of marine life inhabit them. Apart from the fish typical of the area, dolphins, manta rays and whale sharks often make an appearance, and turtles are quite common. The fish population is extremely plentiful and even exceeds that found at Pemba Island, Tanzania, which is well known for its vast numbers of fish.

14 BARRACUDA REEF

★★★★

Location: Further out to the east of Bofa Reef (No. 13). See map.
Access: Approximately 10 minutes by dive boat from Kilifi Creek.
Conditions: Best dived on an incoming tide during the diving season.
Average depth: 20m (65ft).
Maximum depth: 30m (100ft).
Average visibility: 15–20m (50–65ft).
Average water temperature: 25–28°C (80–84°F).
This reef is well known and popular with divers because of the large numbers of good-sized pelagic fish that approach from the deeper waters. As the name denotes, large schools of barracuda may generally be expected to appear out of the blue, and these are often joined by jacks and tuna. The coral on the reef is unspoilt, but appears rather barren, with some small pinnacles. The attraction here is undoubtedly the large number and variety of pelagic fish.

15 KILIFI CREEK

★★ (day dive) ★★★★ (night dive)

Location: Inside the Kilifi Creek area. See map.
Access: By local boat or from shore if permission is granted to go through a residential property.
Conditions: Generally calm and protected inside the creek, but visibility is not always good. Best dived on slack after an incoming tide.
Average depth: 10m (33ft).
Maximum depth: 20m (65ft).
Average visibility: 5m (16ft).
Average water temperature: 25–28°C (80–84°F).
The banks of the creek form a shallow wall, with some overhangs. There are several coral outcrops on the sandy bottom. The soft coral takes the form of small, solitary patches, and the hard corals include pods of attractive basket coral. Because of its status as a protected area, the relatively shallow average depth, and the fact that visibility does not matter much, Kilifi Creek offers excellent night diving opportunities. Night dives offer the opportunity to view large numbers of invertebrates, and are enhanced by the presence of the spectacular Spanish dancer (*Hexabranchus sanguineus*), a species of giant nudibranch previously only recorded off Djibouti in the Red Sea. The creature is so-named because of its bright red colour, a white lacy fringe and its graceful, dance-like swimming movements. Its eggs, clustered together in a red rosette, are often seen during day dives – unlike the animal itself, which is normally only sighted at night.

16 SOUTHERN REEF

★★★★★★

Location: The northern tip of the southern reef, which is located to the south of the Kilifi Creek, approximately 600m (0.25 miles) out. The reef is easy to find because of the shallow surface. See map.
Access: Approximately 20 minutes by dive boat from Kilifi Creek.
Conditions: Best dived on an incoming tide during the diving season. A mild current may be present at times. The dive site itself is fairly close to the waves and care should be taken when diving or anchoring. This dive is not for beginners.
Average depth: 5–15m (16–50ft).
Maximum depth: 40m (132ft).
Average visibility: 15m (50ft).
Average water temperature: 25–28°C (80–84°F).
The reef forms a wall that drops down to the maximum sport-diving depth on the sandy bottom and is adorned with fabulous hard coral in a pristine state. The top of the reef is covered with a variety of colourful soft coral with small tropical fish everywhere. There are dense shoals of picturesque schooling fish, such as yellow snappers, fusiliers and bigeyes, and big schools of pelagic fish often hunt here. Mantas sometimes put in an appearance and may stay around for some time. When they do, Southern Reef could easily be rated a five-star dive.

The appearance of the reef is, in general, similar to Bofa Reef (No. 13). The visibility is variable and the top of the reef may be quite surgy.

17 VUMA CAVES

★★★★★

Location: To the south of the Takaungo Gap. See map.
Access: Approximately 45 minutes from Kilifi and 90 minutes by boat from Nyali Beach.
Conditions: Best dived on slack tide during the diving season. For experienced divers only because of the presence of caves and blowholes.
Average depth: 5–20m (16–65ft).
Maximum depth: 22m (71ft).
Average visibility: 10–30m (33–100ft).
Average water temperature: 25–29°C (77–84°F).
The main attractions of this excellent dive site are the stunning caves and blowholes that can be explored at a relatively shallow depth. Large groupers often hide in the caves, and marine life includes big Napoleon (or humphead) wrasse and a great variety of pelagic game fish, such as schools of barracuda, tuna, jacks (caranx) and the occasional kingfish or wahoo. Turtles are common, and many giant reef and blue-spotted rays are sighted on the bottom. White-tipped reef sharks often make an appearance, and lucky divers have enjoyed exhilarating dives with dolphins – guaranteeing a five-star experience. The fantastic variety of marine life and good visibility make this an ideal site for experienced underwater photographers; a wide-angle lens is recommended.

This reef is a must for serious divers. Because of its distance from the dive centres, a two-dive package is recommended. When there is current present it is possible to do a good drift dive on this dive site.

The nocturnal squirrelfish, shown here concealing a lionfish, spends the days in caves or beneath overhangs.

The North Coast: Regional Directory

How to Get There

Malindi

By air: There are three charter companies that operate daily flights between Mombasa and Malindi. For information contact: Eagle Aviation, tel. Mombasa (011) 434480/316055, or Malindi (0123) 21099; Prestige Air Services, tel. Mombasa (011) 221443/223073 or Malindi (0123) 20860/1; Skyways Airline, tel. Mombasa (011) 221964, or Malindi (0123) 21260.

By road: Take the B8 road north from Mombasa for a distance of 122km (76 miles). The road up to Kilifi is in very good condition, but between Kilifi and Malindi the road is badly patched. The journey takes about 1.75hr by car.

By bus: Three bus companies operate a regular daily service between Mombasa and Malindi and there are several departures each day in both directions. The journey takes about 2.5hr by bus.

By minibus: There are *matatus* (private minibuses) that make the trip in either direction throughout the day. These are very cheap but often overcrowded, noisy and not always the safest way to get around.

By taxi: There are also taxis (where passengers share the fare) between Mombasa and Malindi, which leave in the early morning.

Watamu

By air: The nearest airport is at Malindi, but there is a small airfield on the southern side of Kilifi Creek.

By road: Watamu is 104km (65 miles) north of Mombasa on the Malindi road and 18km (11 miles) south of Malindi. The buses and *matatus* travelling between Mombasa and Malindi pass through Watamu in both directions several times throughout the day, but the buses are often full and *matatus* may be a better option.

Kilifi

Kilifi is 57km (36 miles) north of Mombasa on the Malindi road.

Getting Around

Malindi

By car: There are car hire firms in Malindi near the **Blue Marlin Hotel** on the main street. Bicycles are available for rental and there are quite a few signboards advertising these.

Watamu

By bicycle: Bicycles are available for rental. Enquire at the local hotels.

Dive Facilities

Prices for dives as well as courses are on the whole cheaper than on the south coast, but the standards are very high at most bases.

Malindi

Most of the dive bases are at the hotels along Silversands Road. The longest-established scuba diving organization in this region is Lorenz and Maja Riedl's **Scuba Diving Kenya Ltd,** P O Box 160, Watamu, tel. (0122) 32099, fax. 32430, at the Driftwood Beach Club, as well as Lawfords Hotel, Government Road, and the Eden Rock Hotel, tel. (0123) 20480/2. Standards of equipment, training and dives are excellent. They offer PADI and VDST (German) courses of most levels and know the reefs very well. Highly recommended. (*See* Watamu for further details.)

Kenya Diving Centre 'The Crab' is a Franco Rosso-owned organization at the Tropical Village on the beachfront, with excellent equipment and training standards. All PADI-related courses are on offer, as well as equipment rental and daily boat dives.

Riki Diving Centre, tel. (0123) 20516/21110, offers SSI (Scuba Schools International) courses at the Dorado Cottages and the Coconut Village along Silversands Beach.

Venta Diving, tel. (0123) 21245, is based at the Jambo Village.

Watamu

Steve Curtis's **Aqua Ventures,** tel. (0122) 32008/32288, fax. 32266, is based at Ocean Sports, has extremely high standards and is popular with both residents and visitors. They offer training in PADI as well as BSAC courses and do daily dives out to the reefs. Excellent equipment is available and this base is highly recommended. Courses for beginners are also available.

Lorenz Riedl's **Scuba Diving Kenya Ltd,** (the main base) P O Box 160, Watamu, tel. (0122) 32099, fax. 32430, is located at the Blue Bay Village, P O Box 162, Watamu, tel. (0122) 32626, fax. 32422. They are Watamu's longest-established diving centre and offer excellent and friendly personal service. Their policy is to take only a limited number of experienced divers to ecologically sensitive sites. PADI, VDST and beginners courses are available. (*See* Malindi (at left) for details.)

There is also a PADI facility at the **Turtle Bay Beach Hotel,** tel. (0122) 32622 which offers daily boat dives and equipment rental.

Kilifi

Live-aboard facilities: The very competent and friendly Edmondson brothers, Stephen and John, run highly recommended live-aboard charters aboard the SY *Aristos of Kenya*, a luxury, fully equipped, 17-m (56 ft) ketch accommodating eight guests in comfortable double or twin cabins. Both brothers are qualified marine biologists and PADI instructors. They cruise and dive Pemba, Zanzibar and Mafia islands during the diving season for periods of one week or longer, and have excellent knowledge of the sites and marine life as well as very high standards of both diving safety and catering. Their fees are reasonable when compared to most live-aboard charters, and the excursions offer unbeatable value for money. For bookings and enquiries contact: **Dive Safari Kenya,** P O Box 128, Kilifi, Kenya, tel. (0125) 22222, fax. 22251. During the southeast monsoon, guests are transported to Shimoni, from where the excursions depart. Dive courses and shorter trips may be available upon request in advance.

Dive bases: The quaintly named **Pink Shark Diving Centre** is located at the Kilifi Bay Resort Hotel & Village on the beachfront, north of Kilifi Creek, P O Box 156, Kilifi, tel. (0125) 22511/22258. They offer PADI scuba diving courses.

Where to Stay

Malindi

Malindi is a popular resort, especially with Italian visitors, and the signboards found here are quite evident of the fact. The many first-class hotels of European standard here offer good cuisine and there are diving facilities at a number of them. Accommodation, coupled with scuba diving facilities, can be found at the **Eden Rock Hotel,** P O Box 350, Malindi, tel. (0123) 20480/2, fax. 20333; **Driftwood Club,** tel. (0123) 20155; the **Dorado Cottages,** P O Box 868, Malindi, tel. (0123) 31697; **Jambo Village,** P O Box 444, Malindi, tel. (0123) 21265, fax. 21048; **Tropical Village,** Casuarina Est., Malindi, tel. (0123) 20788. These are all situated along Silversands Road, which runs along the beachfront.

Camping: There are bandas and camping facilities right on the beach at the **Silver Sands Campsite Bar & Restaurant,** Silversands Road, Malindi, tel. (0123) 20336.

Watamu

There are resort hotels at Watamu that offer good accommodation. Hotels which also offer scuba diving facilities, are the **Blue Bay Village,** P O Box 162, Watamu, tel. (0122) 32626, fax. 32422; **Ocean Sports Limited,** P O Box 100, Watamu, tel. (0122) 32008/32288 (very popular with Kenya residents); and the **Turtle Bay Beach Hotel,** tel. (0122) 32622. **Hemingways,** P O Box 267, Watamu, tel. (0122) 32624/32052, fax. 32256, is popular with deep-sea fishermen and locals.

Kilifi

Probably the least touristy destination on the coast, Kilifi has less accommodation than Malindi or Watamu. A popular hotel is the **Seahorse Inn,** left of the Mombasa-Malindi road, north of Kilifi Creek, tel. (0125) 22813. Exclusive accommodation may be found at the **Mnarani Club Hotel,** on the southern side of Kilifi Creek, tel. (0125) 22178. Bookings for both these hotels have to be made through the **African Safari Club,** tel. (011) 485520/485906. Scuba diving is also offered at the **Kilifi Bay Resort Hotel & Village,** P O Box 156, Kilifi, tel. (0125) 22511/22258, on the beachfront north of the creek.

Where to Eat

Malindi

Apart from the restaurants in the hotels, some recommended eating places are **El Pescatore,** tel. (0123) 31198, which serves upmarket seafood dishes alfresco; and **I Love Pizza,** tel. (0123) 20672, in front of the fishing jetty. For lighter meals and snacks, try the **Baobab,** tel. (0123) 31699/20489 on the waterfront. **Hermann's Beer Garden and Restaurant,** tel. (0123) 20533, has cold beer, good food and atmosphere.

Watamu

In season try the lunch buffet at the **Watamu Beach Hotel,** tel. (0123) 32001/32010, or for a good evening meal, the restaurant at the **Hotel Dante,** tel. (0122) 32243.

Kilifi

The best restaurants in Kilifi are found at the **Mnarani Club Hotel,** Kilifi Road, tel. (0123) 2318/9 and the upmarket **Sahani Tamu Restaurant,** Kilifi Entrance, tel. (0123) 22046, located on the northern side of the creek. Bookings are essential in the peak season. The **Kilifi Creek Member's Club,** on the northern side of the creek, is popular at night, and the Mnarani Club Hotel often has a floor show and a band.

Regional Highlights

Malindi

The history of Malindi stretches as far back as the 12th century. As can be expected, there are a number of historical sites to visit. These include the Vasco Da Gama monument – a limestone cross originally erected in 1541 at the site of the Sheikh of Malindi's palace and later re-erected at Vasco da Gama Point – the remains of the Portuguese church and the mosque. There are also some venerable pillar tombs, including that of Sheihk Hassan.

The main attractions of Malindi, however are the watersports, more particularly the Malindi National Marine Park and the excellent deep-sea fishing opportunities. For night-time revellers there are a few popular clubs and an international casino.

Watamu

The famous ruins at **Gedi National Monument,** about 4km (2.5 miles) before Watamu, date back to the 13th century and are well worth a visit when staying in Watamu or Malindi. Located in the Arabuko-Sokoke Forest – Kenya's largest remaining stand of indigenous coastal forest – the walled town includes the excavated remains of the Palace, Great Mosque, tombs and 14 houses. As no mention of it was ever made by the Portuguese when they occupied Malindi, it is thought that it was completely overlooked by them, although it lies a mere 15km (9 miles) to the south of Malindi. The ruins are home to the golden-rumped elephant shrew (a cat-sized mammal that resembles a long-nosed mouse); the red-capped robin chat, which consorts with the shrew; and the Zanzibar duiker. Ghost stories abound and the atmosphere towards late afternoon at the ruins is very conducive to this. Other highlights of the area are of course the excellent diving and deep-sea fishing opportunities.

Kilifi

With its wide variety of watersports and scenic beauty, Kilifi Creek is the main attraction of the town. The beaches are, unfortunately, only accessible through private property and permission must obviously be obtained or a house must be rented. There is a cashew factory to the north of the town where these delicious nuts are available at the cheapest prices in Kenya.

Emergency Measures

The nearest **recompression facilities** are available at the Kenya Navy's base in Mombasa; contact the Staff Officer or Duty Officer at tel. (011) 45 1201 ext. 3308 (24-hour standby availability).

The nearest **hospitals** are the Malindi District Hospital, tel. (0123) 20490; and the Kilifi District Hospital, tel. (0123) 2323. There is no hospital at Watamu.

The international **emergency radio channel** is **#16.**

MOMBASA AND ENVIRONS

When visiting Mombasa – a bustling city with the largest natural deepwater port on the east coast of Africa – it is easy to forget that one is actually on a coral island. Taking the ever-crowded Likoni Ferry to the south is bound to remind one of this. The fact that Mombasa is surrounded by water and is situated only 620km (345 nautical miles) south of the equator accounts for its high humidity and the sweltering heat that greets passengers like a clammy cloth as they step off air-conditioned aircraft. Average humidity is in the high 80s and the temperature stays around the 28°C (82°F) mark, dropping to a more bearable but still humid 24°C (70°F) at night, and reaching a daytime high of 32°C (90°F) in March.

Mombasa is the gateway to the Kenyan coast, and thousands of tourists disembark at Moi International Airport during the peak season. There is a definite lull during the rainy season, which coincides with the beginning of the European summer, and many hotels close during this time. The rainy season on the coast lasts for up to three months. The driest months are January, February and March.

During the Portuguese occupation, Mombasa was known as the 'Island of War'. Fort Jesus, built by the Portuguese in 1593, is one of the oldest buildings on the coast and a popular tourist attraction. The Old Town of Mombasa, with its predominantly Arabic architecture, is influenced by its many Muslim inhabitants, who account for almost 40 per cent of the population. Another place of interest is the Old Harbour, from where dhows sail to Lamu, Pemba, Zanzibar and Dar es Salaam, and which houses the Old Customs House and Wharf. The modern city centre along Moi Avenue displays African curios and mementos.

There are many taxis available to take visitors to any destination in the city or along the coast, but it is prudent to agree on a fee beforehand. It is not wise to make an ostentatious display of wealth, and after dark, the section of Mombasa between the elephant tusks on Moi Avenue and the Mission to Seamen should be avoided.

Left: *Above the busy and picturesque dhow harbour, a minaret pierces the skyline of Mombasa's Old Town.*
Above: *Colourful wrasse live in shallow reef waters, where they prey on the eggs of other fish.*

MOMBASA
Mtwapa Creek
Shimo La Tewa
Dolphin
1 Mtwapa Creek
Plaza Beach
Intercontinental
2 Serena Drop
Serena Beach
3 Bamburi Buoys
Neptune
Severin Sea Lodge
Plaza Beach
Mombasa Marine N.P.
Kenya Beach
Fontana
Bamburi Beach
4 Whitesand Coral Garden
Travellers Beach
Whitesands
Piccolo
Reef
Nyali Beach
Bahari
Nyali
Mombasa Marine Nat.Res.
Tudor Creek
Port Tudor
E949
E982
Miritini
Changamwe
MOMBASA INTERNATIONAL AIRPORT
C110
Mombasa
Port Reitz
Kilindini Harbour
Mkunguni
Lotus
Nyali Beach
5-9
10 Mashimo
11 Turning Buoy Reef
12 Lucky Chance
Mteza Creek
Likoni
Shelley Beach
13 Likoni Reef
C109
Bombo Creek
Shelley Beach
14 The Wall (Part 1)
Savannah Cottages
16
17 Birthday Reef
Mehali ya Papa 18
15 The Wall (Part 2)
Shelley Corner
Waa
Ngombeni
Manjera
Tiwi
Ukunda
Diani Beach
E965
N
0 5 km
0 3 miles
0 1 km
0 0.5 miles
Port Reitz
Kwamwanamweupe Island
Makupa Causeway
Port Tudor
Shimanzi
Makande
Makupa
Tom Mboya
Manyimbo
Kilindini Harbour
Shimanzi
Mwangeka
Lumumba
Swaleh
Nguru
Kwakiziwi
Mombasa Polytechnic
Kilindini
Ziwani
Ronald Ngala
Ras Makamaiwe
Rassini
Makupa Market
Water Sports Club
Liwatoni
Kinyozi
Sidiriya
Narok
Mozambique
Kenya Ports And Ferry Services
Mombasa
Machakos
Baringo
Gatundu
Jomo Kenyatta
Tononoka
Tom Mboya
New Nyali Bridge
MIRAMAR
SAFARI
Ras Kisauni
Kisauni
Coast General
Mvumoni
Mwembe Tayari
Kikowani
Lady Grigg
Ras Kiberamini
Archbishop Makarios
Moi
Haile Selassie
TAJ
Abdel Nasser
Old Nyali Bridge (Closed)
OUTRIGGER
NEW CARLTON
Mzizima
Yacht Club
HERMES
Jain Temple
Mombasa Harbour
Ras Likoni
NEW CASTLE
Little Theatre Club
Digo
HYDRO
MANOR
CENTRAL
Bohra Mosque
Nyali
Mbaraki
NEW PALM TREE
Nkrumah
Fish Market
Mbaraki Pillar
Nyerere
Dedan Kimathi
Cinema
Krapf Memorial
Aga Khan
LOTUS
Vanga
Kaunda
Town Hall
Fort Jesus Museum
Ferry to Shelley Beach
Oceanic
Bokole
Kaunda
SUNSET LODGE
5 Koto Menang Wreck
Mzimle
Golf Course
Mwamba
Lighthouse
Kizingo
FOUR SEASONS
Mama Ngina
Nyali 6
Second Reef
Ras Mzimle
Fort St. Joseph
7
MV Globestar 8
Nyali First Reef
Nyali Coral Garden 9

Mombasa has a grand variety of eating places that cater for every taste. These range from superb European cuisine, to simple but mouth-watering Swahili dishes.

As can be expected from such a popular tourist gateway, accommodation is plentiful and available in and around the city. Hotels range from the ultra-luxurious (which are mainly clustered on the coast north of Mombasa) to the more simple hotels found in the city centre, although a number of budget hotels and guest houses do exist.

The beaches to the north of Mombasa are within easy reach, and the south coast beaches are only some 20km (12 miles) from the Likoni Ferry crossing. Access to the north and the airport is by way of causeways.

DIVING CONDITIONS:

The area to the north of Mombasa was proclaimed a marine national park and reserve in 1968, and there are some excellent four- and even five-star dive sites here. It is not recommended that dives be made in the entrance to the Mombasa harbour, as this stretch of water is frequented by Zambezi sharks that are attracted by the waste dumped off ships. The indiscriminate eating habits of the sharks have severely injured divers in the past.

During the long rains, visibility underwater is hampered by the inflow of silt-bearing inland water from the Mtwapa and Nyali creeks. The fringing reefs along this section of the Kenyan coast are located approximately 800–1 000m (0.5–1.6 miles) offshore, and therefore all dives are done from boats. Most of the popular dive sites are outside of the fringing reef and are accessible through the *mlangos* ('doors', or natural openings) in the reef. Most of the hotels along the coast north of Mombasa offer scuba diving facilities, where full diving gear is available for organized dives.

The imposing ramparts of Fort Jesus controlled the approaches to Mombasa during the Portuguese occupation.

1 MTWAPA CREEK

★★★★

Location: On the southern side of Mtwapa Creek. The reef is buoyed. See map.
Access: A 10-minute boat ride from Nyali Beach.
Conditions: Best dived on slack after an incoming tide during the diving season. Because of the depth, only recommended for divers of intermediate to expert level.
Average depth: 15–20m (50–65ft).
Maximum depth: 25m (80ft).
Average visibility 10–20m (33–65ft).
Water temperature: 25–29°C (77–84°F).
The reef forms a drop-off with several small overhangs. The coral itself is not too spectacular, but the main attraction of this reef is the presence of a large population of pelagic game fish. These include king mackerel, tuna and barracuda that swim in from the open sea to feed, and there is always a good chance of seeing schools of them during a dive. A number of big moray eels and large groupers can also be seen, and the combination of these makes for an exciting and interesting midwater dive.

2 SERENA DROP

★★★

Location: A little to the south of Mtwapa Creek (No. 1). The reef is buoyed. See map.
Access: A 10-minute boat ride from Nyali Beach.
Conditions: Best dived on slack after an incoming tide during the diving season. Because of the depth, it is recommended for divers of intermediate to expert level.
Average depth: 15–20m (50–65ft).
Maximum depth: 25m (80ft).
Average visibility: 10–20m (33–65ft).
Water temperature: 25–29°C (77–84°F).
The drop-off here has some good coral formations. Dense shoals of yellow snappers congregate around the large coral heads that are found here. The snappers are often joined by pelagic fish including tuna, jacks, king mackerel and barracuda.

3 BAMBURI BUOYS

★★★

Location: To the south of Serena Drop (No. 2). The reef is buoyed. See map.
Access: A 5-minute boat ride from Nyali Beach.
Conditions: Best dived on an incoming tide during the diving season.
Average depth: 10–18m (33–60ft).
Maximum depth: 22m (80ft).
Average visibility: 10–20m (33–65ft).
Water temperature: 25–29°C(77–84°F).
This reef stretches for a considerable distance and there are five dive sites to choose from. The reef forms a small drop-off, and the large coral heads attract dense clouds of snappers and other brightly coloured tropicals. Coupled with the proximity of Bamburi Buoys to Nyali Beach, the many fish to be seen here make the site a favourite excursion with dive centres on the north coast.

A soldierfish peeps out from his coral lair while tiny damselfish known as sea guppies swim past.

The hawksbill turtle has a distinctive scaled shell.

4 WHITESAND CORAL GARDEN

★★

Location: Opposite the Plaza Beach Hotel. The reef is not buoyed. See map.
Access: A 5-minute boat ride from Nyali Beach.
Conditions: Calm conditions prevail during the diving season as it is well protected by the fringing reef.
Average depth: 4–6m (13–20ft).
Maximum depth: 8m (25ft).
Average visibility: 5–15m (16–50ft).
Water temperature: 27–30°C (80–86°F).

This reef is mainly used as a training site for first open-water dives because of the shallow maximum depth and its sheltered position. There are lots of brightly coloured tropicals on the few coral patches on the sandy bottom, but is only recommended for experienced divers or when no other sites are can be dived.

5 *KOTO MENANG* WRECK

★★

Location: Opposite Ras Iwatine. See map.
Access: A 10-minute boat ride from Nyali Beach.
Conditions: Best dived on slack after an incoming tide during the diving season.
Average depth: 15–20m (50–65ft).
Maximum depth: 25m (80ft).
Average visibility: 10–20m (33–65ft).
Water temperature: 25–29°C (77–84°F).

This dive site is the wreck of a small cargo vessel that went down in the mid-1970s. Schools of large pelagic fish come in to feed around the wreck. Other typical marine life includes sea turtles and moray eels, which are regularly seen here.

6 NYALI SECOND REEF

★★★

Location: To the south of the *Koto Menang* wreck (No. 5). See map.
Access: A 15-minute boat ride from Nyali Beach.
Conditions: Best dived on slack after an incoming tide during the diving season.
Average depth: 15–20m (50–65ft).
Maximum depth: 18–25m (80ft).
Average visibility: 10–20m (33–65ft).
Water temperature: 25–29°C (77–84°F).

This long stretch of reef starts some 15m (50ft) below the surface, and consists of two parts: the first dive site features predatory fish that regularly come in to feed off the thousands of small tropical fish around the large coral heads (unicornfish and soldierfish are especially plentiful). Turtles are also often seen here. The second dive site is to the north and the coral formations here are dense and unspoilt, with numerous colourful tropicals. The maximum depth on this section is 18m (60ft), making it an easy, relaxed dive suitable for all levels of divers.

7 NYALI FIRST REEF

★★

Location: Farther to the south of Nyali Second Reef (No. 6). See map.
Access: A 10-minute boat ride from Nyali Beach.
Conditions: Best dived on slack after an incoming tide during the diving season.
Average depth: 15–20m (50–65ft).
Maximum depth: 25m (80ft).
Average visibility: 10–20m (33–65ft).
Water temperature: 25–29°C (77–84°F).

Large shoals of small tropical fish, including snappers, fusiliers, emperor angelfish and cardinal fish, hover around this reef. The occasional turtle may be seen here, and there are many moray eels that hide among the coral formations. The reef forms a small drop-off, with large coral heads and some overhangs.

8 THE MV *GLOBESTAR*

★★★

Location: North of Ras Mkungombe. See map.
Access: A 15-minute boat ride from Nyali Beach.
Conditions: Best dived on slack after an incoming tide during the diving season.
Average depth: 10m (33ft).
Maximum depth: 12m (40ft).
Average visibility: 10–20m (33–65ft).

Water temperature: 25–29°C (77–84°F).
The small freighter MV *Globestar* was carrying a cargo of grain when it ran aground in 1976 in shallow water. The wreck rests upright on the sandy bottom and is a favourite hunting place for big schools of pelagic game fish, including tuna, king mackerel, wahoo and jacks (caranx). The hull is in a good state of preservation, with some coral growth, and it is a popular wreck dive. It is also used for the training of advanced diving courses, but because of its shallow depth is suitable for all levels of divers. The size of the wreck allows divers to circumnavigate it twice during the course of a normal dive.

9 NYALI CORAL GARDEN

★★★

Location: Inside the fringing reef north of Ras Mkungombe. See map.
Access: A 15-minute boat ride from Nyali Beach.
Conditions: Generally calm and protected by the fringing coral reef. Best dived on an incoming tide during the diving season.
Average depth: 4–6m (13–20ft).
Maximum depth: 8m (25ft).
Average visibility: 5–15m (16–50ft).
Water temperature: 27–30°C (80–86°F).
This dive site is similar in appearance and conditions to Whitesand Coral Garden (No. 4), but there are more small tropical fish to see which accounts for the higher rating. Ideal for a training dive, and for when conditions on other sites preclude diving.

10 MASHIMO

★★

Location: Slightly to the north of Ras Mkungombe. See map.
Access: A 15-minute boat ride from Nyali Beach.
Conditions: Best dived on an incoming tide during the diving season.
Average depth: 10–18m (33–60ft).
Maximum depth: 20m (65ft).
Average visibility: 10–20m (33–65ft).
Water temperature: 25–29°C (77–84°F).
A peculiarly shaped reef, where the coral forms a circular wall on the sandy bottom and gives the appearance of an extinct underwater volcano. Mashimo also offers a protected haven for numerous fish of differing sizes and varieties, including most of the tropical fish that frequent East African coral reefs.

11 TURNING BUOY REEF

★★★

Location: In the mouth of the entrance to Mombasa port. See map.
Access: A 20-minute boat ride from Nyali Beach.
Conditions: Best dived on slack after an incoming tide during the diving season.
Average depth: 14–20m (47–65ft).
Maximum depth: 23m (75ft).

The plant-like forms of sarcophyton coral are found in shallow water, and colonies can cover large areas of reef.

Butterflyfish live in the shallows around the reefs.

Average visibility: 10–20m (33–65ft).
Water temperature: 25–29°C (77–84°F)
Many interesting caves and overhangs are found here. Big schools of barracuda also often make an appearance and they are joined by other big pelagic game fish.

12 LUCKY CHANCE

★★★★

Location: To the east of Ras Mwa Kisenge. See map.
Access: A 20-minute boat ride from Nyali Beach.
Conditions: Best dived on slack after an incoming tide during the diving season.
Average depth: 20–30m (65–100ft).
Maximum depth: 40m (130ft).
Average visibility: 10–30m (33–100ft).
Water temperature: 25–29°C (77–84°F).
At Lucky Chance, an impressive drop-off with dense shelf and plate coral starts at a depth of 22m (71ft) and falls off to a depth of 40m (130ft). The good depth of the reef attracts larger predatory fish from the deep sea, such as barracuda, king mackerel, tuna and wahoo. The reef is also home to schools of yellow and white snappers and sea turtles.

13 LIKONI REEF

★★★

Location: Immediately to the south of the Likoni Creek. See map.
Access: A 20-minute boat ride from Nyali Beach.
Conditions: Best dived on slack after an incoming tide during the diving season.
Average depth: 5–15m (16–50ft).
Maximum depth: 18m (60ft).
Average visibility: 10–20m (33–65ft).
Water temperature: 25–29°C (77–84°F).
The coral on this reef is spectacular, especially in the shallower depths, and it is not uncommon for divers to spend most of the dive at around 5m (16ft) where the staghorn coral banks are prolific.

This particular variety of coral provides a home to thousands of tiny, beautiful damselfish that hide among the protective branches. The damselfish form a kaleidoscope of darting colour.

14 THE WALL (PART 1)

★★★★

Location: Southeast of the Likoni Creek entrance. See map.
Access: A 25-minute boat ride from Nyali Beach.
Conditions: Best dived on slack after an incoming tide during the diving season. There is often a strong current.
Average depth: 15–25m (50–80ft).
Maximum depth: 30m (100ft).
Average visibility: 10–30m (33–100ft).
Water temperature: 25–29°C (77–84°F).
The reef forms a wall that drops sheer from 12m (40ft) to a maximum depth of 30m (100ft) and is richly adorned with soft corals.

Schools of large pelagic game fish and groupers are common here, and an enormous shoal of resident soldierfish seen against the backdrop of the wall guarantees a spectacular dive.

15 THE WALL (PART 2)

★★★★

Location: A little farther out to the east of dive No. 14. See map.
Access: A 25-minute boat ride from Nyali Beach.
Conditions: Best dived on an incoming tide during the diving season.
Average depth: 15–30m (50–100ft).
Maximum depth: 40m (130ft).
Average visibility: 10–30m (33–100ft).
Water temperature: 25–29°C (77–84°F).
This section of the reef also forms a sheer wall that drops from a relatively shallow depth of 10m (33ft) to a maximum depth of 40m (130ft).

The reef consists almost entirely of solid banks of shelf coral which form a favourite hiding place for lobsters. There is also a large resident Napoleon wrasse that adds to the splendour of this dive site.

16 SHELLEY CORNER

★★★

Location: Directly opposite the Shelley Beach Hotel, south of Likoni. See map.
Access: A 20-minute boat ride from Nyali Beach.
Conditions: Best dived on an incoming tide during the diving season.
Average depth: 15–20m (50–65ft).
Maximum depth: 23m (75ft).
Average visibility: 10–30m (33–100ft).
Water temperature: 25–29°C (77–84°F).

This beautiful and pristine reef is densely covered in hard coral. A number of moray eels hide among the coral growths and sea turtles often put in an appearance. Large shoals of fish abound here. In general, the shape of the reef at Shelley Corner is quite similar to that of the Bamburi Buoys (No. 3).

17 BIRTHDAY REEF

★★★★★

Location: A long distance out to the southeast of the Likoni Creek entrance. Only a few divers know how to locate it. The ones who are willing to take visiting divers there are mentioned in the Regional Directory on the opposite page. See map.
Access: A 25-minute boat ride from Nyali Beach.
Conditions: Best dived on slack during the diving season as strong currents may be present. This factor, coupled with the depth, makes it a site that is exclusively suited to experienced divers.
Average depth: 15–30m (50–100ft).
Maximum depth: 40m (130ft).
Average visibility: 10–30m (33–100ft).
Water temperature: 25–29°C (77–84°F).

Birthday Reef's distinctive name stems from its discovery by the well-known Mombasa diver Conway Plough, who came upon the site on his birthday. (Conway was later badly injured by a Zambezi shark while working on a mooring in the Mombasa port area.) This is one of the most spectacular reefs on the Kenyan coast when conditions are perfect.

Birthday Reef starts at a depth of 27m (86ft) and descends at a steep angle to beyond 50m (165ft). At its narrowest point the reef extends only 2m (6ft) in width, and giant groupers are present in numbers that may exceed a hundred.

Large leopard moray eels, sea turtles and schools of big pelagic game fish are common. There are enormous and extremely dense shoals of red and grey snappers, surgeonfish and even sardines, and white-tipped reef sharks often come into the area to investigate the abundance of food.

18 MEHALI YA PAPA

★★★★

Location: South of Shelley Beach. See map.
Access: A 25-minute boat ride from Nyali Beach.
Conditions: Best dived on an incoming slack tide during the diving season.
Average depth: 15–20m (50–65ft).
Maximum depth: 23m (75ft).
Average visibility: 10–20m (33–65ft).
Water temperature: 25–29°C (77–84°F).

Mehali Ya Papa is in the shape of a small, submerged island, and looks like a tiny oasis in a sandy desert.

The fish life is prolific and several species of varying sizes are found here in large shoals, including barracuda and other game fish. White-tipped reef sharks (*Papa* is the Swahili word for shark) are often encountered during dives on this reef, but they are wary of approaching divers and never present any problems.

The sea cucumber uses its tentacles to gather food.

How to Get There

By air:
Mombasa's international airport is served by international and charter airlines from Europe, South Africa and neighbouring countries. Air Tanzania flies between Dar es Salaam and Mombasa via Zanzibar three times a week in either direction, but schedules and times may change on short notice. Contact: **Air Tanzania,** Corporation ATC House, Ohio Street, Dar es Salaam, tel. (011) 46643/44111.

By road or bus:
From Nairobi: Take the A109 road southeast to Mombasa (487km; 304 miles). The road is often in poor condition and the journey may take more than 7hr by car. It is recommended that driving be done in daylight. There are several daily bus departures to and from Mombasa. Buses leave in the early morning and late evening, and take about 8hr (with meal break). Companies include Coast, Akamba, Mawingo, Goldline and Malaika; offices can be found along Jomo Kenyatta Avenue.
From Dar es Salaam: The A14, the main road to Tanga, crosses the border at Lunga Lunga; the journey takes about 10hr by car and 20hr by bus.The Cat Bus Company departs from Mombasa to Dar es Salaam via Tanga on Mondays, Wednesdays and Fridays at 16:00.

By train:
From Nairobi: The route is well served by rail. Trains between Mombasa and Nairobi in either direction depart at 17:00 and 19:00 hours to arrive at 08:00 and 8:30, respectively. Railway station tel. (011) 312220.

By sea:
From Dar es Salaam or Tanga: There are weekly ferry services between Dar es Salaam and Mombasa via Zanzibar. Passage may be obtained on a dhow. Enquiries at the Dhow Harbour in Dar es Salaam or the Old Port in Mombasa.

Dive Facilities

There are a number of independent dive operators who have diving concessions and dive bases at the tourist hotels along the coast. All relevant dive facilities are offered by the following:

Bruce Phillips of **Buccaneer Diving,** P O Box 10394, Mombasa, tel. (011) 485163, fax. 471763, offers NAUI and PADI training facilities and has excellent experience of the north coast. Some sites are exclusively dived by Buccaneer and daily boat trips are done to the various sites. Standards are high and all equipment is available.

One Earth Safaris, P O Box 82234, Mombasa, tel. (011) 471771, fax. 471349. A PADI facility that offers courses (German and English), day charters and gear rental. Excursions to Pemba Island are arranged by them and may be combined with a land safari. Dive base at the Reef Hotel. Pemba excursions highly recommended. One Earth now has a diving camp at the northern end of Pemba Island.

Barakuda Diving Schools, P O Box 82169, Mombasa; head office at the Severin Sea Lodge, tel. (011) 485001, and operate from several other hotels.

Tropical Diving, tel. (011) 471819, fax. 485900, is run by Mohammed Mawji from the Bamburi Beach Hotel.

Where to Stay

Dialling code (011)
Five-star: **Nyali Beach Hotel,** P O Box 90414, tel. 471567/8; **Intercontinental Hotel,** P O Box 83492, tel. 485811; **Serena Beach Hotel,** P O Box 90352, tel. 485721; **The New Outrigger Hotel,** P O Box 82345, tel. 220822/3.
Four-star: **Whitesands Hotel,** P O Box 90173, tel. 485926; **Reef Hotel,** P O Box 82234, tel. 471771; **Plaza Beach Hotel,** P O Box 88299, tel. 485321.
Three-star: **Neptune Beach Hotel,** P O Box 83125, tel. 485701; **Bamburi Beach Hotel,** P O Box 83966, tel. 485611; **The Manor Hotel,** P O Box 84851, tel. 314643/7; **Manson Hotel,** P O Box 83565, tel. 222356.

Cheaper lodgings are available at the **Cosy Guest House,** Haile Selassie Road, P O Box 83011, tel. 313064.

Where to Eat

Apart from restaurants at the hotels, some exceptional eating places include the **Tamarind Restaurant,** Silos Road, tel. (011) 471729/47, which offers superb seafood and an excellent setting and atmosphere at European prices; **La Terrazza Restaurant** (overlooking Nyali Creek), Mbuyuni Road, tel. (011) 312831/315910, is less pricey but offers excellent cuisine in a nice atmosphere, and a casino. For good, fast-food, the **Blue Room** in Haile Selassie Road, tel. (011) 223499; the **Hard Rock Cafe** in Nkrumah Road, tel. (011) 222221, for good food and music. A popular venue for snacks and lunches, as well as good cakes and coffees, is the **Capri** in Ambalal House.

Regional Highlights

The massive Portuguese bastion, **Fort Jesus,** completed in 1593, is one of the most popular attractions in Mombasa. Its walls stand 15m (50ft) in height. The fort was declared a national monument in 1960. The museum on the eastern side of the fort conveys a good idea of Swahili culture and heritage.

Mombasa's **Old Town** starts next to Fort Jesus. With its gold-topped dome and carved silver doors, the **Jain Temple** in Langoni Road is worth a visit. The dhow harbour now only has a few vessels at a time. Mombasa's floating market is popular with visitors. **Biashara Street** is the place to go when shopping for fabrics and colourful *khangas*. The twice-daily **Tamarind Dhow** trip, which includes a seafood dinner or lunch, is a very popular excursion, especially on moonlit evenings.

The **tourist office** is located at the tusks on Moi Avenue, tel. (011) 311231.

Emergency Measures

Recompression facilities are located at the Kenya Navy's base in Mombasa. Contact the Staff Officer or Duty Officer at tel. (011) 451201, ext. 3308 (24-hour standby availability).

The main **hospitals** in Mombasa are the Aga Khan Hospital, Vanga Road, tel. (011) 312953, and the Coast Provincial General Hospital, Kisauni Road, tel. (011) 24111.

Emergency services: tel. **999.**

The international **emergency radio channel** is **#16.**

THE SOUTH COAST

Strung together by long, brilliant-white, sandy beaches, interspersed with tall palms and majestic baobab trees, the resorts along the Kenyan coast south of Mombasa to Shimoni are some of the most magnificent on the East African seaboard.

Stretching from the Likoni Ferry, just off the island of Mombasa, and including Tiwi Beach, Chale Island, Shimoni, the Mpunguti Islands and Kisite Island, down to the Tanzanian border, the south coast offers some of the most popular, beautiful and accessible dive sites in Kenya. Most of the coastal region features abundant public transport, functional infrastructure and good shopping, recreation and entertainment facilities.

Diving Conditions

The fringing coral reef is located offshore at a distance of only some 600m (0.75 mile) out to sea. It is very much intact in this area and rises right to the surface, often emerging during low tides. This means that the beaches are well protected from wave erosion and the water between the reef and the shore is relatively shallow, very clear and safe for swimming and all other watersports.

All scuba dives are done from boats and the most popular and well known sites are buoyed to protect the reef from damage. Dives are generally done under the guidance of experienced instructors who orientate new divers to the reefs. During the peak holiday seasons in December and January, as well as around Easter, the sites can become quite crowded with dive boats and their passengers.

There are few rivers running into the sea along this section of the coast, and only very heavy rains will affect visibility in a few places such as off the mouth of the Tiwi River. Lots of plankton in the water can, however, reduce visibility even when surface conditions are perfect. The best visibility is almost always experienced on an incoming tide.

Left: *Palm trees shade the inviting sands of Tiwi Beach along Kenya's south coast.*
Above: *The nosestripe anemonefish lives in symbiosis with a large anemone.*

SOUTH COAST
KENYA
Kwale
Shimba Hills National Reserve
Shimba Hills Lodge
Mkongani
Majimboni
Njele
Lukore
Shimba Hills
Mwanayamala
Kikoneni
Mafisini
Msambweni
Mrima
Ramisi
Majoreni
Kisiwani Island
Ngowa Island
Mkokoni Island
Vanga
Funzi Island
Funzi Bay
Funzi
Kisimachande
Gazi
Gazi Bay
Tiwi
Ukunda
Muhaka Mbavu
Mwabungu
Diani Beach
Demweni
Mwachema
Mtawa
Mkurunuji
Mkanda
Lovu
Mkundi
Mwena
C106
C108
A 14
E965
1 The Waa Wreck
El Caprichio
Maweni Cottages
Tiwi Beach
Tiwi Villas
Coral Cove
Tiwi Sea Castles
2 Tiwi Reef
3 Bilango Reef
Indian Ocean Beach
Southern Palms
Sheraton Golden
Diani Reef
Warrandale
4 Kongo Reef
Trade Winds
Two Fishes
Africana Sea
Jadini Beach
Nomao Beach
Safari Beach
Paradise Ocean
5 Galu Reef
6 Kinondo Reef
7 Mavovo
Chale Reef
8 Snorkelling Reefs
Chale Point
Chale Island
9 Chale Reef
Black Marlin
Beachcomber
Seascapes Villas
10 Msambweni Reefs
Msambweni Reef
Pemba Channel Fishing Club
Shimoni
Shimoni Reef
Wasini Channel
Wasini Island
SEE PAGE 75
11-19
Kisite-Mpunguti Marine National Park
INDIAN OCEAN
N
0 10 km
0 5 miles
C106
El Caprichio
Tiwi Reef 2
Tiwi Beach
Bilango Reef 3
4 Kongo Reef
Tiwi
Tiwi River
Ukunda
Warrandale
Diani Beach
E965
Robinson's Club Baobab
Muhaka Mbavu
Mwabungu
5 Galu Reef
A 14
Neptune Paradise
Galu Beach
7 Mavovo
6 Kinondo Reef
Chale Reef
Gazi Bay

Tiwi Beach

This is the first beach south of Mombasa where scuba diving facilities are offered and a range of comfortable accommodation is readily available. Tiwi is also popular with overland travellers, and the atmosphere here is quite different to the much more tourist-oriented Diani Beach to the south. Tiwi offers one of the only diveable wrecks on the south coast and Tiwi Reef (No. 2) is one of the region's best dive sites.

1 THE WAA WRECK

★★★

Location: To the northeast of Tiwi River Mouth. See map.
Access: Ten minutes by dive boat from Tiwi or 35 minutes from Diani Beach.
Conditions: Best dived on an incoming tide during the diving season as the inflow of river water, as a result of heavy rains, may disturb visibility.
Average depth: 20–24m (65–79ft).
Maximum depth: 24m (79ft). Buoyed with the bottom at 22–25m (73–80ft) depending on the tide.
Average visibility 10–20m (33–65ft).
Average water temperature: 25–29°C (77–84°F).
The actual name of this wreck is not known, and so it has been named after the small coastal village of Waa, which is situated a few kilometres before reaching Tiwi from the north. How long it has lain at the bottom of the sea is also unknown, but it is believed to have sunk quite recently because there is such a small amount of marine flora growing on it. As it is the only easily accessible wreck in the area, it is a popular site for divers who are keen to include a wreck dive, and it is also used for advanced training courses. The wreck lies upside down in an east–west direction, which is not altogether the most interesting position, but there are nevertheless some big groupers that can be seen with the aid of an underwater light on the southern side. It is a small wreck of around 30m (100ft) in length and can be easily circumnavigated a few times during the course of a single dive. There is a fair amount of marine life on and around the wreckage and at the bottom of the mooring, which is anchored to some engine parts. There is a family of lionfish and some large and unwary slatey sweetlips (*Diagramma pictum*) which can be approached very closely. Together with the remains of the engine, they make quite interesting photographic subjects. Stingrays are often seen in the vicinity and small and colourful fish are plentiful. Some big pelagic game fish often make an appearance, on the lookout for food around the wreck, and tuna and barracuda in particular are common.

The anchor may be seen when swimming to the south of the wreck and there is always some fish life in the vicinity. For advanced and adventurous divers the wreck makes for an atmospheric and eerie dive but because of the depth this should only be attempted by experienced divers, who can organize this with Tiwi Scuba Divers. The upside-down hull is fairly smooth, so the wreck is not very photogenic, but there are some colourful soft coral growths which may be good for macrophotography. It is not one of the most exciting wrecks to dive on, but the lack of other wrecks in the area makes it worth a visit.

The cleaner shrimp removes parasites from fish.

2 TIWI REEF

★★★★

Location: Opposite the Tiwi River mouth, where the reef forms a tongue jutting out to the north. See map.
Access: By dive boat from Tiwi or Diani Beach. From Diani it takes approximately 30 minutes to reach the reef.
Conditions: Not to be attempted during the rainy season or after periods of heavy rainfall, as visibility will be severely reduced by the resultant outflow of the Tiwi River. The top of the reef can be surgy when large swells are running, but generally calm at depth. Best dived on an incoming tide.
Average depth: 12–15m (40–50ft); top of the reef is at a depth of 5m (16ft).
Maximum depth: 22m (71ft). Buoys at 11m (36ft) and 13m (43ft).
Average visibility: 15m (50ft); up to 40m (131ft) on very good days.
Average water temperature: 27°C (80°F).
When diving conditions are good, Tiwi Reef is one of the better dive sites on the East African coast. The top of the reef starts at about 5m (15ft) and the reef wall forms a shallow drop-off to around 18m (60ft), after which it levels out to a sandy bottom. The reef runs parallel to the coast for quite some distance and is buoyed roughly in the middle at a depth of 11m (36ft). It then swings away to the east to form the northern tip; the second buoy is fixed here at a depth of 13m (43ft). The coral growths on the reef form crags, pinnacles, swim-throughs and gullies

Gorgonian fan, soft coral and sponges.

and the wall is covered with a variety of splendid hard and soft coral formations. Literally every nook and cranny is crammed with some form of marine life and this makes every dive an interesting one – even on days when visibility is poor. Apart from a multitude of general marine life of the area, huge shoals of scissor-tailed fusiliers (*Caesio caerulaureus*) often form a solid fish ceiling. Lionfish and scorpionfish are plentiful, together with sizeable moray eels, and the elusive green mantis shrimp (*Odontodactylus scyllaris*) is often found here. Whale sharks cruise past and manta rays have been seen here on occasion. A particularly interesting feature of Tiwi Reef is the white-spotted garden eels (*Gorgasia maculatus*) that peep out from the sandy bottom, only to vanish comically as a diver approaches. They blend in well with their environment, but can be seen on the sand to the northwest of the southern buoy. The reef lends itself to excellent photo opportunities. Wide-angle lenses are best for clear days, but macro- or close-up photography can be as rewarding on dives with poor visibility. An underwater light will add colour and illuminate the many small caves and overhangs. Tiwi Reef is also a good site for night dives, where coral formations are dramatic, and the reef teems with marine life.

3 BILANGO REEF

★★

Location: To the southwest of Tiwi Reef. See map.
Conditions: Usually dived on when visibility or conditions at Tiwi do not allow diving. As it is closer to shore, surge can be heavy when big swells are running.
Access: Approximately 25 minutes by dive boat from Diani Beach.
Average depth: Around 20m (65ft).
Maximum depth: 24m (77ft).
Buoys: Two: at 10m (33ft) and 12m (40ft).
Average visibility: 15m (50ft).
Average water temperature: 27°C (80°F).

The reef is partly named after Billy Mwanza, the first black Kenyan PADI instructor. It is not as well-known as most of the other popular sites, but offers rewarding diving when conditions are good (mainly October to April). Do not attempt after rains, when visibility is poor.

The reef slopes gently from the shallowest depth of 10m (33ft) to a maximum of 24m (77ft) with good, unspoilt coral formations of great variety. Fish abound, and big sea turtles and moray eels are frequently seen.

4 KONGO REEF

★★

Location: Opposite the old Kongo Mosque south of the Tiwi River mouth. See map.
Conditions: Generally calm during the diving season.
Access: Approximately 20 minutes by dive boat from Diani Beach.
Average depth: Around 12–15m (40–50ft).
Maximum depth: 18m (60ft). Not buoyed.
Average visibility: 15m (50ft).
Average water temperature: 27°C (80°F).

Kongo Reef, which is flat and slopes gently to the seaward side, is covered with small coral growths, interspersed with some larger coral heads.

Marine life consists mainly of the small, tropical varieties, with a number of lionfish hiding under the coral ledges. There are quite a few stingrays to be seen and turtles have also been sighted here.

Diani Beach

Diani Beach has been called the 'Miami Strip' of Kenya and the lovely, long, white beaches are bordered by tightly packed tourist hotels of international standard. Most of Diani Beach is geared for and aimed specifically at the tourist industry and there is lots to do for topside divers and their companions. The diving facilities are excellent and all dive-related services are available here, with the exception of independent gear rental (only for charters). There are no dive shops. The dive sites are popular and the many dive boats are packed to capacity during the peak season. There are a number of independent dive centres that work from the hotels, providing transport to and from dive sites, although diving with the hotel's concessionaire is also an option.

5 GALU REEF

★★★

Location: Opposite Galu Beach south of Robinson's Club Baobab at Diani Beach, immediately outside the fringing reef after crossing through Robinson's *mlango*. See map.
Access: Approximately 20 minutes by dive boat from Diani Beach.
Conditions: Normally calm, with fairly clear visibility in the diving season. Can be surgy when big swells are running and a current may be present. Plankton blooms inside the reef often reduce visibility considerably; best dived on an incoming tide.
Average depth: 10–15m (33–50ft).
Maximum depth: 18m (60ft). Buoys at 11m (36ft) and at 14m (45ft).
Average visibility: 10–20m (33–65ft).
Average water temperature: 27–28°C (80–82°F).
Galu Reef is a popular site for training dives with dive centres operating from Diani Beach. The conditions found here are generally conducive to relaxed diving, and the site is well buoyed and not very deep. There are two anchor buoys permanently attached to the reef to prevent anchor damage to the coral formations and to facilitate descents and ascents.

The reef itself is round and flattish in appearance and gradually slopes to a maximum depth of 18m (60ft), where the coral growth gives way to a sandy bottom. The top of the reef also appears stripped of much of the coral, presumably because of heavy wave action during the stormier months. Galu Reef does, however, hold some delightful surprises, mainly in the form of turtles, big tiger groupers and some very large stonefish. There are some resident moray eels, and a family of tame spotted stingrays (*Dasyatis kuhlii*) can be found on the top of the reef on the shoreward side. Some really big pufferfish also make an appearance, and small shoals of yellow snappers hover around. Though this reef is not too spectacular as far as coral formations are concerned, it offers rewarding diving for the careful observer. There is of course always a chance to see the gigantic whale shark. Dolphins are often seen in the vicinity. Galu Reef is also an excellent site for night dives.

6 KINONDO REEF

★★★★

Location: To the south of Diani Beach on the seaward side of the fringing reef. See map.
Access: By boat only, through the *mlangos* in the fringing reef. An experienced skipper is essential to negotiate these safely.
Conditions: A strong, unpredictable current can at times be present and a trail line is always a good idea. A plankton bloom at the surface can reduce visibility drastically, but this generally clears up further down.
Average depth: 12–20m (40–65ft).

A hawksbill sea turtle and beautiful fusiliers glide over hard rose coral formations.

THE CROWN-OF-THORNS STARFISH

A voracious feeder that devours coral, the crown-of-thorns starfish (*Acanthaster planci*) posed a serious threat to Australia's Great Barrier Reef from 1962 to 1967, when it destroyed a high proportion of coral. In 1980–81 a lesser outbreak destroyed approximately 500km (300 miles) of reef.

It is not certain whether these outbreaks form part of a natural cycle, or whether they are caused by the interference of human beings, who have removed thousands upon thousands of the crown-of-thorns's natural predator, the giant triton (*Charonia tritonis*), for its attractive shell. Reefs in New Guinea, Palau, Truk, Fiji, Tahiti, the Tuamotos and, lately, the Maldives, have been affected by the starfish to varying degrees. Countermeasures include collecting and killing them individually by the injection of compressed air, or removing them from the water, burning and then burying them.

When prodded underwater these predators undergo a colour change and curl into a protective ball and are really quite attractive. Unfortunately, the far worse damage wrought by humans on reefs has not elicited the same outrage and response as the feeding habits of this natural predator.

Maximum depth: 30m (100ft).
Buoys: Three: at 19m (57ft), 16m (54ft) and 13m (52ft).
Average visibility: May be as good as 30m (100ft), but averages 10–20m (33–65ft).
Average water temperature: 27–28°C (80–82°F).

Kinondo Reef is, apart from Nyulli Reef at Shimoni, probably the best dive site on this section of the coast to spot large pelagic fish. The coral formations are varied and fairly dense to a depth of approximately 28m (84ft) on the northern and eastern side, where the reef gives way to a sloping sandy bottom. On the shallower depths large plate coral tables are common. These formations offer great hiding places for fish, as well as good settings for photography.

There are almost always dense clouds of yellow snappers hovering around the buoylines; these fish allow divers to get really close. Dark blue triggerfish (*Odonus niger*) swarm around the buoylines and display distinctly territorial behaviour. Barracuda often make an appearance, either singly or in schools of smaller ones, which cause the snappers to congregate even closer. A few exceptionally large moray eels coil in and around the coral, and there is one honeycomb moray (*Gymnothorax favagineus*) often found below the middle buoy that allows itself to be stroked. This is best left to experienced dive guides as the wrong moray may not take kindly to this display of affection from an unknown visitor. Whale sharks and dolphins are often seen from the surface, and from down below, by the very lucky divers. Kinondo is a popular reef amongst local and visiting divers and a dive here is almost always worth the effort.

7 MAVOVO

★★★★★

Location: Inside the fringing reef, directly across from the Neptune Paradise Hotel. See map.
Access: By boat from Diani Beach and can be reached by a 20-30-minute snorkel swim; this option is not recommended for the unfit or for those with a full scuba kit.
Conditions: Best dived on an incoming tide for the clearest water.
Average depth: 8–10m (25–33ft).
Maximum depth: 10m (33ft). Not buoyed.
Average visibility: 5–15m (16–50ft).
Average water temperature: 25–29°C (77–84°F).

As the site is positioned on the shoreward side of the reef, dive boats do not have to cross the reef. It is mostly dived on when conditions outside the reef are not favourable or when crossings are too rough. The coral formations are interspersed with bare sandy patches, and for this reason it is a good location for training dives. Visibility is generally best on an incoming tide when clear water is pushed in, or during neap tides when waters inside the reef are placid and clear.

Small tropicals abound and small morays, lionfish and stonefish frequent the coral outcrops. Powder-blue surgeonfish are plentiful, and fluorescent, patterned sea urchins and bright red sea stars inhabit the bottom. Occasionally the crown-of-thorns starfish *(Acanthaster plancii)* can be seen on the coral. (*See* box at left). Because of the depth and because it is not necessary to cross the reef, Mavovo is a good location for night dives, as well as an interesting snorkelling reef.

Glass-bottom boats are available from Neptune Paradise Hotel to take snorkellers out to the reef. A fair fee should be negotiated in advance.

Chale Island

Tiny Chale Island is only 600m (0.3 mile) in length, and is situated some 12km (7.5 miles) south of Diani Beach, off the tip of Chale Point at the very southern end of the Diani coastal road.

No casual visitors are allowed on the island, as most of it is privately owned. There is a lodge, however, with 25 bungalows and an open-air restaurant. A hefty fee is charged to visit the island, but the price includes a very good lunch. A party is regularly held at the lodge at each full moon. Day excursions (including snorkelling, lunch and an island tour) and overnight stays are available (*see* the Regional Directory at the end of this chapter for details). To get to Chale Island by vehicle, take the coastal road to the south (turn right at the T-junction from Ukunda) and follow this road past the beach hotels to where the resurfaced road starts. From here it is another 12km (7.5 miles) to Chale Point.

8 SNORKELLING REEFS

★★★★

The shallow reefs are located close to the island and are reached by boat from the restaurant area. The depth varies with the tides, but the water is richly inhabited by most of the colourful varieties of tropical marine life.

9 CHALE REEF

★★★

Location: To the south of Chale Island.
Access: By boat from either Diani Beach or Chale Island. See map.
Conditions: Best dived from October to April.
Average depth: 12m (40ft).
Maximum depth: 18m (60ft).
Average visibility: 10–20m (33–65ft).
Average water temperature: 27–28°C (80–82°F).

The reef formation, which runs in a north-south direction, is somewhat similar in shape and formation to Tiwi Reef (No. 2). The coral growths are unspoilt, and filled with gullies, small caverns and pinnacles.

A shoal of vibrant sweetlips.

Marine life is plentiful and manta rays have, on the odd occasion, been sighted here. Chale Island is a breeding haven for sea turtles.

Msambweni

Msambweni is a busy village between Ukunda and Shimoni and the name is Swahili for 'the place of the sable antelope'. Unfortunately, there are no more antelope to be seen here, but there is a lovely, long beach and some good accommodation and eating places. This beach has also become popular with upcountry Kenyan residents who have built their holiday homes here. The famed Shimoni cave, reputedly a 17th-century slave pen, can be visited here.

Offshore and to the south of the village are the fringing reefs, which offer good diving opportunities. There are scuba diving facilities available at one of the clubs, and dive excursions are sometimes organized by dive centres from Diani.

10 MSAMBWENI REEFS

★★★★

Location: To the southeast of Msambweni village, outside the fringing reef.
Access: Approximately 45 minutes by dive boat from Diani Beach or 5–10 minutes from Msambweni village. See map.
Conditions: Best dived during the months of October through April.
Average depth: 12m (40ft).
Maximum depth: 20m (65ft).
Average visibility: 10–20m (33–65ft).
Average water temperature: 27–28°C (80–82°F).

The Msambweni reefs are long, and run in a north-south direction parallel to the shoreline. The reefs form a shallow drop-off to the east, where the walls are covered with a profusion of coral growth. The coral is mostly intact and inhabited by the rich variety of marine life found in this area.

The Msambweni reefs are not often dived on as they lie almost halfway between the reefs of Diani Beach to the north, and Wasini Island to the south. Lucky divers have seen whale sharks cruising past, however, and some of the bigger pelagic game fish often visit the area in search of smaller prey.

Shimoni and Environs

Near the Tanzanian border, the tranquil fishing village of Shimoni (Swahili for 'place of the hole'), nestles on a small peninsula. The name comes from the coral cave that, legend has it, served as a holding pen for slaves awaiting shipment to the Arabian markets. It was also, reputedly, used by locals to hide from Maasai raiders.

The area is renowned for deep-sea fishing and the beautiful coral reefs that surround its islands. There are a growing number of diving and deep-sea fishing operators who organize excursions across the Pemba Channel, and live-aboard dive charters to Pemba Island off the coast of Tanzania.

It is the offshore islands, however, with their surrounding coral reefs, that have become Shimoni's most popular tourist attraction. In 1978 the Kisite Marine National Park, covering 28km^2 (10 sq miles), and the Mpunguti Marine National Reserve, covering an area of 11km^2 (4 sq miles), were jointly declared the Kisite-Mpunguti Marine National Park and Reserve. Subsistence fishing is allowed inside the reserve, but no fishing or collecting of marine life is allowed within the park.

Inexpensive dhow excursions (*see* feature on page 76) take divers and snorkellers to the reefs, after which they are treated to excellent cuisine on Wasini Island. Across the channel from Shimoni Jetty (the home of hundreds of swallows) lies the Wasini Marine National Park.

Wasini Island, a mere 17km^2 (6.5 sq miles) in area, hosts a fantastic variety of bird life, a small authentic Muslim village where 'undiluted' Swahili culture may still be observed, a fossilized and exposed coral garden close to the village and extensive mangrove swamps – the home of the saltwater mangrove crab (*Scylla serrata*). These delicious crustaceans are steamed in ginger and served as the first course of a delicious Swahili-style seafood lunch at the well-known Wasini Island Restaurant. Because of the excellent diving in the area, the author has established a diving base with the Wasini Island Restaurant on Wasini Island. All modern diving facilities are available from here, and divers are transported to the reefs by Lamu dhow for diving, after which they may join snorkellers for a seafood lunch at the restaurant. The good news for divers is that almost all the reefs in this area (including the five-star Nyulli Reef) are diveable throughout the year, and afford excellent diving during the warm sunny days that are common even during the rainy season. The reasons for this fortunate phenomenon are that there are, unlike along most of the coastline, no fringing reefs to cross, and there is always a leeward (or land) side to the islands where the water should be calm and clear.

The attractive lionfish has 13 poisonous dorsal spines.

11 NYULLI REEF

★★★★★

Location: 04°40.70'S; 39°25.62'E. Due east of the Wasini Channel, approximately 30 minutes by dhow from the Shimoni jetty. Nyulli Reef falls outside the marine parks. To the east of the reef marked on charts as 'Lockyer Patches'. See map.

Access: About 30 minutes by dhow or 15 minutes by fast dive boat from Shimoni.

Conditions: The best time to dive this reef is on the turn of the tide (slack tide) when the current should be much less noticeable. This reef is diveable during the rainy season when weather conditions allow. For experienced divers only as there is often a strong current present. A drift dive with a tender boat following divers equipped with SMBs (surface marker buoys) is recommended. The depth is also a factor which excludes novice divers. At the time of writing the reef was buoyed, but an experienced skipper, dive guide or Global Positioning System (GPS) equipment are essential to find the reef.

Average depth: Top of the reef at 20m (65ft), down to 30m (100ft).

Maximum depth: 40m+ (130ft+).

Average visibility: 15–40m (50–131ft).

The reef, which runs in a northeasterly direction, rises to a depth of 20m (65ft) and drops sharply to depths approaching 50m (165ft). The coral formations on the steeply inclined wall are spectacular, and gorgonian fan corals and coral whips adorn the deeper sections of the wall. Nyulli Reef offers a large selection of big pelagic fish, and giant groupers (*Epinephelus lanceolatus*), which often exceed 2m (6ft) in length, frequent the walls.

Gigantic shoals of five-lined snappers (*Lutjanus quinquelineatus*) appear everywhere and seem to almost envelop divers, whilst the less common spotted sweetlips (*Plectorhincus picus*) are also seen. Moray eels and lionfish inhabit the coral growths against the spectacular background of the drop.

Barracuda often school together to form compact reflecting walls of silver, and big Napoleon wrasse are frequently sighted. Reef sharks are also common visitors to the deeper sections of the reef, and large zebra sharks (*Stegostoma fasciatum*) have been seen here.

Mpunguti Islands

There are two islands, Upper Mpunguti (or Pungutiayuu) and Lower Mpunguti (or Pungutiachini), in this group. The area around the two islands has been proclaimed a

national marine park and is protected by the park rules and regulations. There are a few excellent but relatively shallow reefs around the island.

12 CORAL GARDENS (PINK REEF)

★★★★

Location: 04°41.99'S; 39°25.30'E. Approximately 300m (1 000ft) out, northwest of Inner Mpunguti Island. See map.
Access: About 35 minutes by dhow from Shimoni or 15 minutes by fast dive boat.
Conditions: Generally clear and calm, with little current present during the diving season. Also diveable in fair weather during the rainy season.
Average depth: 10m (33ft).
Maximum depth: 12m (40ft).
Average visibility: 10–30m (33–100ft).
Average water temperature: 25–29°C (77–84°F).

Pink Reef is a small round reef that owes its distinctive name to the veritable flower garden of pink and lavender soft coral that flourishes here. If any reef deserves to be called pretty, this is definitely the one – hundreds of rainbow-coloured anthias (flamebacks), goldies, angelfish and butterflyfish paint a kaleidoscope of contrasting colours against the background of the breathtaking lavender, blue, pink and purple coral formations.

This section of the reef lends itself splendidly to both macro- as well as wide-angle photography. After exploring the wonders of Pink Reef, divers may take a bearing of 30° northwest and head towards an extension of the reef that forms an arm jutting out in the same direction. The start of this reef is reached after a short distance of 50m (165ft) or so. This reef continues for a considerable distance in the same direction and the top of the reef is at a depth of only around 3–5m (10–16ft) below the surface, while the shallow wall bottoms out at around 15–17m (50–55ft).

The hard corals that are found here are in pristine condition, and are richly interspersed with soft coral bushes. Turtles often put in an appearance, and white-tipped reef sharks have been observed here on occasion. Giant sweetlips hover conspicuously above the coral, often accompanied by large and dense schools of four-striped yellow snappers. Emperor angelfish, pufferfish, large white snappers and thousands of small tropicals appear everywhere amongst the coral growths. Tame-looking blue-spotted stingrays glide lazily past, affording ample proof of the protection provided by the marine park for its inhabitants. Because of the relatively shallow depths, both Pink Reef and its extension can easily be covered during a single dive and may be explored in either direction.

The excellent coral formations that are found on top of the reef provide four-star snorkelling conditions during low tide for more experienced swimmers.

While a larger vessel undergoes repairs, a small dhow takes shape at a beachside shipyard.

A magical cruise on an authentic Arabian dhow is an experience that should be included on any visit to the East African coast. 'Dhow' is a general term used to describe Arabian wooden sailing vessels of ancient design. With their graceful lines and lateen (triangular) sails, dhows have plied the trade routes from the Persian Gulf, across the Indian Ocean and down the East African coast for more than 4 500 years.

The Arabs themselves never use the word dhow, but employ more specific names to describe vessels of differing shape and size These include the *boom*, from Kuwait; the *baggala* (she-mule), from India; the *sambuk,* from Sur, Somalia and the Red Sea; the *shu'ai*, which is an elegant small dhow; the *ganja*, which has a high poop deck that is intricately carved and decorated; and the *zarook*, the *jaliboot* and the *belem*, which refer to smaller types of fishing boats. To confuse things even further, the names of boats are often spelled differently and may have an entirely different name in Swahili.

The boom, a double-ended type of dhow, and the sambuk are today the commonest of these vessels. The largest are known in Swahili as *jahazi*, whilst the smaller ones found around the Lamu Archipelago are called *kijahazi*.

All dhows are broad-beamed, with a shallow draught that permits them to load as much cargo as possible. All feature one or two lateen sails, which in the days of Solomon and Sheba were square and fashioned from palm fronds. On the smaller fishing vessels, the sails often fly from the fragile-looking but resilient masts fashioned from the branches of the casuarina tree. The size of a dhow varies from the large ocean-going traders of 400 tonnes (the booms), down to the smaller vessels of 40 tonnes or less which sail between the islands. They all have a low, curved stem and a high, built-up square stern.

The first dhows were stitched together with cord made from coconut husk fibre, as it was believed that there were great mag-

nets at the bottom of the ocean which would pull the nails from the planking. Most of the *jahazi* have woven coconut fibre matting attached to the hull to reduce splash and provide protection, and the tail-boards are often beautifully carved and decorated. All dhows have 'eyes' – wooden disks which are often decorated with the Islamic crescent moon, to enable them to see the way. They often have a toilet hanging from the stern. The boats built around Lamu have perpendicular bows, whilst those from Zanzibar have sloping bows. Today many of the *jahazi* are motorized, and the small *kijahazi* or *belem* are called *motaboti* ('motor boaty'). The *kijahazi*, apart from being smaller, have a narrower hull and only one sail. In a good wind they are remarkably fast, but a lot of tacking is often involved to get to the destination. This type of dhow is often employed to sail tourists, but is more traditionally used to ferry cargo – anything from spices to cattle – between the islands. Another common type of small dhow, which is mainly used for fishing, is the dugout canoe known as *ngalawa*. These are often rigged with outriggers to prevent them from capsizing.

The *nakhoda*, as the captain of a dhow is called, often wears a full length one-piece garment called a *dish-dash*, with his head swathed in a turban. Some captains still wear magnificently carved silver daggers called *khanjars* fastened to their belts. The boatswain of a dhow goes by the name of a *serang*, and the crew of a big dhow will also include a cook.

With the wind filling its triangular lateen sail, a dhow sails past the harbourfront of Stone Town, Zanzibar.

A multitude of damselfish, including the chocolate dip, mingle with sea goldies.

13 CAPTAIN HASSAN'S REEF

★★★★

Location: 04°49.99'S; 39°25.30'E. To the east of Outer Mpunguti Island. See map.
Access: Approximately 40 minutes by dhow from Shimoni or 20 minutes by fast dive boat.
Conditions: Generally clear and calm with little current present during the diving season. Also diveable in fair weather during the rainy season.
Average depth: 10m (33ft).
Maximum depth: 16m (52ft).
Average visibility: 10–30m (33–100ft).
Average water temperature: 25–29°C (77–84°F).

The reef itself runs in a generally north-south direction and the coral cover is delicate and unspoilt. Strikingly beautiful lilac-blue soft corals are to be found along most of the reef's length.

The coral formations on Captain Hassan's Reef are often inhabited by exquisitely contrasting orange fairy damselfish. Turtles have been spotted resting among the coral growths, and brightly coloured angelfish and surgeonfish abound.

Further to the west there are some isolated coral heads that attract bigger fish, such as inquisitive jacks (caranx) and some large slatey sweetlips, which rest lazily on the bottom.

The reef is extremely scenic and ideal for a relaxed and easy dive – almost reminiscent of a Sunday afternoon stroll through the park.

14 DOLPHIN POINT

★★★★★★★

Location: 04°42.50'S; 39°24.94'E. Slightly to the south-east of Outer Mpunguti Island. See map.
Access: Approximately 45 minutes by dhow from Shimoni or 25 minutes by fast dive boat.
Conditions: Generally clear and calm during the diving season, and also diveable in fair weather and during the rainy season.
Average depth: 10m (33ft).
Maximum depth: 12m (39ft).
Average visibility: 10–30m (33–100ft).
Average water temperature: 25–29°C (77–84°F).

This dive site owes its name to the playful dolphins that often put in an appearance here. Many lucky divers have spent exhilarating moments at Dolphin Point.

The fringing reef runs along the eastern side of the island and swings away to the east off the southern side. The top of the reef lies at a shallow 3m (10ft) on the island side and inclines at approximately 40° down to the sandy bottom, which is found at 12m (40ft). The coral growths are splendid and undamaged, and bigeyes and squirrelfish abound. There are exquisite varieties of lionfish and turkeyfish, and dense clouds of yellow-striped snappers float above and around the coral heads. Large multicoloured parrotfish feed off the coral, but not many other big fish seem to frequent this particular reef. On the sandy bottom the bizarre outline of the head of the predatory flatfish (*Aurelia aurita*) may be distinguished as it lies in ambush for unsuspecting prey. The animal moves off in a peculiar flip-flopping fashion when it is disturbed. The entire area covered by this dive falls within the Kisite-Mpunguti Marine National Park and Reserve, so park fees are payable before entering or diving.

15 CHOP SUEY REEF

★★★★★★

Location: 04°42.80'S; 39°24.42'E. Near and to the northwestern side of Outer Mpunguti Island with the light tower seen on the tip of the island. See map.
Access: About 35 minutes by dhow from Shimoni or 15 minutes by fast dive boat.
Conditions: Generally clear and calm, as it lies on the lee side of Outer Mpunguti that is protected from both the summer and winter monsoons. It is for this reason also diveable in fair weather during the rainy season.
Average depth: 8m (25ft).
Maximum depth: 12m (40ft) on the sandy side.
Average visibility: 10–30m (33–100ft).
Average water temperature: 25–29°C (77–84°F).
Chop Suey Reef makes an ideal site for novice divers, as well as for night dives. It runs in a 60° northwesterly direction along the northwestern side of Inner Mpunguti Island. The coral formations consist mainly of the less spectacular brown pillar variety, which forms a small wall with some large mounds. There is, unfortunately, considerable damage evident, which may be attributed to indiscriminate anchoring in the past. There is nevertheless some very interesting marine life to be found here, including tiny, very light-coloured and delicately formed lionfish, which should make superb subjects for macrophotography.

Colourful ascidians (sea squirts) and a yellow sea fan.

Wary garden eels peek out from the sandy bottom in places, as well as really big and darkly coloured turkeyfish, some small moray eels and small stonefish. As it is a fairly long reef, Chop Suey is good for a drift dive. Because of its very sheltered position and shallow depth, it is an ideal site for spectacular night dives.

Kisite Island

Diminutive Kisite Island is flanked by a partially submerged sand bank (*fungu* in Swahili), a shallow coral reef on the western side and a deeper coral reef on the eastern side. Kisite offers unbeatable snorkelling conditions, as well as great scuba diving opportunities. It was in fact here that the famous ichthyologists, the late Dr J.L.B. Smith and his wife Margaret, of Rhodes University, South Africa, carried out much of the research for their invaluable fish identification volumes. The island is protected, as it forms a roosting place for thousands of birds. Access is allowed to within only 20m (65ft) of the island and no one may set foot on land without a special permit. Kisite is a favourite snorkelling destination for the extremely popular daily dhow trips that are run by the Wasini Island Restaurant and others. Scuba diving excursions by dhow are now also available.

16 KISITE POINT

★★★★★★★★

Location: Around the eastern point of Kisite Island. See map.
Access: About 50 minutes by dhow from Shimoni or 30 minutes by fast dive boat.
Conditions: Diveable throughout the year. Usually calm except when the northeast monsoon blows. Visibility is generally good.
Average depth: 12m (40ft).
Maximum depth: 14m (46ft) on the sandy bottom. There is a permanent mooring at the site, the bottom of which is at 11–12m (36–40ft).
Average visibility: 10–20m (33–65ft).
Average water temperature: 27–30°C (80–86°F).
This dive site has been the favourite one for divers from Robinson's Club Baobab in Diani for more than five years, and with good reason. The great attractions on this superb reef are the large numbers of extremely tame fish of every imaginable tropical variety, as well as the good coral formations and the calm conditions. The coral reef forms a shallow wall that rounds the eastern point, and there are some deep holes near the bottom in which large lobster and rockcod hide. The reef is mostly in a pristine state, but close to the top some past damage caused by wartime target practice and careless anchoring is evident. The fish are not at all bothered by divers and seem to enjoy escorting them on a dive. Big surgeonfish and unicorns are almost always present, and some very

A royal angelfish passes over a bed of hard rose coral, which forms a hiding place for another fish.

big snappers as well as rockcod frequent the top of the reef. A resident school of spadefish *(Ephippus orbis)* often accompany divers and may approach relaxed divers very closely. There are a number of garden eels on the sandy bottom off the reef, and close to the mooring the comical jawfish *(Opistognathus muscatensis)* sticks its froglike head out of a neatly constructed hole. The tameness of the fish provides excellent photographic opportunities, and this dive is ideally suited to divers of all levels. On a number of occasions, the author has enjoyed the thrilling experience of diving on this reef in the company of inquisitive and playful dolphins. It is advisable to keep a good lookout to avoid missing this – a highlight in any diver's life, and one that naturally turns the dive into a five-star experience.

17 OUTER KISITE

★★★★★★★

Location: 04°43.45'S; 39°22.56'E. To the eastern (seaward) side of Kisite Island. See map.
Access: About 50 minutes by dhow from Shimoni or 30 minutes by fast dive boat.
Conditions: Diveable throughout the year, except in very stormy conditions accompanied by strong winds.
Average depth: 10m (33ft).
Maximum depth: 12–14m (40–45ft) on the sandy seaward side. There are two mooring buoys.
Average visibility: 10–30m (33–100ft).
Average water temperature: 25–29°C (77–84°F).

The corals on this reef, which runs in 30° northwesterly direction for a considerable distance, are in excellent condition and the marine life is tame and abundant.

The reef gets better towards the northwestern end, where the coral formations are larger and more spectacular. During most dives there are many turtles present (some extremely big), which often allow divers to get quite close. There are also schools of pufferfish, large white snappers, emperorfish, brightly coloured wrasse and big parrotfish. Filefish, yellow snappers, and numerous bigeyes and cardinal fish swim everywhere and large moray eels inhabit some of the isolated coral outcrops on the sandy bottom.

The top of the reef is below the surface at around 3m (10ft), and features beautiful hard coral – in particular the enormous sheets of plate coral. Here several varieties of angelfish and butterflyfish are found, along with big schools of white snapper.

The soft coral growths are dense and prolific, and together with the numerous giant anemones, house a great variety of damselfish, dominos and clownfish. Big lionfish are quite common and some are of the dark-coloured turkey variety.

The slight current on this reef lends itself ideally to an extended and relaxed drift dive.

18 INNER KISITE

★★★★★★★★★

Location: 04°42.80'S; 39°22.39'E. To the western (leeward) side of Kisite Island. See map.
Access: About 50 minutes by dhow from Shimoni or 20 minutes by fast dive boat.
Conditions: Diveable throughout the year. Inner Kisite is almost always calm and clear as it lies on the leeward side of the island and sandbank.

Average depth: 6m (20ft).
Maximum depth: 10m (33ft) on the sandy bottom. There are two mooring buoys on the site.
Average visibility: 10–30m (33–100ft).
Average water temperature: 27–30°C (80–86°F).

This pristine reef makes a good spot for snorkelling because of its shallow depth and the variety of superb, colourful coral formations. Some scuba divers may scoff at the depth, but the four-star rating for diving is awarded particularly for the huge, very tame and brilliantly hued parrotfish which allow photographers to get in really close, and for the large leopard morays that sway and yawn in holes and arches in the colourful coral formations on the sandy bottom.

As many as three morays, sometimes of different varieties, are often found together, accompanied by dense swarms of almost transparent glassies. All the small tropicals may be found here in their thousands, making this an exciting and colourful snorkel and dive. There is some coral damage evident in places, but this may be attributed to careless anchoring in the past, and the reef seems to be recovering well. The excellent light penetration affords ample natural light for photography and conditions are ideal for night dives.

19 MAKOKOKWE REEF

★★★★★

Location: 04°43.89'S; 39°19.77'E. To the south of Wasini Island, close to the Tanzanian border. See map.
Access: About 60 minutes by dhow from Shimoni or 40 minutes by fast dive boat.

Open coral polyps make a spectacular display at night.

Conditions: Strong currents may be present but the water is normally very clear.
Average depth: 8–10m (25–33ft).
Maximum depth: 12m (40ft). There are no buoys.
Average visibility: 10–30m (33–100ft).
Average water temperature: 25–29°C (77–84°F).

There is unfortunately still a lot of dynamite damage evident on this site, inflicted before Makokokwe Reef was incorporated into the marine reserve. The coral growths are not very large, but seem to be making a good recovery. The fish that inhabit this reef are mainly small tropicals and there are quite a number of beautiful and regal angelfish around. There are also many unicornfish and schools of yellow snappers that hover around the reef. This reef is not as popular as many of the others in the area, as it is quite a long distance from Shimoni and not too spectacular.

20 KITUGAMWE REEF

★★★★

Location: To the south of Wasini Island, close to the Tanzanian border. See map.
Access: About 90 minutes by dhow from Shimoni or 50 minutes by fast dive boat.
Conditions: Strong currents may be present but the water is normally very clear.
Average depth: 15m (50ft).
Maximum depth: Beyond 40m (130ft). No buoys.
Average visibility: 15–40m (50–130ft).
Average water temperature: 25–29°C (77–84°F).

This mid-water atoll, which must once have been quite spectacular, is now unfortunately nothing more than a sad monument to the devastation that can be wrought by relentless dynamite fishing. As this reef lies close to the border of Kenya and Tanzania, it is hard (and not the purpose of this guide) to establish blame, but the fact remains that this large reef has been almost irreversibly damaged by fishermen.

All that remains of the hard corals at Kitugamwe are the widely scattered fragments, though the soft corals seem to be making a remarkable recovery at depths of between 12 and 18m (40–60ft). The entire food chain appears to have been disturbed here, and there are no signs of the big schools of pelagic fish that are usually associated with similar mid-ocean deep reefs. There are still many small tropicals, which include the quaint little fire goby *(Nemateleotris magnifica)*. The only big fish is the lyretail grouper *(Variola louti)*, of which some magnificent specimens are still evident, but these are shy and elusive when approached by divers. The site used to be well known for reef sharks, but there is not much that remains to attract them to this underwater coral graveyard. Until the reef recovers, there is not much reason to make the journey, except to witness the devastation caused by explosive blasting.

The South Coast: Regional Directory

How to Get There

By road, train and air:
Mombasa's international airport is efficiently served by trains and buses from Nairobi. Access to the south coast from Mombasa is via the Likoni Ferry (free for pedestrians and a small charge for vehicles). Taxis are available at the airport and railway station and charge a set fee (a bit of bargaining may be successful). Rental cars are available at the airport or in Mombasa. *Matatus* (minibuses) are available after crossing the ferry and serve most coastal hotels. Matatus are cheap, but often crowded and noisy.

(Travel times are approximated below)
Tiwi Beach: Approximately 30 minutes to the Tiwi Beach turnoff, 21km (13 miles) south of the Likoni Ferry.
Diani Beach: Approximately 40 minutes to the Diani Beach turnoff at Ukunda village, 35km (22 miles) south of Likoni. There is an airstrip for light aircraft between Ukunda and Diani Beach.
Shimoni: Approximately 90 minutes to the turnoff from the main road, at 84km (53 miles) from Likoni, and 15km (9 miles) by dirt road to Shimoni. Wasini Island Restaurant runs a daily bus service for clients from hotels on the north and south coast. There are *matatus* from Ukunda to Shimoni (early morning and late afternoon) for budget travellers.

Recommended car-hire firms include **Diani Car Hire & Safaris,** P O Box 412, Ukunda, tel. (0127) 3163/4 or 3152 (home); office at the Diani Bazaar Shopping Centre. They can arrange tours, travel deals and camping safaris, and have a taxi service at the airport.

Dive Facilities

Tiwi Beach
Tiwi Scuba Divers, tel. (0127) 51054, owned and run by Bob Thomas. PADI and SSI qualification courses. Daily boat dives, and all diving equipment (including air fills) available for rental.

Diani Beach
There are a number of independent dive operators who have concessions and dive bases at the hotels along the coast.

Kenya Diving Centre 'The Crab', tel. (0127) 3400, fax. 2218, owned by Franco Rosso, is a PADI five-star resort facility which offers courses in English, Italian and German, and all diving-related services. Excellent and spacious dive boats do daily trips to dive sites. Bases at many of the top hotels on Diani Beach. Highly recommended.

One Earth Safaris, P O Box 82234, Mombasa, tel. (011) 471771, fax. 471349. A PADI facility offering courses in German and English, day charters and gear rental. Arrange excursions to Pemba Island (highly recommended), where they have a camp for scuba divers; this may be combined with a land safari. Dive bases located at all the Reef Hotels.

Diani Marine, P O Box 340, Ukunda, tel. (0127) 2367/3451, fax. 3452, is the only diving resort on the coast that offers accommodation to divers. All PADI courses and related diving services are available. Dive bases at a number of hotels, with mostly German-speaking clientele. Tuition in German and English.

Robinson's Club Baobab, P O Box 32, Ukunda, tel. (0127) 2623, fax. 2032, is a PADI dive base that caters on a club basis mainly for German-speaking guests. Most diving facilities are available. Tuition in German and English.

Coral Marine, Neptune Paradise Hotel, Diani, tel. (0127) 3620, fax. 3019, offer PADI courses, gear rental and daily boat trips to the reefs and Chale Island. Swiss-owned; tuition in German, French and English.

Diani Diving, P O Box 353, Ukunda, tel/fax. (0127) 3122. A PADI training facility; tuition in German and English. Most facilities available six days a week.

Msambweni
Club Green Oasis, P O Box 80, Msambweni, tel. (0127) 52205/6, fax. 52099, has a PADI facility catering exclusively for guests of the resort, which operates on a club basis mainly for German-speaking visitors.

Shimoni
Wasini Island Diving, P O Box 281, Ukunda, tel. (0127) 2331, fax. 3154, with a diving base on Wasini Island. A customized Arabian dhow that comfortably accommodates up to 20 divers departs daily from the Shimoni Jetty to the best dive sites off the south coast. Excursions include transport from and to Mombasa and hotels on the north and south coasts. Snorkelling arranged for non-divers. A two-dive trip is usual; includes lunch on the island. Accommodation arranged for groups or individuals. Highly recommended.

One Earth Safaris, Shimoni Reef Lodge, tel. Shimoni 9, has a dive base at the hotel offering PADI dive courses; tuition in German and English. Pemba Island excursions depart from here. Air fills, gear rental and daily boat trips to the reef available. Recommended.

Live-aboard dive charters
These depart from Shimoni to Pemba on a regular weekly basis, during the months of September to April, for live-aboard dive charters of varying duration.
Pemba Diving Limited, P O Box 1475, Ukunda, tel. (0127) 2331/3155, fax. 3154, for bookings on the MY *Kisiwani,* a 67ft (20m) twin-screw diesel motor yacht equipped with all diving facilities for cruises to Pemba Island. Five twin air-conditioned cabins with showers, saloon, bar, and video and reference library. Two-day scuba diving courses available. UK booking agent Don McGichrist, tel. 44 (1334) 472504, fax. (1334) 479221. Reasonable fees. Highly recommended.

Where to Stay

Some establishments close for part of the rainy season during May and/or June. Dialling code is 0127.

Tiwi Beach
Minilets, tel. 51054, has a popular beach bar with curry lunches on Sundays and a dive centre.

Twiga Lodge, tel. 51210, welcomes budget travellers and overlanders. Camping facilities available.

Diani Beach
Prices mostly in the top bracket, but standards are world class. A wide range of first-class hotel accommodation is available and recommended ones are:

The Leisure Lodge Club, P O Box 84383, Mombasa, tel. 2620, fax. 2046 with luxury air-conditioned units, swimming pools, bars, restaurants and TV and video in all rooms. There are tennis courts, a casino, windsurfing, a nine-hole golf course and a dive base.

Nomad Beach Hotel, P O Box 1, Ukunda, tel. 2727/2155, fax. 2391. double and two-bedroomed cottages. An excellent seafood restaurant, beach and snack bar, and very popular Sunday curry lunch with live jazz. Deep-sea fishing; dive base on the premises.

LTI Kaskazi Beach Hotel, P O Box 135, Ukunda, tel. 3170-9, fax. 2233. Large hotel, with restaurants, swimming pool and most sport and entertainment facilities. Dive base on the premises. Caters mainly for German package tours.

Neptune Paradise Hotel, P O Box 697, Ukunda, tel. 3620, fax. 3019. Air-conditioned units, pool, restaurants, bars and live entertainment. Casablanca Nightclub is across the road. Facilities for windsurfing and deep-sea fishing, as well as a scuba diving base.

Protea Pinewood Village, P O Box 90521, Mombasa, tel. 3720, fax. 3131, offers luxury air-conditioned private villas, each with cook and all catering facilities. There is a swimming pool with snack bar, bar, restaurant, TV and video lounge, conference room, squash, tennis and table tennis. Booking facilities for scuba diving and deep-sea fishing.

Budget accommodation: Dan's Trench campsite behind the Tradewinds Hotel, tel. 2016/9. The **Diani Beachalets,** tel. 2180, offers reasonable self-catering accommodation.

Chale Island

Chale Island Lodge, tel. 3235/6, fax. 3319/20. Upmarket luxury bungalows, and a good restaurant popular with day-trippers. Snorkelling trips are also arranged by the restaurant.

Msambweni

Club Green Oasis, P O Box 80, Msambweni, tel. (0127) 52205/6, fax. 52099, caters mainly for German package tours, but all visitors are made welcome. Set in pleasant surroundings, with a swimming pool. Diving facilities located on the premises.

Shimoni

Shimoni Reef Lodge, P O Box 82234, Mombasa, fax. (011) 471349 or Shimoni 9. Luxury accommodation with swimming pool and scuba diving base.

Pemba Channel Fishing Club, P O Box 86952, Mombasa, tel. (011) 313749 or Shimoni 2, fax. (011) 316875, caters mainly for deep-sea fishing enthusiasts. Separate cottages; meals served in the club dining room. Diving and live-aboard charters can be arranged from here.

Budget accommodation: The Kenya Wildlife Service's **Eden Bandas;** self-catering. Tel. Shimoni 3.

Wasini Island

Budget accommodation includes **Mpunguti Lodge,** also known as **Masoud's,** which offers traditional Swahili fare and basic accommodation (no electricity or telephone) in atmospheric rooms overlooking the sea. There are also camping facilities.

Where to Eat

Tiwi Beach

The Sunday curry lunch at **Minilets,** tel. 51054, is highly recommended.

Diani Beach

Gallos Restaurant & Bar at the Diani Shopping Centre, tel. 3150. Superb seafood and international cuisine. Open daily for lunch and dinner.

The Maharani Restaurant, Diani Beach Road, tel. 2439/2421. Excellent Indian and international fare in an Eastern-style building. Open daily for lunch and dinner.

Nomad's Seafood Restaurant, Nomads Beach Hotel, Diani, tel. 2155, offers a superb à la carte menu for dinner, set menu on Friday evenings. There is a Sunday curry lunch.

For inexpensive Swahili-style fare, try the informal **Sundowner Restaurant** at the Galu / Kinondo Shop.

Shimoni

Wasini Island Restaurant and **Kisite Dhow Tours,** run by Sally and Steve Mullens for the past 10 years, P O Box 281, Ukunda, with an office at the Jadini Beach Hotel, Diani Beach, tel. 2331, fax. 3154, arrange an unbeatable day outing that includes snorkelling or diving excursions by dhow and centres around a Swahili-style seafood lunch.

Wasini Island

Pilli Pippa Dhow Tours, P O Box 84045, Mombasa, tel./fax. 2401, owned and operated by Bruce and Pippa Trzebinsky, offer snorkelling trips by dhow and five-star cuisine.

For good Swahili food try **Masoud's** restaurant on Wasini Island (no alcoholic beverages are served).

Regional Highlights

At Tiwi Beach, there are beautiful beaches, and the 18th-century **Kongo mosque** on the Tiwi River.

Near Diani Beach lie the remains of the **Jadini Forest,** which teems with monkeys, including the black-and-white colobus, vervet and Sykes monkeys, and yellow baboons. Squirrels, hornbills and small duikers may also be seen. The entrance to the forest is opposite the Nomads Beach Hotel. Not far from Diani Beach is the **Shimba Hills National Reserve.** Inexpensive bungalows and camping facilities are available from the Kenya Wildlife Service in Mombasa; tel. (011) 312744 for bookings.

Chale Island, 12km (8 miles) south of Diani, is worth a day trip; the entrance fee includes lunch. (*See* 'Where to Stay'.) In Shimoni village, just before the entrance to the jetty, is the cave or 'hole' from which the village got its name. Across the channel, Wasini Island is a bird-lover's paradise. The **Kisite-Mpunguti Marine National Park and Reserve** offers some of the best diving on the East African coast.

Emergency Measures

Recompression facilities are available at the Kenya Navy's base in Mombasa, contact the Staff Officer or Duty Officer at tel. (011) 45 1201 ext. 3308 (24-hour standby availability).

The nearest **hospitals** are in Mombasa (*see* page 65).

Ambulances can be contacted at (0127) 2021 or (0127) 2435/6.

The **international emergency radio channel** is **#16**.

INTRODUCING TANZANIA

Tanzania is rich in natural splendours. These include the perpetually snowcapped Mount Kilimanjaro, highest peak in Africa; a substantial part of Lake Victoria – Africa's largest and the world's second largest freshwater lake – which drains into the Nile River to the north; and the Selous Game Reserve – the biggest game reserve in Africa, sheltering one of the single largest elephant populations remaining in the world. Around Tanzania's main islands are incredibly beautiful coral reefs, some of which drop off to form precipitous walls that plunge to depths well beyond 600m (2 000ft).

The Natural Environment

Tanzania appears to have it all. But there is still more. The country also boasts several lesser known, but no less stunning, natural wonders in the form of Mount Meru – the fifth highest mountain in Africa; Lake Tanganyika – the bottom of which is the lowest point on the African continent, at 4 566m (14 990ft); the northern waters of the spectacular Lake Malawi, known as the Lake of Stars, and two other World Heritage sites (apart from Selous) – Serengeti National Park and the Ngorongoro Crater Conservation Area. Taken together, these three parks host nearly a quarter of all the game found in Africa.

It is easy to see that Tanzania represents a wonderland for nature lovers. A safari to one of the country's nature reserves – among the world's last remaining true wilderness areas – is an experience that cannot be duplicated anywhere else. It is, however, beneath the waters of the Indian Ocean, around the beautiful islands of Pemba, Zanzibar and Mafia, that divers may discover some of the most dramatic diving conditions in the world. The Tanzanian coastline stretches an enormous distance of approximately 800km (500 miles), from Lunga Lunga, at the border with Kenya in the north, to Mtwara, near Mozambique in the south.

Previous pages: *A pair of small dhows ply the waters off Zanzibar Island, with a wooded island in the distance.*

Left: *Seen from the road to Arusha, lofty Mount Kilimanjaro rears high above the Serengeti plain.*

Above: *A Swahili fisherman at Kiuyu, Pemba Island.*

Viewed from the rim, the floor of Ngorongoro Crater presents a spectacular vista.

CURRENTS AND CLIMATE

Not far south of the border with Mozambique, the South Equatorial Current divides into the south-flowing Mozambique Current and the north-flowing East African Coastal Current. The latter, with an average temperature of 27°C (80°F), washes the Tanzanian coast.

Tanzania's climate is hot and humid throughout the year, but between June and September cool sea breezes help to dissipate the stifling heat. Humidity levels peak from January to March. Maximum rainfall is received during the long rains, from March to the end of May. The short rains fall in November and December. The islands receive a higher rainfall than the mainland, generally in the same periods. The annual rainfall at the coast and on the islands is 1 150–2 000mm (45–78in). Humidity averages 78% year-round.

Inland Tanzania is dominated by savanna plains, and by the Maasai Steppe, which includes the Serengeti. This is divided from the Central Plateau, which receives an annual rainfall of only 500mm (20in), by the eastern section of the Great Rift Valley, which is about 100km (60 miles) wide here.

WHAT TO SEE AND DO: AT THE COAST

The Pemba Channel, together with Mafia Island, is a famous deep-sea fishing destination, and many record-breaking catches have been made in these waters. There are organized charters available from Dar es Salaam.

The top hotels in and to the north of Dar es Salaam all have swimming pools, some have tennis courts and most offer in-house entertainment in the form of bands, discotheques and traditional dancing. However, muggings occur frequently along the beaches outside of hotels, so be sensible at all times. There are casinos in Dar es Salaam.

There are some good restaurants at the hotels and in Dar es Salaam. Cuisine varies from local Swahili fare to international dishes. Wine from around the world is available and reasonably priced. Supermarkets are well stocked with local and imported products.

The smaller coastal towns, such as Bagamoyo, are rich in historical background and worth a visit if time allows. Zanzibar Island is highly recommended. Superb diving may be combined with one of the numerous topside attractions (*see* feature on page 118).

WHAT TO SEE AND DO: INLAND

Comfortable accommodation is available in government-owned lodges and camps in Tanzania's many parks and game reserves. Luxury camps, too, guarantee superb service and unrivalled wildlife experiences. The best known of the country's 15 reserves are:

Selous Game Reserve: This is the world's largest wildlife reserve, covering an area of 55 000km^2 (21 230 sq miles). An abundance of wildlife is found here. There are four tented camps to accommodate visitors. The TAZARA railway line from Zambia to Tanzania crosses through part of the reserve.

Mikumi National Park: Just to the west of Dar es Salaam, it is divided by the main road from Tanzania to Zambia. Lion, elephant, rhino, buffalo, kudu, giraffe, zebra, hartebeest, bushbuck, baboons and monkeys are just some of the myriad animals to be found here. There is a government-owned luxury lodge, a tented camp and campsites.

Ngorongoro Conservation Area: Lies in an extinct volcano crater, and teems with lion, rhino, hyena, cheetah, hippo, baboons and gazelles. There are three luxury lodges situated right on the rim of the crater, and campsites can be found throughout the area.

Serengeti National Park: Bounded on the west by Lake Victoria, and to the north by the Mara River and Kenya's well-known Masai Mara reserve, the Serengeti National Park is home to the 'big five' and to unrivalled herds of game. The Serengeti is the gathering place of some two million plains zebra, wildebeest and Thomson's gazelles that annually migrate from the plains across the Mara River in search of water. Accommodation is available in the luxury lodges of Serorena and Lobo, as well as nine campsites.

Arusha National Park: A tiny reserve close to the magnificent Mount Meru. Elephant, buffalo, bushbuck, red forest duiker, and the rare black-and-white colobus monkeys – identifiable by their white 'collars' – are found here. There is one government-owned tourist lodge, and mountain huts and campsites in the park.

A starry pufferfish rests on a bed of algae, Pemba Island.

Lake Manyara National Park: Two thirds of the park is covered by the waters of Lake Manyara. Elephant, hippo, buffalo, lion, leopard, giraffe and zebra are plentiful, and substantial herds of wildebeest congregate here during the dry season. Accommodation is available in the form of one first-class hotel, a hostel, self-catering bandas and campsites.

Mount Kilimanjaro National Park: Beautiful scenery and changing vegetation zones are inhabited by leopard, elephant, buffalo, bushbuck, eland, the rare Abbot's duiker, and monkeys. Accommodation on the mountain and along the climb to the top is very good. Some 67 000 people attempt to climb Kilimanjaro every year. (*See* box on page 24).

HIGHLIGHTS OF NEIGHBOURING COUNTRIES

Eight countries share borders with Tanzania. To the north lie Kenya and Uganda; to the west, Rwanda, Burundi, Zaïre and Zambia; and to the south, Malawi and Mozambique. The main overland route leads southward through Tanzania, but if you are planning a visit to Mozambique, it is advisable to check on road safety conditions. Due to political instability, it is unwise to visit Rwanda, Burundi or Zaïre at present. A trip along the magnificent shores of Lake Malawi, or directly through Zambia where the route crosses the Great Rift Valley, are tempting options. As tourism in Tanzania outgrows its infant stage, the country is bound to become one of the most popular and worthwhile travel destinations in the world.

TRAVELLING TO AND IN TANZANIA

Tanzania's tourist infrastructure is still relatively undeveloped, and the country will take some time to catch up with some of its neighbours in this regard. A visit to the country, therefore, requires some effort in planning to make the most of your trip. Scuba diving is, unfortunately, almost an unknown activity other than around the islands of Pemba, Zanzibar and Mafia. Diving off the mainland, and to a lesser extent on the islands (with the exception of the west coast of Zanzibar) is still mostly done on a small-scale or independent basis, and all live-aboard excursions are operated from Kenya. Wildlife safaris are, on the whole, well organized and efficiently catered for, and bookings and itineraries for these can be arranged from within one's country of origin.

Red tape and bureaucratic corruption still present major headaches in Tanzania, especially at Dar es Salaam airport. Officials often give visitors to the country the impression that they would rather not have them or their much-needed foreign currency in Tanzania. This is an unfortunate hangover from the suspicious days of socialism, and an attitude which a country desperately trying to attract tourism can sincerely do without.

ENTRY REQUIREMENTS

Entry visas are required by most passport holders, and these should be obtained before leaving your country of origin. The visa is valid for a period of three months, but is good for only one entry. Visas may be obtained from the Tanzanian High Commission. In Kenya, a visa can be obtained in Nairobi or Mombasa without any undue delays and normally only takes a few hours.

Visas are also required for entering Zanzibar (or any of the main islands), but these may be obtained at the point of entry. Fees range from US$10 to US$50. It is strongly advised that visitors check on entry requirements before leaving their home countries.

Left: *The rain forest between Marangu and Mandara marks the first stage in any ascent of Mount Kilimanjaro.*

Above: *The radianthus anemone grows to 25cm (10in) across, and uses its poisonous tentacles to trap fish.*

A valid passport is required by all visitors. Visitors are advised to check this in their home countries before departure. A visitor's pass that is valid for a maximum of three months may be issued on arrival, but it is usually necessary to produce an onward or return ticket, and proof of funds sufficient to sustain you for the intended length of your visit. A valid yellow fever vaccination certificate is obligatory. As a precaution, visitors arriving from cholera-infected areas should bring proof of inoculation. Note that a tourist fee of US$25 per person is payable by passengers on live-aboard dive boats. Immigration and customs procedures are generally hassle-free, and the officials are on the whole friendly and helpful.

MAJOR ENTRY POINTS

By air

Most major airlines operate regular scheduled flights to Tanzania. The main entry point is Dar es Salaam International Airport, which is 16km (10 miles) outside the city centre. Airport tax (about US$20) is payable upon departure.

By road

Only some five per cent of Tanzania's 82 000-km (51 000 miles) road network is paved. The busiest overland route is the one that runs from Nairobi to Dar es Salaam via Arusha, and which crosses the border at Namanga. From Mombasa to Tanga or Dar es Salaam, the road crosses into Tanzania at Lunga Lunga. From Zambia the border crossing is at Tunduma, and from Malawi over the Songwe Bridge between Karonga and Mbeya. The road into Uganda is not often used due to its extremely poor condition. This route crosses the border between Bukoba and Masaka. Opening times at the border post may change, so it is advisable to check before setting off.

By live-aboard boat or ferry

Dar es Salaam is East Africa's second largest port, and there are customs and immigration posts in the port area. The ferry services to and from Pemba, Zanzibar and Mafia islands operate on a daily basis. The other ports of entry on the Tanzanian coast are Tanga to the north, and Kilwa and Mtwara to the south. On Lake Tanganyika, ferry routes run between Mwanza and Bukoba in Tanzania and Port Bell in Uganda. There is also ferry service, aboard the historic MV *Liemba,* running between the Tanzanian port of Kigoma and lake-side towns in Zambia and Burundi.

By rail

The TAZARA railway line joins Kapiri Mposhi in Zambia with Dar es Salaam. There are weekly trips with an 'express train' service between the two countries. After an interval of 18 years, rail links have been re-established between Kenya and Tanzania. A train leaves Voi on the Kenyan side at 05:00 on Saturday mornings, and arrives at Moshi in Tanzania at 11:00 the same morning.

CUSTOMS AND IMMIGRATION

Customs and immigration officials are on the whole helpful but this may depend entirely on the individual. The import of firearms and of agricultural and horticultural produce is forbidden. Temporary permits (valid for three months on request) are issued for the import of personal possessions and vehicles and a fee of around US$60 is charged for this. Duty-free imports of 200 cigarettes, 50 cigars, one litre of alcohol and 250ml of perfume are allowed. There is a duty-free shop for departing visitors at the Dar es Salaam International Airport.

WHEN TO VISIT

Tourism in Tanzania is not dependent on season, as the country enjoys a tropical climate. Peak periods are during the European winter holidays (November, December and January). The diving season stretches from September through March, when the northeast monsoons prevail. The rainy season (March to May) often adversely affects diving conditions because of the increased flow of river water into the ocean. The best times to visit the game parks in northern Tanzania are between November and March and from June to October. A visit to the southern reserves should be planned between July and November.

PUBLIC HOLIDAYS

January 1	New Year's Day
January 12	Zanzibar Revolution Day
February 5	Founding of the CCM Party
April 26	Union Day
May 1	International Worker's Day
July 7	Peasant's Day (may be repeated on August 8)
December 9	Tanzania Independence and Republic Day
December 25	Christmas Day
Variable dates:	Good Friday
	Easter Monday
	Idd-ul-Fitr (end of Ramadan)
	Islamic New Year
	The Prophet's Birthday

Preparing to dive off Zanzibar.

TIME ZONE

Tanzanian time corresponds with East African Standard Time, which is three hours ahead of Greenwich Mean Time. The sun rises at around 06:30 and sets at around 18:45.

GETTING AROUND

By air

The national carrier, Air Tanzania, offers domestic services from Dar es Salaam to the following places: Arusha and Moshi (Kilimanjaro Airport), Dodoma, Mwanza, Kigoma, Songea, Iringa, Bukoba, Tabora, Tanga, Mtwara / Lindi, Mafia, Zanzibar, and Pemba. These flights leave several times a week. Enquiries should be made at the head office in Dar es Salaam. Light aircraft can be chartered from Dar es Salaam airport. Air Tanzania offers direct flights to and from Mombasa twice weekly.

By taxi, car or bus

Taxis are abundant. It is recommended to agree on a firm fee before taking a taxi, as fees vary drastically according to the driver's judgment of the means of the customer.

Cars are available for hire at the airport, and a few hotels provide a transport service. Driving is done on the left-hand side of the road, but it is at times difficult to adhere to this rule because of the poor condition of the roads: giant potholes appear unexpectedly, and a journey demands concentration and caution. A famous Tanzanian saying is: 'They who drive straight had too much to drink!' It is not advisable to drive at night because of the condition of the roads, not to mention that of some of the other vehicles that share it.

With the day's work done, Zanzibaris enjoy the twilight on the stretch of beach fringing the dhow harbour.

There are regular bus services from Dar es Salaam to the other major towns, such as Arusha, Tanga and Mbeya. It is advisable to enquire about road and travel conditions before setting off as some roads may be attempted by four-wheel-drive vehicles only.

By boat

There are regular ferry services several times a day from Dar es Salaam to Zanzibar and back. There is also a weekly sailing to Mafia Island via Mtwara. Dhow trips to the islands and Mombasa are dependent on the reigning monsoons and enquiries should be made at the dhow harbour next to the container section. A ferry service operates to and from Mombasa.

By train

Most of the main towns are linked by rail, except for Arusha, Bagamoyo, and Kilwa. There are three classes of travel, but only first class can be recommended. The TAZARA Express, crossing from Kapiri Mposhi in Zambia to Dar es Salaam, affords splendid views of the Great Rift Valley. The train crosses the Selous Game Reserve in the early morning on the way to Dar es Salaam, and in the late afternoon on the return journey to Zambia.

HEALTH AND SAFETY

Medical services are available and cheap in Dar es Salaam and Zanzibar, but it is strongly advised that visitors take out comprehensive medical (and travel) insurance.

Malaria is endemic throughout the country and particularly rife during the rainy season. Prescribed prophylactics should be taken for the recommended times before (up to one week) and after (usually for six weeks) a visit. If you exhibit any flu-like symptoms during this period, a blood test for malaria should be taken, just to be on the safe side. Be aware that the incidence of HIV infection is high in Tanzania.

Dental care is available in Dar es Salaam and Zanzibar, and there are well-stocked pharmacies. Most prescription drugs are available in Dar es Salaam or can be ordered.

Tap water is unsafe and should be avoided at all costs, unless it has been boiled and filtered. The safest option is to buy bottled mineral water, which is readily available. Be very choosy about where you eat – stick to hotels and well-known restaurants.

The proximity of the equator guarantees *kali* (fierce) sunrays. All exposed body parts (especially the face) that are unaccustomed to a tropical sun should be covered or treated with a strong sunscreen. Make use of a hat or peaked cap and sunglasses at all times when outdoors. Remember that the glare on beaches and the water will increase the burning effect and it is possible to burn even in the shade. Beware of sunburn when snorkelling as the rays penetrate at least 1m (3ft) into the water.

The per capita income in Tanzania is still one of the lowest in the world, and robbers, muggers and confidence tricksters are rampant. Beware of walking alone or in small groups on any deserted beach, even in broad daylight, and do not carry any visible valuables, even within a few metres of hotel premises. Beware of watch-snatchers, who will take the watch

Women strolling in their colourful khangas, *Zanzibar.*

off your arm through the window of a car. Do not walk around Dar es Salaam at night, especially near the beachfront. It is wise not to leave a vehicle unattended or any clothing on the beach when taking a swim. Do not change money with street dealers or at border posts as they have the ability to make even the most seasoned of travellers part with their money. Let common sense prevail, and when in doubt, ask for advice from trustworthy local residents.

CURRENCY AND INSURANCE

The monetary unit is the Tanzanian shilling, which is divided into 100 cents. Notes are printed in shilling denominations of 1000, 500, 100, 20 and 10. Coins have values of 20, 5 and 1 shilling, and 50, 20, 10 and 5 cents. Foreign traveller's cheques and cash in hard currency may be exchanged at any of the many bureaux de change or banks.

Credit cards are not accepted, and therefore cash cannot be withdrawn in this way. A few hotels accept major credit cards as payment for hotel bills, but it is advisable to make sure before checking in. Ensure that you are covered against theft and loss of personal property before leaving home.

Exchange control regulations have been relaxed extensively, and foreign transfers to Tanzanian banks do not present any major problems. These can be done without having an account at a bank. The National Bank of Commerce is the major bank in Tanzania, and there are branches of the Meridian Bao and Standard Chartered banks. Normal banking hours are: Monday to Friday 08:30–15:00; Saturday 08:30–12:30. Banking hours are often subject to change on short notice, so it is best to check.

COMMUNICATIONS

Post offices are open daily from 08:00–16:30, except for Saturdays when they close at 12:00. The telephone system is a nightmare. Telephones with a direct satellite link are fairly reliable, and the best place from which to make international calls is the Extelecomms House on Bridge Street in Dar es Salaam, south of the Askari Monument off Samora Machel Avenue. Faxes or telexes may also be sent from here or received at reasonable rates. Hotel rates for all calls are horrendously expensive.

The postal system is reliable and letters generally turn up. All parcels have to clear customs and are opened on a public counter, much to the delight of curious bystanders.

ELECTRICITY AND FUEL

The electricity supply is 230 volts (50 cycles AC) and some hotels may supply adaptors. Power peaks or surges occur frequently, which may severely damage electronic appliances without a protector. Power cuts are frequent and rationing is often introduced during the dry season, when power cuts occur daily and may last all day long. Petrol, diesel and kerosene fuel is readily available, and there are many filling stations at reasonable intervals along the main routes. The main islands often experience shortages of fuel. Almost all types of batteries are available, but they are expensive, so bring a good supply of spares with you.

THE PEOPLE, LANGUAGE AND CUSTOMS

An estimated 26 million people were living in Tanzania in 1990, mainly represented by Africans. The inhabitants of Pemba and Zanzibar islands are mostly of Arabian, Shirazi and Comoran descent. The official languages are English and Swahili, and many phrase books are available. There are more than 120 tribal tongues, with the most common ones being from the Bantu family of languages.

Freedom of religion is practised in Tanzania, and the Muslim faith accounts for about 35% of the population. Christianity is represented by 33% of the inhabitants, and the remaining 32% are traditional believers. Overt displays of affection are frowned upon in predominantly Muslim communities, as is topless bathing. In Muslim villages women are advised to wear a wraparound over shorts to avoid giving offence.

PHOTOGRAPHY

The photographing or video-recording of all government buildings, military installations and police stations is taboo. Film is readily available but very expensive. Developing of slide film (transparencies) is not done in Tanzania. Cameras are an all-time favourite in the robbery stakes, so take extra care of yours.

HOTELS, GUEST HOUSES, RESORTS AND CAMPSITES

The best hotels are found on the coast to the north of Dar es Salaam and in and around the city. Guest house accommodation is also available, but standards vary drastically and should be investigated personally. There are several popular camping sites situated throughout Tanzania. A number of luxury camps and lodges cater for wildlife safari guests.

Flower gardens surround a small hotel at Dangwe on Zanzibar.

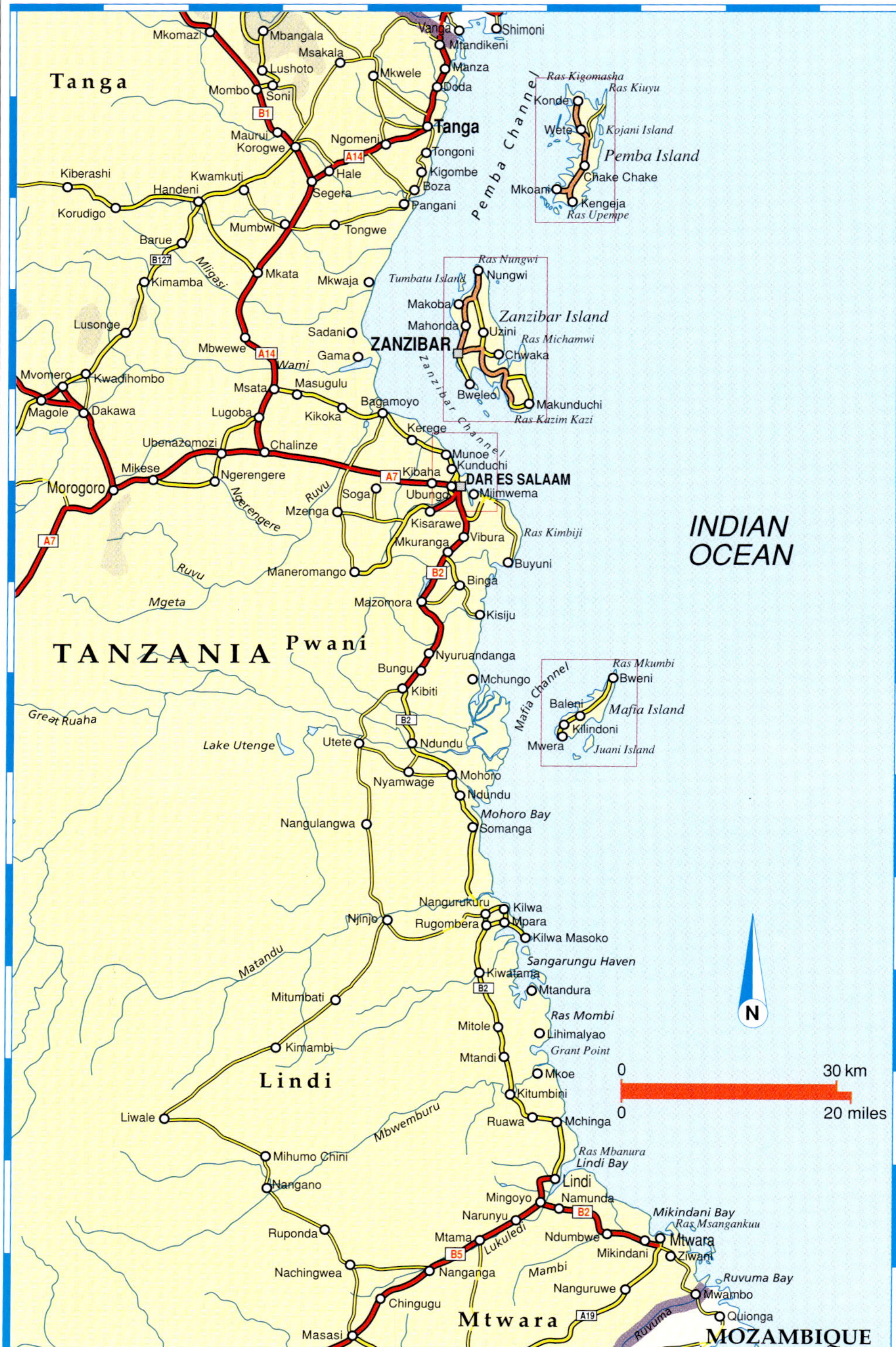

Tanga
TANZANIA
Pwani
Lindi
Mtwara
MOZAMBIQUE
INDIAN OCEAN
ZANZIBAR
DAR ES SALAAM
Pemba Island
Zanzibar Island
Mafia Island
Pemba Channel
Zanzibar Channel
Mafia Channel
Tanga
Morogoro
Lindi
Mtwara
Bagamoyo
Kilwa Masoko
Mohoro Bay
Lindi Bay
Mikindani Bay
Ruvuma Bay
Sangarungu Haven
Lake Utenge
Great Ruaha
Ruvu
Wami
Mgeta
Matandu
Mbwemburu
Lukuledi
Ruvuma
0 30 km
0 20 miles
N

INTRODUCING THE DIVING REGIONS OF TANZANIA

The Tanzanian coastline is some 320km (200 miles) longer than that of Kenya, but the country's lack of a developed tourism infrastructure precludes organized diving along most of the coast. For this reason almost all diving activities and facilities are at present centred around the main islands, and around Dar es Salaam, Tanzania's capital city. Any other recreational diving activities will, for the time being, have to be totally independent excursions involving a great amount of advance planning and logistical support. Preparation for such excursions will require boats, all equipment, compressors, food and accommodation, as well as contingency plans in the event of an emergency.

For these reasons the dive sites in these regions are not described in detail, but any worthwhile reefs are mentioned, together with possible sources of information. For the purposes of this guide, the diving regions of Tanzania can be grouped into the following areas:

The Main Islands:
Pemba, Zanzibar and Mafia

The Mainland:
Dar es Salaam

It is undoubtedly the waters around the islands of Pemba, Zanzibar and Mafia that have the best dive sites off the coast of Tanzania. This fact is evident from the enormous influx of divers who are on the lookout for new and unspoilt world-class diving destinations. Before these islands became known for their excellent diving and game fishing conditions, they were mainly renowned for their scenic splendour and for their rich history and culture; Pemba and Zanzibar, both famed for the cultivation of fragrant spices, particularly cloves, are known as the 'Spice Islands'.

The diving regions of Tanzania are divided into two main regions, namely the main islands and the mainland, because of various factors that influence diving conditions in these areas. Waters around the islands are almost always sheltered on the leeward (land) side, where diving conditions will be superior during a particular time of the year, depending on the prevailing monsoon wind.

Topographic features, such as the vertical undersea cliffs off Pemba Island, also greatly influence diving conditions. The cliffs are exposed to currents, and consequently attract large numbers of fish. The islands off the Tanzanian coast also lie in the path of the southeast monsoon winds, which means a higher rainfall than on the mainland. This obviously influences diving conditions, as is the case with the outflow of river water from the larger rivers on the mainland.

The accessibility and infrastructure of the islands and the mainland also vary drastically in most cases (with the exception of Zanzibar), and more careful planning and preparation is required for a successful diving excursion to the islands.

PEMBA ISLAND

Pemba Island is known as the 'clove capital of the world', as it is the world's largest producer and exporter of cloves. Still relatively untouched by tourism, Pemba's increasing fame as a first-class diving destination is bound to boost its popularity. One can only hope that the influx of tourists will not spoil the untouched beauty and breathtakingly pristine coral reefs of this tropical island paradise.

Other than the live-aboard excursions from Kenya, Pemba can be reached from Dar es Salaam and from Zanzibar. Air Tanzania flies three times a week from mainland Tanga to Chake Chake airport on Pemba.

If conditions or circumstances are not perfect for scuba diving, snorkelling or deep-sea fishing, a visit to the clove-impregnated interior of the island is well worth the effort. Signs of modern society are found in a double highway leading up to the coastal town of Mkoani. Lovely old Bedford trucks travel up and down the highway, but ox-drawn carts show that life here continues at its centuries-old pace.

When a storm destroyed two-thirds of Zanzibar's clove trees in 1872, plantations multiplied on the richer soils of Pemba. Today there are approximately three and a half million clove trees, and almost as many palms, on the island, which was once covered by a primeval forest, of which today only the Ngezi Forest in the north remains.

Pemba's main town is Chake Chake, which boasts an 18th-century Muslim fort which has been converted into a hospital, some modern administration buildings and a few shops. Arab influence is evident in the architecture, particularly the remains of tombs and mosques.

The island's population of approximately 250 000 is widely distributed, lending Pemba the air of a 'Robinson Crusoe' setting. The many exquisite, small islands that surround the main island offer superb snorkelling conditions, and afford splendid opportunities for simply relaxing in the sun, searching for shells and enjoying evening barbecues on the beaches.

Left: *Looking from Pemba to Njao Island, with a live-aboard diving vessel visible in the distance.*
Above: *Flatworms attain a length of up to 5cm (2in), and feed at night on small invertebrates.*

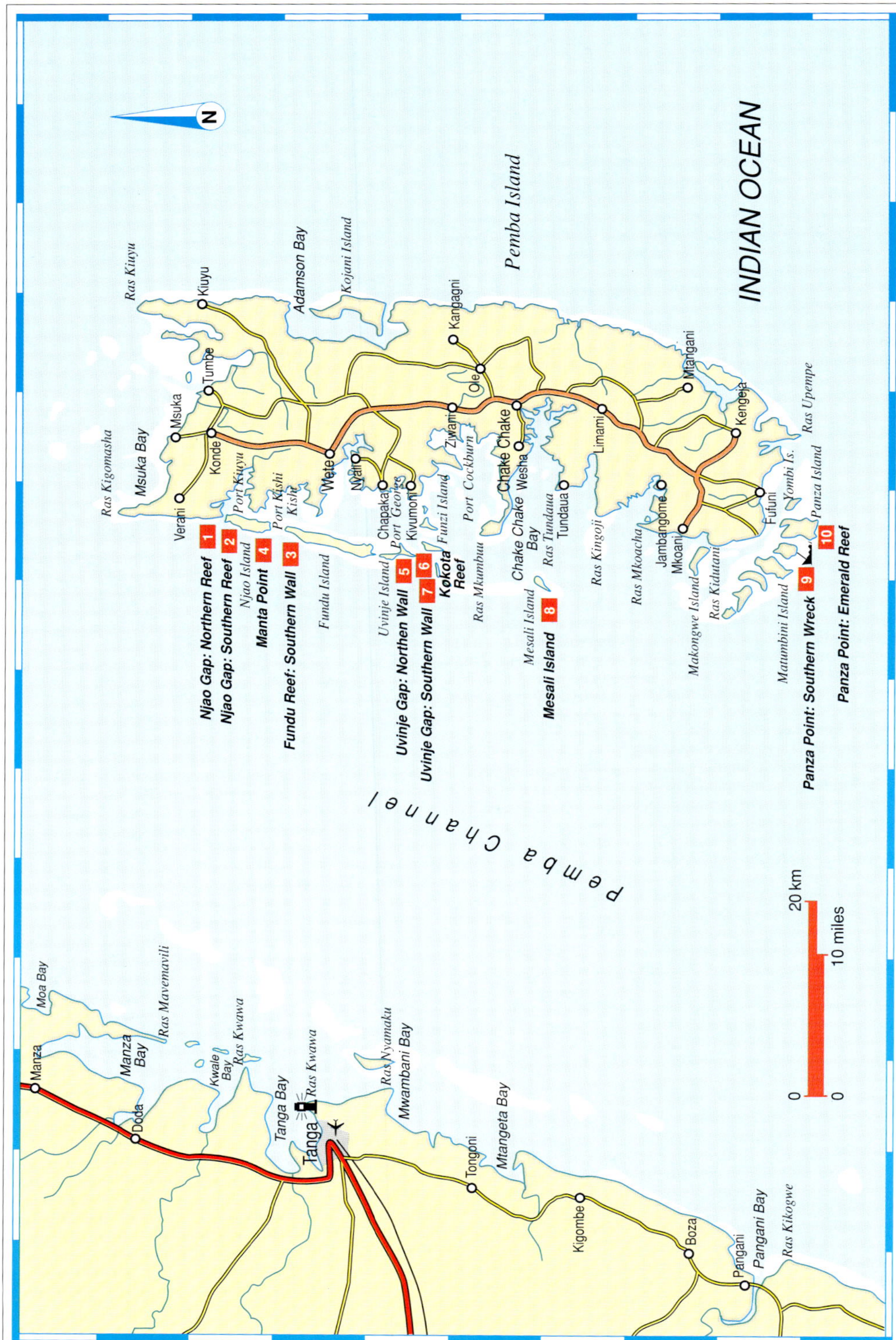
N
INDIAN OCEAN
Pemba Island
Pemba Channel
Njao Gap: Northern Reef 1
Njao Gap: Southern Reef 2
Fundu Reef: Southern Wall 3
Manta Point 4
Uvinje Gap: Northern Wall 5
Kokota Reef 6
Uvinje Gap: Southern Wall 7
Mesali Island 8
Panza Point: Southern Wreck 9
Panza Point: Emerald Reef 10
Ras Kiuyu
Kiuyu
Adamson Bay
Kojani Island
Ras Kigomasha
Msuka Bay
Msuka
Tumbe
Konde
Verani
Port Kiuyu
Njao Island
Port Kishi
Kishi
Wete
Fundu Island
Nyali
Chapaka
Port George
Kivumoni
Uvinje Island
Funzi Island
Ziwani
Kangagni
Ole
Port Cockburn
Ras Mkumbuu
Chake Chake
Wesha
Chake Chake Bay
Mesali Island
Ras Tundaua
Tundaua
Limani
Ras Kingoji
Ras Mkoacha
Jambangome
Mkoani
Mtangani
Kengeja
Makongwe Island
Ras Kidutani
Fufuni
Yombi Is.
Panza Island
Ras Upempe
Matumbini Island
20 km
10 miles
0
0
Moa Bay
Manza
Manza Bay
Ras Mavemavili
Doda
Kwale Bay
Ras Kwawa
Tanga Bay
Ras Kwawa
Tanga
Ras Nyamaku
Mwambani Bay
Tongoni
Mtangeta Bay
Kigombe
Boza
Pangani
Pangani Bay
Ras Kikogwe

DIVING CONDITIONS

Pemba lies some 50km (31 miles) north of its sister island, Zanzibar. The surrounding waters offer divers dramatic and exciting experiences in warm water that reaches depths in excess of 800m (2 640ft). Pemba is surrounded by numerous small islands, and fringed by coral cliffs that drop off to a depth of more than 300m (1 000ft). At present, only the west coast of Pemba Island has been explored, because it is close to the mainland. The western side forms the leeward side during the northeast monsoon, making diving conditions on this side of the island more favourable. The majority of dives are done from live-aboard vessels that operate from the Kenyan coast. There are plans in the offing for land-based diving operations, although logistics still present a considerable problem.

Pemba's lush, brilliant green tropical palm forests have given rise to the nickname of the 'Emerald Island'. Offshore, the island hosts a fascinating, and often unique, array of colourful marine life that swarms on the pristine coral reefs. Steep walls drop off to undiveable depths, and the water stays deep and dark blue to within a few metres of the shore. The bottom then rises dramatically to form almost vertical cliffs topped by a shallow shelf, where the colour of the water becomes turquoise.

Spectacular shore dives do not always necessitate a long, cumbersome swim, and the shallows afford superb snorkelling conditions. In shallower waters – mostly above 20m (66ft) – the walls are densely covered in coral growths and formations of every description; below that, colourful sponges and huge gorgonian sea fans adorn the sides.

In the deeper waters, the lush coral gardens often stretch as far as the eye can see; underwater visibility averages around 40 metres (130ft), and sometimes reaches up to 60m (200ft). Here the big pelagic game fish – shoals of barracuda, kingfish, wahoo, tuna and jacks (caranx) – hunt together with large Napoleon wrasse (also known as humphead wrasse), graceful manta rays and sharks. The shallower waters are the playground of smaller tropical fish, including almost every variety of Indo-Pacific marine fauna. The Napoleon wrasse and giant groupers often reach lengths of 2m (6ft), and the wingspan of the manta rays sometimes exceeds 5m (16ft). The small, rare yellow-edge chromis damselfish (*Chromis pembae*) is named after the island. Pemba is indeed an underwater naturalist's dream, and the opportunity to discover, and even name a new species, is always present in this marine paradise.

The dive sites described on the following pages are all located off the western and southern coast of the island. At present, dives are generally done from live-aboard boats. Day excursions from the Kenyan south coast are scheduled on an irregular basis, and their frequency depends mainly on the unpredictable weather and sea conditions that prevail in the Pemba Channel, some 35km (22 miles) in width. Weekend camping excursions are organized from time to time by the Dar es Salaam Yacht Club, which is much further away.

PEMBA'S MAGICAL WORLD

The incredible natural kingdom beneath the waters around Pemba Island was first encountered, and described to the world, by the crew of Jacques Cousteau's *Calypso* when the ship dropped anchor off the island on April 29, 1967, for repairs. In his book *Life and Death in a Coral Sea* (London: Cassel, 1971), Cousteau described some of Pemba's wonders: *'The divers working under the hull, discovered a treasure trove of marine life: fish with what appeared to be horns on their heads, and an unusual species of red and grey starfish armed with stingers, which seemed carved out of wood, and then painted. They also saw giant cucumbers, and a green crustacean five or six inches [125mm] long that resembled a praying mantis and had eyes that could be divided into four parts. In addition it had two false eyes on its head.'* (Author's note: The fish with 'horns on their heads' must have been the unicornfish (*Naso annulatus*) that is commonly found here. The 'green crustacean resembling a praying mantis' was almost certainly the mantis shrimp (*Odontodactylus scyllarus*).

Njao Gap seen from the deck of a small coastal ship.

For these reasons Pemba's dive sites are largely unexplored – the east coast in particular lies waiting for adventurous divers who can look forward to the thrill of diving where no one else has ever dived before. A new wreck was discovered recently and one can never tell what other exciting finds may be hiding in the deep blue waters.

Most dives are carried out as drift dives, as there is almost always a current present. For this reason it is recommended that groups of divers always carry a surface marker buoy (SMB), and that each individual always stash a delayed SMB in their buoyancy jacket to facilitate being spotted on the surface by the boat.

Visibility: The best visibility is almost always experienced on an incoming tide, when clear water is pushed in. On an outgoing tide the greenish, plankton-rich water is drawn from the shallow bays surrounding the main island, and visibility deteriorates. Average visibility ranges from 20 to 40m (66–100ft), increasing in some instances to 60m (200ft), especially in the south, where the north-flowing current is split by the islands. Though the plankton may disturb visibility, a concentration of it attracts the big filter-feeders such as manta rays and whale sharks.

Experience: Because of the great depths and strong currents, diving on Pemba is restricted to experienced divers, or must be done with a competent and experienced dive master. There are, however, a few sites which are more suitable to inexperienced divers, and conditions on these could be checked out before the dive.

Snorkelling: One of the greatest snorkelling thrills is to swim over the drop-off and experience the feeling of hovering in free-flight over a cliff, especially on days when the visibility is good and big fish can be seen cruising below.

Care should always be taken with currents, and it is a good idea to make use of a surface marker buoy, which also serves as a warning to other boats and makes a useful device to hang on to when you wish to rest.

Climate: Pemba enjoys mainly hot and dry days from December to March; the months of June to October are cool and dry (an average of 25°C; 75°F). Between March and the end of May, and in June and July, as well as during November, the rainfall is heavy, with humidity averaging around 78 per cent.

Water temperature: The average water temperature is around 27–28°C (80–82°F) but may drop as low as 24°C (75°F) during some months. The temperature stays constant to depths exceeding the maximum sport-diving limits, but thermoclines can be expected at almost any depth. It is advisable to wear a 3mm (⅛in) wetsuit.

The best months to dive Pemba Island are from October through to March, after which the seas become quite rough and unpredictable, with an accompanying deterioration in visibility and the presence of strong currents. The best time of year to see manta rays is from December to early February.

1 NJAO GAP: NORTHERN REEF

★★★

Location: 04°52'S; 39°41'E; outside and northwest of Njao Gap (Port Kiuyu). See map.
Anchorage: There is a splendid and picturesque anchorage inside the gap at Port Kiuyu.
Access: By live-aboard diving vessels from Kenya, dive schools in Zanzibar, own boat or Manta Reef Camp on North Pemba.
Conditions: Best dived on an incoming tide in the afternoon. Should a current be present, the dive can be completed as a relaxed drift dive.
Average depth: 12–15m (40–50ft).
Maximum depth: 30m (100ft).
Average visibility: 15m (50ft) on average, but can reach 40m (131ft).
Average water temperature: 27°C (80°F).
The top of the reef starts at 8m (27ft) and declines at a 60° angle to a maximum depth of 30m (100ft). The coral is profuse and mainly unspoilt, but in places damaged by anchors and dynamite fishing. In some parts, remarkable tabletop coral is stacked in shelves against the incline, where yellow and blue royal angelfish abound.

The best depths to dive on this reef appear to be at around 12–15m (40–50ft) because of the pristine state of the coral, the amount of colourful tropical reef inhabitants and the abundance of natural light.

Fish school in huge numbers off Pemba Island.

2 NJAO GAP: SOUTHERN REEF

★★★★

Location: 04°57.6'S;39°39.65'E; to the southwest of Njao Gap and about 500m (550 yards) out. See map.
Access: By live-aboard diving vessels from Kenya, dive schools in Zanzibar, own boat or Manta Reef Camp on North Pemba.
Conditions: Strong currents may run across the face of the wall. The best time to dive is in the afternoon when more light is available, and on an incoming tide that clears the water.
Average depth: 12–20m (40–65ft).
Maximum depth: Beyond maximum sport-diving depth.
Average visibility: 30–40m (100–130ft).
Average water temperature: 27°C (80°F).
The top of the reef ranges from 20m (65ft) in the north to about 12m (40ft) in the south and drops steeply beyond maximum sport-diving depths. The reef runs in a southeasterly direction. In the north, the top forms a sandy plateau, after which the coral-encrusted wall drops off to great depths to the south. The steep wall forms dramatic overhangs and the sections below 20m (66ft) are covered with sea whips and large gorgonian sea fans. At depths of around 30m (33 yards), some giant groupers, large Napoleon wrasse and sea turtles may be seen, as may big red snappers, large spadefish, unicorns and big titan or moustache triggerfish (*Balistoides viridescens*). Towards the south the top of the reef rises at a shallow incline to about 12m (40ft) where profuse coral growths are inhabited by prolific varieties of small tropical marine life. On the sandy sections around 10m (33ft) depth, shy garden eels peer out of their hides like periscopes.

3 FUNDU REEF: SOUTHERN WALL

★★★★

Location: 05°00,5+S; 39°39,2+E.
To the south of the Fundu Gap and approximately 200m (660ft) out in a southwesterly direction. See map.
Access: By live-aboard diving vessels from Kenya, dive schools in Zanzibar, own boat or Manta Reef Camp on North Pemba.

Conditions: The best time to dive this reef is on an incoming tide with an afternoon sun. Strong currents can be present, necessitating a drift dive. Closer to the gap where the reef forms a shoulder to the east, the reef drops out of sight far beyond maximum sport-diving depths. Towards the gap the current normally picks up speed as it approaches the fairly narrow channel.
Average depth: The top of the reef is at 5m (17ft) and slopes down at an angle of approximately 60°.
Maximum depth: 25m (82ft) in the south and drops to far below 40m (131ft) closer to the gap to the north.
Average visibility: 20–40m (65–131ft) depending on tides and plankton concentrations.
The coral formations are superb, with shallow caverns, overhangs and sheer walls. The shallower depths are covered with large plates of leaf (rose) coral and soft corals, which are undamaged.

Fish life is plentiful, with dense masses of yellow and/or blackspot snappers, sweetlips and damselfish, interspersed with blue humphead parrotfish (*Scarus syanescens*), Napoleon wrasse, large triggerfish and other big pelagic fish such as kingfish and jacks (caranx). Large schools of sheepshead (*Archosargus probatocephalus*) hover in the shallower sections of the reef, which is adorned with small yellow sea fans. Below depths of 25m (82ft) large red gorgonian sea fans are found. Due to the shallower maximum depth of the reef to the south, it is a good site for an orientation dive and buoyancy checkout for first-time divers to Pemba, after which a swim towards the gap will provide a foretaste of the deeper dives to follow.

MANTA RAYS

For divers, the gentle and graceful manta ray *(Manta birostris)* is one of the most sought-after of all marine animals. These giants have a wingspan of up to 6.5m (21ft), and the creature's effortless, flapping glide, coupled with an inborn curiosity, often brings it quite close. An encounter with a manta ray will cause any diver to experience sheer exhilaration.

Mantas have disc-shaped bodies with sharply angular wings and a thin whiplike tail, the length of which roughly equals body width. The colouration is blue-black on top with a creamy white underbelly, which is sometimes marked by dark spots, with the gill ventricles clearly visible. The large head ends in two paddlelike projections called cephalic horns or fins, which funnel copious quantities of water containing zooplankton, fish fry, tiny crustacea larvae and small squid into the toothless mouth of the ray. Young are born live and about 30cm (12in) in diameter. They reach sexual maturity at around 100cm (40in). Despite their great weight (up to two tonnes), they are often seen leaping and cartwheeling right out of the water. Mantas inhabit tropical waters around the globe and frequent mid-water either singly or in groups. They tend to return to the same reefs quite frequently. (*See* Manta Point; No. 4.)

4 MANTA POINT

★★★★★

Location: 05°00'S; 39°40'E; approximately 300m (1 000ft) outside and slightly to the northwest of Fundu Gap. See map.
Access: By live-aboard diving vessels from Kenya, dive schools in Zanzibar, own boat or Manta Reef Camp on North Pemba.
Conditions: The best time to dive Manta Point is on an incoming tide when clear waters are swept in. A strong current may be present at times and it is then best to treat the dive as a drift dive.
Average depth: 10–30m (33–100ft).
Maximum depth: Beyond 40m (131ft).
Average visibility: 20m (65 feet) on average , but can reach 40m (131ft).
Average water temperature: 27°C (80°F).
It is undoubtedly the sight of the majestic giant manta rays *(Manta birostris)* that turns Manta Point into an exhilarating five-star dive – an experience which is hard to beat anywhere in the world. More than 15 big mantas have been seen during a single dive – either singly or in groups. They often appear out of the blue at depths that range from just under the surface to below 30m (100ft). The shallower sightings are generally best because of the proximity of the mantas and the good lighting conditions. They cannot exactly be considered tame, but are curious enough to come really close to divers, and to hover for a while. They reputedly frequent the pinnacle that reaches within 9m (30ft) of the surface, to scratch their underbellies on the coral. This of course offers fantastic photo opportunities, and it is advisable to save some frames for what may be the best shot yet. Early mornings or late afternoons are the best times to see mantas, when they normally swim past against the current. Even if these gentle creatures do not grace the dive, it is still a five-star experience as there are lovely coral formations and a steep drop-off on the western side. One could not wish to see more fish of so many varieties.

The pinnacle itself is densely covered with shoals of small goldies, among which hundreds of trumpetfish hunt. It is fascinating to watch them suck in their prey like giant pipettes, and they are often joined in the hunt by larger predators such as jacks, tuna, kingfish and barracuda, which cause the fish to scatter and congregate in big flowing clouds of oranges and yellows. An entire dive may be spent just around the pinnacle, waiting for the mantas to appear, and watching the variety of clownfish – hiding in giant anemones – lionfish, moray eels, titan triggerfish, and just about every variety of Indo-Pacific tropical marine life, including the well-camouflaged spotfin frogfish (*Antennarius nummifer*). Further down the drop-offs, the deeper sections of the wall are adorned with delicate gorgonian sea fans, and walls of brittle leaf coral line the shallower sections. Napoleon wrasse hover below 20m (65ft), and white-tipped reef sharks have also been spotted here. On the northeastern side of the pinnacle the reef slopes down to approximately 20m (65ft), with beautiful sandy 'beaches' among valleys of coral.

One cannot, of course, be guaranteed the presence of mantas, but Manta Point is, nevertheless, one of the best dive sites on the entire East African coast. An itinerary should be planned to include more than one dive on this wonderful site, if time allows.

5 UVINJE GAP: NORTHERN WALL

★★★★

Location: 05°09.2'S; 39°38.9'E; located off the southwestern tip of the reef to the north of the Uvinje Gap. See map.
Access: By live-aboard diving vessels from Kenya, dive schools in Zanzibar, own boat or Manta Reef Camp on North Pemba.
Conditions: Calm, especially on a slack tide, but can turn rough with strong currents in windy conditions.
Average depth: The top of the reef is found at 8m (27ft) to 12m (40ft) deep.
Maximum depth: Beyond 40m (131ft).
Average visibility: 20–30m (65–100ft) on average, but may increase to 40–50m (131–165ft).
Average water temperature: 27°C (80°F).

The coral formations on this reef are excellent and consist of a tremendous variety, including very large sheets of tabletop coral and solid banks of delicate leaf (lettuce) coral interspersed with exceptionally large anemones and their clownfish guests. The most impressive features of this reef are the superb coral growth and sheer drop-offs with ledges at 40–50m (131–165ft). Triggerfish are plentiful and small white-tipped reef sharks may be found sleeping underneath the coral shelves. The shallows teem with impressive coral heads, which are richly inhabited with swarming reef life, and covered with colourful sponges and other forms of invertebrate life.

6 KOKOTA REEF (Night Dive Site)

★★★★

Location: 05°09.4'S; 39°38.2'E; inside Uvinje Gap and west of Kokota Island. See map.
Access: By live-aboard diving vessels from Kenya, dive schools in Zanzibar or own boat.
Conditions: As it is on the leeward side of Kokota Island, which has a fairly high profile, the sea conditions here are generally calm. Together with the shallower depths, this makes it an ideal night diving site, and it is therefore described as such.

Tiny orange goldies are oblivious of the presence of a crescent-tailed rockcod.

Average depth: The top of the reef starts at 8m (25ft).
Maximum depth: 20m (65 feet).
Average visibility: 30–40m (100–131ft) and may increase to more than 50m (165ft).
Average water temperature: 28°C (82°F).
The shallow but steep wall can be enjoyed by drifting along with the current, which is generally not too strong. Kokota Reef makes for an extremely colourful dive (by the light of underwater torches, of course) with many brittle stars (*Crinoids*), giant clams, large starfish and box stars, hermit crabs and cleverly camouflaged sponge crabs (*Petalomera lateralis*) to be seen. All these creatures venture out of their daytime hides to feed in the dark. There are also many slate pencil urchins (*Heterocentrotus mammilatus*) and large radiant urchins (*Centrostephanus coronatus*). The fish life includes squirrelfish and a few colourful parrotfish.

The best feature of a night dive in this part of the world is, of course, the sight of the beautiful Spanish dancer (*Hexabranchus sanguineus*). This glorious creature, which is a member of the nudibranch family, undulates gracefully when picked up and released. This should be done very gently, however, and great care must be taken not to harm the animal. Spanish dancers make superb subjects for photography, but are too big for most close-up attachments and this should be kept in mind when selecting photographic gear for a night dive. Usually bright red in colour (East African specimens vary from orange to red), the dancer's flowing 'skirt' is laced with a delicate white fringe, and its graceful movements are reminiscent of a flamenco dancer. Even its eggs are clustered together in attractive red or pink rosettes, which can often be seen during daytime dives, clinging to coral branches or sponges. The sight of a Spanish dancer invariably turns a dive into a five-star experience.

A night dive off Pemba Island should be included at least once in a diving itinerary of the island (on live-aboard vessels a night dive can be done almost every night) and sufficient torches, batteries and light sticks should be carried. It is, of course, always a good idea to check out conditions and, if possible, to mark the site with a buoy during daylight hours.

An alternate protected and good night dive site is on the Kokota Plateau, with location at the following co-ordinates: 05°08.2'S; 39°37.6'E.

Rose and staghorn corals on Pemba's reef.

7 UVINJE GAP: SOUTHERN WALL

★★★★★★★★

Location: 05°08.5'S; 39°37'E; on the southern side of the Uvinje Gap where the reef forms an elbow that swings into the gap. See map.
Access: By live-aboard diving vessels from Kenya, dive schools in Zanzibar or own boat.
Conditions: Plan to do this dive in the afternoon with the sun to the west and on an incoming tide for maximum available light and clear water.
Average depth: The top of the reef is only 6m (20ft) below the surface, which makes it ideal for snorkelling when conditions allow.
Maximum depth: Beyond 40m (131ft), and indicated on charts as an impressive 810m (2700ft).
Average visibility: 30–40m (100–131ft); may increase to more than 50m (165ft).
Average water temperature: 27–28°C (80–82°F).
With good sunlight and clear water conditions this must surely rate as one of the more spectacular dives on the western side of Pemba Island. The sheer wall forms breathtaking overhangs, pinnacles and swim-throughs in which large black coral bushes grow. Among their branches hide a multitude of fish, such as royal angelfish, bluebanded surgeonfish, butterflyfish of many varieties, moorish idols and many others.

The deeper sections of the reef are frequented by Napoleon wrasse, large groupers (*Plectropomus laevis*), which hide under the coral bommies (heads), and other good-sized pelagic fish. In the shallows the most remarkable of the multitude of tropical fish are the schooling coachmen (*Heniochus diphreutes*), powder-blue surgeonfish, garden eels, large stonefish, moray eels and octopus. The coral formations in the shallows are equally impressive, with big soft coral bushes and large coral heads dominated by thousands of goldies. This side of Uvinje Gap is excellent for making a deep dive down the

Starfish on a night dive.

wall followed by a leisurely return to the shallow surface sections. This rules out the need to hover in one spot to complete a safety stop.

8 MESALI ISLAND

★★★★★★★★★★

Location: 05°14'S; 39°36'E. See map. The main dive sites are on the western and northwestern sides of the island and approximately 100m (333ft) outside and in a line with the small exposed rocky islet.
Access: By live-aboard diving vessels from Kenya, dive schools in Zanzibar or own boat.
Conditions: Generally calm water conditions prevail during the diving season, with the clearest water on an incoming tide. The leeward side of the island is sheltered, with placid waters. Care should be exercised on this dive site because the clarity of the water makes the immense depths misleading.
Average depth: 10–15m (33–50ft) in the shallower sections towards the island.
Maximum depth: Far below 40m (131ft). The walls plunge down vertically to depths of more than 600m (2 000ft).
Average visibility: 40m (131ft), often increasing to 60m (200ft).
Average water temperature: 28–30°C (82–86°F).
The first and lasting impression of Mesali Island is the colour of the water, which ranges from a vivid turquoise in the shallows to a deep indigo blue where the land falls away. When swimming westward (it can be done from shore by fit divers), the first dense coral formations appear at depths of 5–8m (16–25ft). This section of the reef runs for a considerable distance to the north and south and is eminently suitable for snorkelling. The reef then slopes down to depths of approximately 20m (65ft), where beautiful sandy gullies are encountered. These gullies can be seen from the surface on snorkel – when the water is clear enough.

After the gullies, the coral walls drop vertically and sheer to great depths. On the wall's edge are solid banks of delicate leaf (rose) coral, crowned by huge mushroom coral heads under which fish of every variety play hide and seek. The wall is in pristine condition and the coral seems untouched by anchor damage, nets or dynamite fishing. The entire length of this considerable wall presents a fairytale dive in superb coral gardens, the beauty of which can match the best in the world.

Small frogfish can be seen hiding between blue pipe sponge tubes and offer excellent opportunities, together with colourful, tiny nudibranchs, for macrophotography. The deeper sections of the reef are the hunting grounds of the big game fish – barracuda, kingfish and tuna – and huge Napoleon wrasse often hover in mid-water, together with large longfin batfish (*Platax teira*).

Because of the calm and extremely clear waters, this reef is ideally suited to photographers' needs and great panoramic shots can be obtained. It only takes the sight of sharks, mantas, or other big fish to turn this dive into a five-star experience, although coral enthusiasts will already have rated it so.

The waters around the island itself are a paradise for snorkellers, where the surrealistic Picasso triggerfish (*Rhinecanthus aculeatus*) hides among isolated coral. Beautiful empty shells may be collected in the shallow waters, even without the aid of a mask, but care should be taken not to remove any live or inhabited ones. Remember that the removal of any shell takes away a potential home for a hermit crab.

The island is a good place to have a beach barbecue and watch the exquisite sunsets, but beware of sand fleas. Leave the island as you found it. Mesali Island will (as is the case with most of the reefs) make an ideal subject for a conservation area in Tanzanian waters, as its present pristine state needs all the protection it can get.

9 PANZA POINT: SOUTHERN WRECK

★★★★

Location: 05°29.11'S; 39°38'E; inside the reef to the west of Panza Point. See map.
Access: By live-aboard diving vessels from Kenya, dive schools in Zanzibar or own boat.
Conditions: A very strong north-flowing current may be present and can rip through some sections of the wreck. As with any wreck dive, care should be taken, and it may be a good idea to wear gloves in case it becomes necessary to hold on to the wreck.
Average depth: 3–10m (10–33ft).
Maximum depth: 10–12m (33–40ft).

Spanish dancer photographed on a night dive.

Average visibility: More than 30m (100ft) and may increase to 60m (200ft).

Average water temperature: 28–30°C (82–86°C).

The topmost part of the wreck is exposed during low tide, making the wreck clearly visible from the surface. The vessel is lying on its side with the stern pointing to the east, and is oriented in a southeast to northwesterly direction. The wreck should be visible even at high tides when you use a mask.

The wreck has not been identified, but it looks like a 1950s iron freight steamer that probably hit the reef and sank. A great length of thick anchor chain is draped on the reef of Panza Point and it is possible that the anchor came adrift and the swift north-flowing current probably did the rest.

Unlike many other wrecks this one is extremely photogenic, and the clarity of the water and good lighting conditions contribute to dramatic shots. The deformed shapes create dramatic and interesting angles which are covered with colourful marine growths, soft corals, and sponges. The funnels create interesting tunnels to swim through, in which large fish such as groupers often hide. They also afford good hiding places for photographers to capture elusive fish on film. The large steam condenser can also be seen and the freight masts point forlornly towards the surface.

The Spanish dancer's eggs form a 'skirt', or sea rose.

The marine life is plentiful and includes large emperor angelfish, unicorns, sweetlips, groupers, triggerfish, surgeonfish, and a great variety of brightly coloured small tropical reef fish.

This may be an excellent five-star night dive for experienced divers in calm conditions.

10 PANZA POINT: EMERALD REEF

★★★★★

Location: 05°29.3'S; 39°38.35'E; the southernmost tip of Pemba Island, marked on charts as Ras Mugani. The reef runs in a westerly direction for approximately 1km (0.6 mile). See map.

Access: By live-aboard diving vessels from Kenya, dive schools in Zanzibar or own boat.

Conditions: The current flowing from Zanzibar to the south splits here and can be very strong, so drift dives are suggested.

Average depth: Ranging from 3–30m (10–100ft).

Maximum depth: Reached at a sandy, sloping bottom at 30m (100ft).

Average visibility: 40m (131ft) and may increase to 60m (200ft).

Average water temperature: 28–30°C (82–86°F).

The name 'Emerald Island' may well be given to Pemba because of this reef. Emerald Reef is covered in a green coral, which lends an intense hue to the entire reef, and creates the illusion of floating in a fairytale garden of dramatic, soft coral trees backed by huge coral heads. The coral formations are pristine and unspoilt, and the reef lends itself ideally to great drift dives because of its length and immense beauty, coupled with the fact that the water is crystal clear.

One should not become too absorbed in the reef scenery only, as the greatest show may be passing behind in the form of a wall of hundreds of glittering, silver barracuda. The ghostly outline of a shark may be seen cruising silently through deep blue water. Lots of bigeye emperorfish (*Monotaxis grandoculis*) mix with unicorns and surgeonfish, bigeye trevally (*Caranx sexfasciatus*) and thick-lipped Napoleon wrasse. This reef seems to attract the big pelagic game fish and these encounters, coupled with the spectacular reef scenery, create a dive not to be missed at any expense.

At a depth of 12m (40ft) there is an extensive length of thick anchor chain – probably belonging to the Southern Wreck (No. 9) – draped across the reef. The coral has, in places, completely surrounded the chain.

How to Get There

By air:
Air Tanzania, tel. Pemba 2162, flies from Zanzibar and Tanga (on the Tanzanian mainland) to Chake Chake on Pemba Island three times a week. Air Zanzibar may be contacted for charter flights from Zanzibar or Dar es Salaam. For bookings and enquiries contact **Coastal Travel Limited,** Upanga Road, Dar es Salaam, tel. (051) 37479/80, fax. (051) 46045.

By sea:
It is possible to take a **dhow** from Mombasa, Tanga or Zanzibar to Pemba Island. This depends on the availability of a ship and on the winds, and so is very much a hit-and-miss arrangement. Make enquiries in the ports in these places. The dhows are very basic and sleeping is done on deck. Passengers should bring with them all food, drinking water and bedding. Ablutions are done over the side, and there is usually a cantilevered 'toilet'. These trips are only for adventurous travellers who do not mind roughing it. Fares are extremely cheap in comparison to other modes of transport, but the length of the journey cannot be guaranteed as contrary winds often entail a lot of tacking. Some dhows are motorized and so are less dependent on wind conditions.

Live-aboard charters
During the diving season (October to April), several live-aboard options are available from the Kenyan coast:

From Shimoni
For more information and bookings on the MY *Kisiwani* contact: **Pemba Diving Limited,** P O Box 1475, Ukunda, tel. (0127) 2331/3155, fax. 3154. (*See* Directory on page 80 for more details

From Kilifi
For bookings and enquiries about the SY *Aristos of Kenya*, contact **Dive Safari Kenya,** P O Box 128, Kilifi, tel. (0125) 22222, fax. 22251. During the southeast monsoon, guests are first transported to Shimoni, from where live-aboard excursions depart. Dive courses and short trips are available on request in advance.

Dive Facilities

Equipment is catered for in varying degrees on the live-aboard vessels (*see* above) and it is best to enquire beforehand from the agents or operators as to what is available and what should be brought. At time of writing there was one land-based diving facility: **Manta Reef Camp** on the northern tip of the island caters for divers in luxury tented accommodation. All dives on the neighbouring reefs are done from here. For details and bookings, contact **One Earth Safaris,** P O Box 82234, Mombasa, tel. (011) 471771, fax. 471349. This is a PADI facility that offers courses, day charters and gear rental. Excursions to Pemba Island are arranged by them and this may be combined with a land safari.

How to Get Around

Transport between the main towns is available in *matatus* (minibuses) or wooden-sided trucks with bench seats. There is a lack of public transport off the main roads which makes it difficult to get around and explore. There are no car-rental firms, but taxis may be hired.

Where to Stay

Wete
(No street addresses or dialling codes.)
The **Hoteli ya Wete,** tel. Pemba 4301, is the main accommodation in the town. It is government-owned, and located at the top end of the main street. The rooms are clean, self-contained and have a fan. One single or double rate, which includes breakfast, lunch, dinner and cold beer, is available.

The **Sharouk Guest House,** tel. Pemba 4386, in the centre of town, offers more basic but friendly accommodation in the form of five clean rooms, one of which is self-contained. Dhows to Zanzibar, Dar es Salaam and Tanga can be secured by the owner.

Chake Chake
The **Hoteli ya Chake,** tel. Pemba 2069 or 2189; located in the centre of town and the only place to stay. It is government-run, and all facilities and prices are exactly the same as the Hoteli ya Wete in Wete. Outside town are the guest house **Nassir** at Machomane (no telephone) and the **Star Guest House** (no telephone) opposite the stadium.

Mkoani
The only hotel, the **Hoteli ya Mkoani** (no telephone), offers exactly the same facilities and rates as the hotels in Wete and Chake Chake.

Camping
All camping excursions should be fully self-sufficient and permission should first be sought from the authorities in the nearest town.

Where to Eat

At any of the hotels in the main towns (*see* Where to Stay). Restaurants tend to have no names. Food may be bought in the small, colourful *dukas* or stores alongside the roads. Fresh fish and fruit are often brought to the boats by local fisherman and it is a good idea to have some spare Tanzanian shillings handy.

Regional Highlights

The main towns are interesting to visit, if only to see a lifestyle still very much untouched by Western influence. During the hot months of December, January and February, there are bullfights in the Portuguese tradition (in which the bulls are not killed) in Chake Chake. The tourist office is next to the Hoteli ya Wete, tel. Pemba 2121.

Emergency Measures

The nearest **hospitals** are: Chake Chake Hospital, tel. Chake Chake 2311, Mkoani Hospital, P O Box 201, Mkoani, tel. Mkoani 6075 / 6011; and Wete Hospital, tel. Wete 4001.

The airport in Chake Chake will be the obvious evacuation point in case of an emergency.

The nearest **recompression chamber** is in Mombasa at the Kenya Navy's base, tel. (011) 451201 ext. 3308 (24-hour standby availability).

The international **emergency radio channel** is **#16**.

ZANZIBAR ISLAND

The island of Zanzibar brings images of idyllic tropical holidays to mind, and proves to be as fascinating as the travel brochures and history books promise. It has for many years been a favourite travel destination for those in the know, but has only recently become known as a superb diving destination. Zanzibar's reefs are shallow in comparison to those of Pemba Island, but the water here is clear and generally calm. Coral is mostly unspoilt and teems with large numbers of tropical marine inhabitants. South of Bokibu (No. 9) are the Kizimkazi and Pungume patches, and Pungume Island, reputed to offer excellent diving but as yet pretty well unexplored. These sites may prove worthwhile for those who can get there. The infrastructure on the island is well developed and it offers a great variety of top-side attractions. Entry is at Zanzibar's busy port or international airport on the west coast.

Diving Conditions: The West Coast

October and November are the best months for diving near Zanzibar. The western side of the island is well protected, making diving enjoyable for most of the year. There are a number of small islands and sand banks not far from Zanzibar, and supposedly some 200 wrecks resting on the bottom of Stone Town harbour. Diving conditions here are not good, but if you are keen to dive a wreck, it can be done. Facilities in and around Stone Town are modern and all dive-related needs are well catered for. All dives are done by boat and NAUI and PADI dive courses of all levels are taught.

Diving Conditions: The East Coast

There are a few diving operations at hotels on this section of the coast, and the diveable fringing reef that stretches out beyond the shoreline is still virtually unexplored. It is, however, possible to rent equipment from some of the diving centres on the west coast. Local motorized fishing or sailing craft also transport divers to the reefs from the villages.

Left: *Local fisherman prepare to venture out into the turquoise waters around Zanzibar Island.*
Above: *A beautifully coloured wavy aperture identifies the giant clam, which uses projecting lobes to filter algae.*

ZANZIBAR ISLAND
N
1 Leven Bank
Ras Nungwi
Nungwi
Ras Kinunduni
Tumbatu Island
Popo Island
Mnemba Fishing Club
Mwemba Island
2 Mwemba Island
Potowa
Jongowe
Shirazi Ruins
Mwanahaza
Matemwe
Matemwe Bungalows
Mkokotoni
Mkwajuni
Ras Uso wa Membe
Makoba
Pwani Mchangani
Bumbwini
Kinyasini
Mahonda
Kiwengwa
Mangapwani Slave Caves
Kichwele Forest
Pongwe
Chuini
Ndagaa
Mawimbini Hotel Village
Persian Baths
Tamarind
Uroa
Kibweni Palace Ruins
Kidichi
Uzini
Changuu Island
Persian Baths
Changuu Island Resort
Mtoni
Ruins
Ras Michamwi
Michamvi
Chapani Island
Dunga
Bawi Island 3
Dunga Ruins
Chwaka
ZANZIBAR
Stone Town
4-9
Chwaka Bay
Fuoni
Tunguu
4-9
4. Nyange
5. Pange
6. Pwakuu
7. Murogo
8. Mwamba Ukombe (Outer)
9. Bokibu
Chukwani
Bwejuu
AIRPORT
Ukanga Is.
Jozani Forest
Kikungwi
Jozani
Paje
Chumbe Island
Kiwani Bay
Kitogani
Stingray Alley
Pete
10
11
Fumba
Bweleo
Muungoni
Jamblani
Jambiani Reef (Unicorn Reef)
Miwi Island
Uzi Island
Pete Inlet
Kwale Island
Menai Bay
Zanzibar Channel
Vundwe Island
Shirazi Mosque
Makunduchi
Pungume Island
Kufile
Kizimkazi
Mtende
Ras Kazim Kazi
Zinga
Kerege
INDIAN OCEAN
Munoe
Kunduchi
Oyster Bay
0
15 km
A7
Kibaha
DAR ES SALAAM
0
10 miles
Ubungo
Mjimwema

Fusiliers are always found in large groups near reefs.

The West Coast

1 LEVEN BANK

★★★★★

Location: North of Ras Nungwi on the northern tip of Zanzibar Island. It is not always easy to find and a local skipper is needed to pinpoint the exact location. The site is not buoyed. See map.
Access: Approximately 30 minutes by dive boat from Ras Nungwi.
Conditions: Conditions do not always allow diving and there is generally a strong north-flowing current present. This site is best dived on a high slack tide. It is best to treat this dive as a drift dive when a current is present.
Average depth: 17m (55ft).
Maximum depth: 40m (130ft).
Average visibility: 25m (80ft).
Average water temperature: 25–29°C (77–84°F).
The great depth and strong currents found here mean that this dive is exclusively the domain of experienced divers, who can be guaranteed one of the best dives in the region. The coral growths are not profuse, mainly because of the strong currents and depth, but the variety includes pillar and honeycomb coral, interspersed with soft coral. All of these are unspoilt, and richly inhabited by small marine life. The reef is round in shape and quite flat. It angles off at a shallow incline towards the north. The greatest attraction on this reef is its prolific fish life, particularly the large fish, which include giant guitarfish (*Rhynchobatus djiddensis*), huge stingrays and big honeycomb moray eels, giant groupers as well as small rockcod and king mackerel.

2 MWEMBA ISLAND

★★★★★★★★

Location: Southwest of Ras Nungwi. The site is not buoyed. See map.
Access: Approximately 15 minutes by dive boat from Stone Town.
Conditions: There is generally a current present, and divers should be prepared for a drift dive, so some experience is needed. This site is best dived on a high slack tide. The best diving is found on the south side of the island where big swells may be present.
Average depth: 14m (45ft).
Maximum depth: 30m (130ft).
Average visibility: 20m (80ft).
Average water temperature: 25–29°C (77–84°F).
The reef drops off at an incline to the bottom and is mostly covered with soft coral growths. All the coral formations are in a pristine state, and the hard corals include pillar, honeycomb and warty coral. Small and colourful tropical fish abound and large schools of snappers hover around vast clouds of glassies or batfish.

There are a number of large honeycomb moray eels, and turtles are often encountered. Big reef fish such as groupers and rockcod inhabit the reefs and large game fish are often seen.

3 BAWI ISLAND

★★★★★★★

Location: West of Stone Town. The site is buoyed. See map.
Access: Approximately 15 minutes by dive boat from Stone Town.
Conditions: This site is best dived on a high tide. A mild current is usually present. The east side of the island offers the best diving.
Average depth: 10m (33ft).
Maximum depth: 18m (40ft).
Average visibility: 11m (36ft).
Average water temperature: 25–29°C (77–84°F).
Bawi Island is a small reef that rises from a sandy bottom at 18m (40ft) to form an incline with overhangs and pinnacles, and consists mainly of unspoilt hard and soft coral varieties. In the shallower parts, brain coral predominates, with the gorgonian sea fan type found in the deeper sections.

Large shoals of yellowback fusiliers congregate around the coral formations, joined by big twinspot snappers (*Lutjanus bohar*) and a variety of pufferfish. Sand sharks are often seen on the bottom, together with many blue-spotted stingrays.

Yellowtail goldies live on the outer reef slopes.

4 NYANGE

★★★★★★★★

Location: Southwest of Stone Town. The site is not buoyed. See map.
Access: Approximately 20 minutes by dive boat from Stone Town.
Conditions: This site is best dived on a high tide. A mild current may be present. The best diving is done on the eastern side of the reef.
Average depth: 12m (40ft).
Maximum depth: 16m (52ft).
Average visibility: 11m (36ft).
Average water temperature: 25–29°C (77–84°F).
The reef forms a shallow incline that is covered with big plate and staghorn corals in the shallow depths, with mushroom corals and sea fans in the deeper water.

A large pinnacle that forms a delightful swim-through is filled with thousands of glassies. There are also some big resident groupers, as well as batfish and coachmen.

Typical marine life on this very good reef includes stonefish and scorpionfish, garfish, goldies, groupers and twinspot snappers.

5 PANGE

★★★★★★

Location: Southwest of Stone Town. The site is buoyed. See map.
Access: Approximately 20 minutes by dive boat from Stone Town.
Conditions: This site may be dived at any time throughout the year. There is hardly ever any current present, and it is an easy and safe dive which is suitable for all levels of divers.
Average depth: 10m (33ft).
Maximum depth: 14m (45ft).
Average visibility: 10m (33ft).
Average water temperature: 25–29°C (77–84°F).
The reef is covered with staghorn, honeycomb, fire and mushroom corals, which form overhangs and pinnacles. The coral formations are inhabited by surgeonfish, triggerfish, unicorns, cowfish, pufferfish, parrotfish and a remarkable number of blue emperor fish.

6 PWAKUU

★★★★★★★

Location: Southwest of Stone Town. The site is not buoyed. See map.
Access: Approximately 25 minutes by dive boat from Stone Town.
Conditions: This site may be dived at any time throughout the year. There is hardly ever any current present and it is a dive suited to all levels of divers. All areas of this reef provide good diving.
Average depth: 15m (50ft).
Maximum depth: 28m (90ft).
Average visibility: 14m (45ft).
Average water temperature: 25–29°C (77–84°F).
The reef is in an unspoilt condition and the incline forms overhangs, swim-throughs and pinnacles with a great variety of corals, including brain, staghorn, plate, mushroom, honeycomb and peacock, which are interspersed with soft coral bushes. These are covered with small marine life of every kind. The larger fish species typically found here include Napoleon wrasse (on the deeper sections), moray eels, blade fish and turtles.

7 MUROGO

★★★★★★★★

Location: Southwest of Stone Town. The site is not buoyed. See map.
Access: Approximately 25 minutes by dive boat from Stone Town.
Conditions: The best time to dive this site is on a low tide in the early morning. A mild current may be present, and it is an easy dive suited to all levels of divers. The best corals are found on the northern side of the reef.
Average depth: 15m (50ft).
Maximum depth: 22m (71ft).
Average visibility: 10m (45ft).
Average water temperature: 25–29°C (77–84°F).
This big reef forms a drop-off which offers some of the most spectacular corals in the region. The stunning formations are in a pristine state. The hard coral that domi-

nates Murogo Reef includes plate, acropora, brain and abundant staghorn coral. There are also many large soft coral growths present. Overhangs, swim-throughs, pinnacles and gullies add to the dramatic impact of the dive. Small and large marine life is present in copious numbers, adding colour to the splendid beauty of the corals on this excellent, top-rated reef.

8 MWAMBA UKOMBE (OUTER)

★★★

Location: South of Stone Town. The site is not buoyed. See map.
Access: Approximately 30 minutes by dive boat and 2hr by dhow from Stone Town.
Conditions: This site may be dived at any time throughout the year. A mild current may be present. This dive is suited to all levels of divers. The western side of this reef (outer side) offers the best diving. From time to time a large number of jellyfish may be encountered on the surface, but these are generally easy to avoid.
Average depth: 16m (52ft).
Maximum depth: 28m (90ft).
Average visibility: 10m (33ft).
Average water temperature: 25–29°C (77–84°F).
Outer Mwamba Ukombe Reef forms an incline that is covered with hard coral formations in an unspoilt state. The reef offers good hiding places for lobsters and big rockcod, and big parrotfish and turtles swim among the myriad small tropicals. The western side of the reef is decorated with many large vase sponges.

9 BOKIBU

★★★★

Location: Southwest of Stone Town. The site is not buoyed but is easily found on low tide when the sandbank is visible above the surface. See map.
Access: Approximately 40 minutes by dive boat and 2hr by dhow from Stone Town.
Conditions: This site can be dived at any time throughout the diving season. A mild current may be present and it is an easy dive suited to all levels of divers. The eastern side of the sandbank is the most densely populated with marine life.
Average depth: 16m (52ft).
Maximum depth: 28m (90ft).
Average visibility: 18m (45ft).
Average water temperature: 25–29°C (77–84°F).
The coral formations on the eastern side of the sandbank consist mainly of soft varieties interspersed with hard brain, mushroom and honeycomb corals.

Typical marine life found on this reef includes shoals of pelagic fish, with schools of juvenile tuna and jacks, blade fish, small groupers and turtles. Napoleon wrasse and white-tipped reef sharks are also seen.

The crown-of-thorns starfish has flourished because its natural predator, the giant triton, is collected by humans.

Stone Town's buildings include the House of Wonders, whose clock tower is visible at right.

The name Zanzibar may have its origins in the Persian words *zang* (Negro or black) and *bar* (coast), although the Arabs claim that the name comes from the phrase *zayn za'l barr*, which means 'fair is the island'. The more appropriate of the various options is a Swahili name meaning 'heavenlike'.

Zanzibar, in actual fact, only covers the magisterial district of the town, and Unguja is the proper name for the island. For most visitors, however, the name of the island firmly remains Zanzibar.

Market scene in Zanzibar.

The island possesses a fascinating and often turbulent history. It was first mentioned as early as A.D. 60, in a Greek mariner's guide. The Bantu were the first inhabitants of the island, but Zanzibar was known to seafarers from distant Phoenicia, Egypt, Sumeria, Arabia, China and India. Later came explorers and traders from European countries such as Portugal, Holland and Britain.

Zanzibar's first traders were Arabs, who began to settle on the island in the 9th century. These enterprising seafarers plied the coastal waters of East Africa in resplendent wooden dhows pushed along by the monsoon winds. They brought with them the Muslim religion, the influence of which is still prevalent today. By A.D. 1200, the Shirazi arrived from Persia, adding their contribution to the island's rich mixture of Arab and Bantu blood, and giving rise to the origins of the Swahili race.

The Portuguese arrived in 1498 under the command of Vasco da Gama. Portugal maintained a presence on the island until 1652, when Zanzibar was sacked by the Omani Arabs.

Until 1740, the island's exports consisted mainly of ivory, spices, gum copal, copra, cowrie shells and hides. However, when Sultan Sayyid Said moved his court from Oman to Zanzibar in 1740, the miserable trade in human slaves became the mainstay

of Zanzibar's economy. These pitiful creatures were shackled and transported for long distances on foot from the interior of Africa and piled into dhows in the port of Bagamoyo, from where they were shipped across to the slave market of Zanzibar. The 'fortunate' ones that survived the short but treacherous crossing in disease-infested vessels were then sold to work in the clove plantations on the island, or shipped off to the Far East to work as domestic labourers. The export of slaves was banned in 1873 after interference by the British, who applied pressure to the new sultan, Sayyid Bargash. Together with Pemba Island to the north, Zanzibar became a British protectorate in 1890.

After Zanzibar gained independence from Britain in December 1963, a violent revolution in 1964 led to the removal of the Arab population. On 24 April 1964, Zanzibar and Pemba joined Tanganyika to form the new state of Tanzania.

Tourism is still in its infancy in Zanzibar, but the number of visitors is rapidly increasing. Many new hotels and guest houses have opened their doors to visitors and a number of new dive centres now cater for divers. Zanzibar's superb diving conditions have been much publicized, and more and more divers are discovering the unspoilt reefs around the island. For divers and non-divers alike, the island offers a wealth of interesting things to see and do. Apart from relaxing under a palm tree or *makuti* shade on the white coral beaches, visitors can opt for a walking tour through the narrow streets of Zanzibar's old Stone Town. There are numerous guide books available for this purpose or one can easily hire an informative guide, after a fee has been agreed on.

Zanzibar is one of the most secure places in East Africa, but even so, visitors are advised not to wander off into remote areas after dark as the occasional mugging has taken place. The beaches are quite safe and long, leisurely walks can be enjoyed. Do not make an ostentatious display of wealth.

The inhabitants of Zanzibar are a colourful and friendly people with a good sense of humour. Care should be taken to respect their culture and religion. Permission should always be sought before taking photographs. Avoid public displays of affection, such as kissing, or nudity on beaches.

Nobody should be bored on Zanzibar. The island is bound to leave the visitor with treasured memories from both above and below the waters of the 'black coast'.

The green shore of Zanzibar seen from Prison Island.

The East Coast

Nungwi, Matemwe, Jambiani and Makunduchi – these are some of the melodious names of the small villages that nestle along the magnificent and serene snow-white belt of beaches, lapped by an azure Indian Ocean, on the eastern shore of the island of Zanzibar. Although the east coast is only two hours away from Stone Town on the west coast, it retains an engaging atmosphere of isolation and languor.

Cheap, informal but comfortable accommodation can be found almost anywhere along these shores. The east coast of Zanzibar has understandably become a very popular destination with overland travellers and backpackers, but there is also more sophisticated accommodation available. This stretch of coastline must surely rate as one of the safest in East Africa. Here visitors can enjoy long, leisurely walks on the sugary beaches, and languidly observe the unhurried activities of the friendly local people without having to worry about the threat of mugging or the hassling of beach boys – as one is forced to do on parts of the Kenyan coast.

East Coast cuisine is mainly Swahili fare, with strong Arabian influences. After the expensive and elaborate offerings of the tourist resorts, the low prices and the simple dishes make a welcome change. Fresh prawns, large east coast lobster, succulent fish and tasty, tender octopus are always available on the amusingly written menus. These dishes are usually accompanied by coconut-flavoured rice.

10 STINGRAY ALLEY

★★★★

Location: Inside and approximately halfway out to the fringing reef in a direct line with the Shehe Guest House. See map.
Access: Approximately 20 minutes by local boat (*motaboti*).
Conditions: Almost always very clear and calm with only a slight current, as the dive site falls within the protective outer fringing reef.
Average depth: 15m (50ft).
Maximum depth: 18m (60ft).
Average visibility: 10–40m (33–130ft).
Average water temperature: 25–29°C (77–84°F).

Stringray Alley forms part of a deeper channel that cuts through the sandy plateau inside the reef. The sides are lined with lovely coral formations which are inhabited and frequented by a myriad of fish and other interesting marine invertebrates.

Although this will be quite a spectacular dive under normal circumstances, it owes its four-star rating and name to the many graceful and beautiful stingrays that inhabit the sandy floor of the gully. Here fortunate divers can experience the incredible sight of seeing hundreds of stingrays darting in every direction like a startled flock of low-flying birds. The slightest movement by a diver causes greater numbers of stingrays to ascend from their sandy hides. The rays are blue-spotted and vary in size. It is not certain whether this phenomenon takes place throughout the year, or if this was a one-of-a-kind sight. The author recorded this particular phenomenon during the winter month of July. The calm water and excellent visibility to be enjoyed at this time are the crown on the top of an unforgettable diving experience.

Sponges and soft coral formations.

11 JAMBIANI REEF (UNICORN REEF)

★★★★

Location: Immediately outside and about 100m (330ft) north of the rocky finger jutting out of the reef opposite Jambiani Beach. See map.
Access: Approximately 30 minutes by local boat.
Conditions: Generally calm in the early mornings when the wind is still. Strong winds push up the swells, which will make diving unpleasant.
Average depth: 15m (50ft).
Maximum depth: 18m (60ft).
Average visibility: 10–40m (33–130ft).
Average water temperature: 25–29°C (77–84°F).

The water on the east coast of Zanzibar is generally a clear, dark prussian blue, with excellent visibility. The reefs are undamaged and exquisite, with dense clusters of brain, large tabletop and lettuce coral.

The fish are abundant but somewhat shy, and include large schools of unicorns, and numbers of big game fish such as tuna, kingfish and barracuda. The coral is densely inhabited by small tropical fish of every imaginable variety and colour, and there are many lovely royal and emperor angelfish among them.

Regional Directory: Zanzibar Island

How to get There

By air:
Zanzibar boasts an international airport, and Air Tanzania flies here directly from Mombasa three times a week. There are daily flights to and from Dar es Salaam airport, and Gulf Air flies here direct from Muscat in Oman.

By sea:
There are occasional dhows that sail from Dar es Salaam. These may be willing to take on passengers, but dhow trips are only for the adventurous. A much quicker and more comfortable way to reach Zanzibar by sea is to take one of the daily ferries that cross between Zanzibar and Dar es Salaam. The fare varies according to the crossing times and level of comfort, and the choice is up to the individual traveller.

The ***Sea Express*** is a fast, Russian-built hovercraft that speeds across in 1.25hr, but is a bit like being inside an aircraft and much of the atmosphere of the crossing is lost. Bookings through **African Shipping Corporation,** tel. (051) 33414, fax. (051) 30560.

The other two slower ferries, which include the **MV *Flying Horse*** and the **MV *Mungano,*** complete the crossing in about 3hr and allow one to enjoy a leisurely journey in the open air. Bookings and tickets for all these vessels are obtained at the waterfront offices next to the port opposite the old post office and the Lutheran Church.

Dive Facilities

There are a few dive centres and schools in Stone Town that offer all dive-related services and courses, as well as air fills and equipment rental. Highly recommended are:

Indian Ocean Divers (next to the big tree), Mizingani Road, P O Box 2370, Zanzibar, tel./fax. 33860. They offer PADI dive courses of all levels, as well as daily boat charters. Equipment and boats are modern and standards are high. They will also take interested divers on a protected wreck, where artifacts can be seen (but not collected).

One Earth Safaris, P O Box 82234, Mombasa, tel. (011) 471771, fax. 471349. A PADI facility that offers courses, day charters and gear rental. Excursions to Pemba Island are arranged, and this can be combined with a land safari. Dive base at the Reef Hotel. Pemba excursions highly recommended. Tuition in German and English. Other dive centres in Stone Town are located next to the port entrance and under the Africa House Hotel on the southern section of the beach front.

Where to Stay

The island offers an excellent choice of accommodation. Taxis operate on commission and will often take visitors to a few of the hotels at no charge. A few of the recommended ones include:

Stone Town
Masons Hotel, tel. (054) 33476, where Gulf Air crews stay; and the **Hotel International,** tel. (054) 33182, which caters for package tourists.

The Stone Town Inn, Shangoni Street, tel. (054) 33658, for authentic Zanzibarian atmosphere.

One of the best and cheapest places to stay is the **Malindi Guest House,** tel: (054) 30165, close to the port exit.

East Coast
The Shehe Guest House, Jambiani Beach, tel: (054) 33188; **The East Coast Visitor's Inn** (no telephone) and **The Horizontal Inn** (no telephone).

Where to Eat

Restaurants are plentiful, and excellent seafood and traditional Swahili dishes are served. A superb and cheap early evening meal can be enjoyed in the night food market in the **Jamituri Gardens,** located on the beachfront of Stone Town, where the air is thick with the mouth-watering aromas of barbecued octopus, fish, liver, lamb or beef kebabs (*mishkaki*). **The Fisherman's Restaurant** (with a bar), tel. (051) 33101, on the waterfront, offers superb seafood dinners; **Le Pecheur** (no telephone) next door is open daily till late. Many of the hotels on the island do not serve alcohol and the public watering holes often close early.

Regional Highlights

There are an incredible number of places to visit and things to do while on Zanzibar. Numerous excellent guide books are available for this purpose. Among the highlights are the **spice tours,** which take visitors by taxi or minibus to the spice farms. Tours stop at the **Mtoni Palace,** and further to the north at the **Marahubi Palace** ruins, as well as the **Persian Baths** at Kidichi.

If time allows, a visit to the unspoilt east coast of Zanzibar is a must. The east coast is not as explored by divers as the west coast, but there are exquisite reefs that slope down to greater depths than the reefs on the western side. On the way, a recommended stop is the **Jozani Forest Reserve,** one of the last sanctuaries of the red colobus monkey. The animal is often spotted near the road.

Stone Town, Zanzibar's historic old quarter, offers too many worthwhile sights to describe in detail. It is suggested that visitors consult one of the excellent guide books on Zanzibar, or hire an informed local guide. There are a few discotheques in Stone Town which start and stay open late. The best sundowner terrace is at the rather dilapidated **Africa House Hotel.** The **tourist office** has a branch in Livingstone House, tel. (054) 32344.

How to Get Around

Taxis and public transport abound but be sure to settle on a fee beforehand. A highly recommended, knowledgeable taxi operator who will also arrange spice tours or excursions to the east coast is **Seif Kipingwa** who can be contacted at the Bwawani Hotel, tel. (054) 30200 or residence (054) 33629.

Emergency Measures

There is one **hospital** in Stone Town: V.I. Lenin Hospital, P O Box 672, Zanzibar, tel. 31071.

The nearest **recompression chamber** to all the islands is in Mombasa at the Kenya Navy's base, tel. (011) 451201 ext. 3308 (24-hour standby availability).

The international **emergency radio channel** is **#16.**

MAFIA ISLAND

Mafia Island is, geographically, less accessible than Pemba or Zanzibar. Although the island offers some of the best diving off the East African coast, organized diving is still very much in its infancy, and excursions to Mafia entail careful planning. For those with the time and inclination to visit this diving and fishing paradise, where pristine reefs teem with big game fish, it should prove to be well worth the effort.

The island lies opposite the mouth of the Rufiji River delta on mainland Tanzania. Its sinister-sounding name is not derived from the Italian crime syndicate, but most likely has its origins in the Arabic word *morfiyeh*, or group, describing the archipelago of Mafia, which is today administered from the mainland.

Diving Conditions

Most of the coral reefs off the south of Mafia Island are unspoilt, largely because dynamite fishing was never practised here as intensively as it was on some of Tanzania's other reefs. It is believed that Mafia's reefs may serve as 'seed banks' for reefs in Tanzania and the coastal waters to the north, and its marine life is distributed by the action of the East African Coastal Current. The diversity of marine life includes more than 380 species of fish and more than 45 different kinds of coral genera. Green and hawksbill turtles breed here in significant numbers. Unfortunately the status of the endangered dugong *(Dugong dugon)*, once frequently seen in the waters around Mafia Island, cannot be verified with certainty until fieldwork in the Rufiji area has been completed. The southern region of the island was declared a marine park and reserve in 1995, and this should contribute greatly toward the preservation of the wonderful marine environment in this part of Tanzania.

The waters around the island are normally very clear, and visibility averages from 20-40m (65–130ft) during the best diving months (October to the end of March). Average water temperature is 27°C (80°F) during the diving season, and only a thin wetsuit is required.

Left: *The overgrown remains of a coastal fort lend an air of mystery to Chole Island, southeast of Mafia.*
Above: *The Napoleon or humphead wrasse, the largest in the wrasse family, can be quite tame and friendly.*

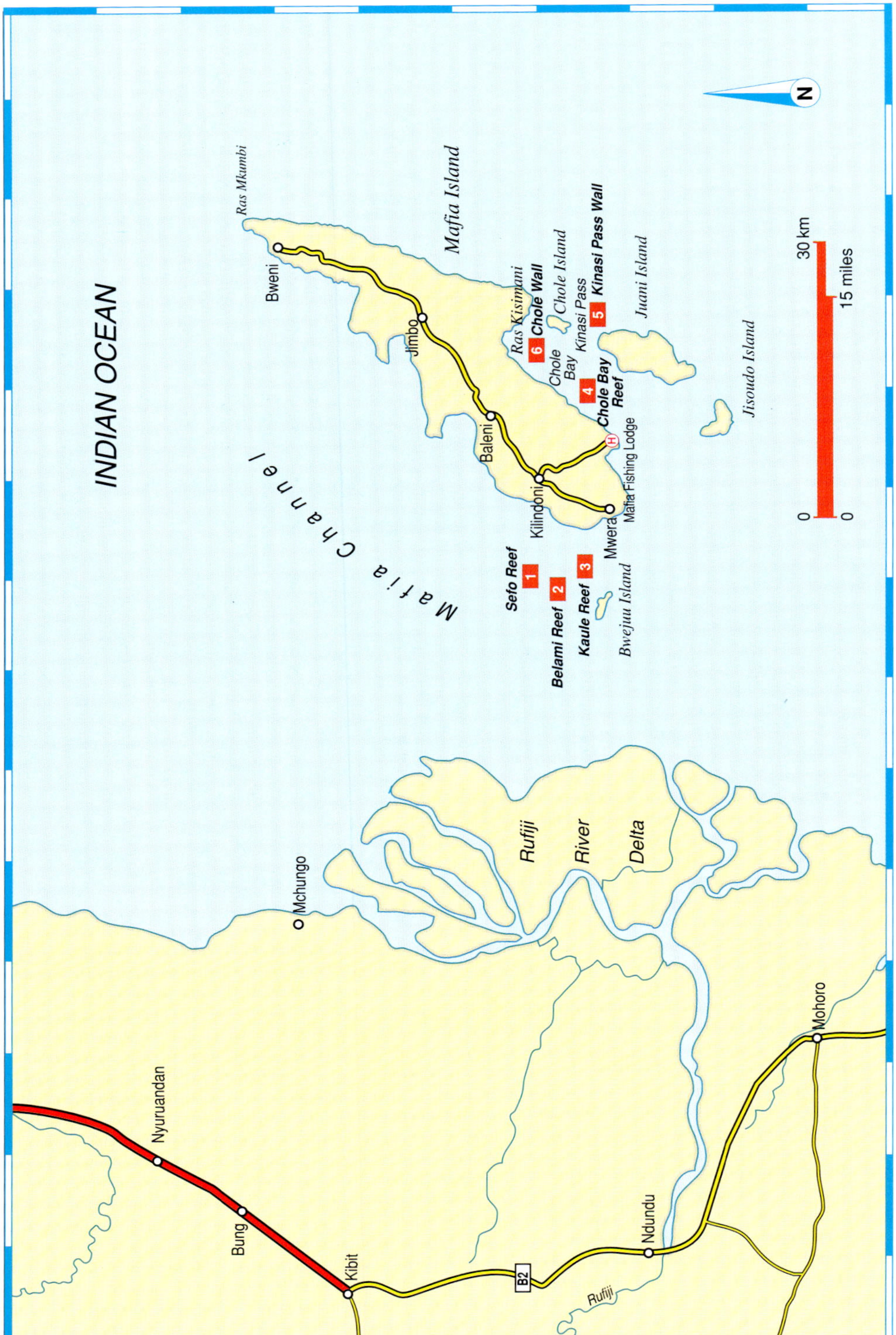
INDIAN OCEAN
Mafia Channel
Mafia Island
Ras Mkumbi
Bweni
Jimbo
Baleni
Kilindoni
Mwera
Mafia Fishing Lodge
Ras Kisimani
6 Chole Wall
Chole Island
Chole Bay
Kinasi Pass
5 Kinasi Pass Wall
4 Chole Bay Reef
Juani Island
Jisoudo Island
1 Sefo Reef
2 Belami Reef
3 Kaule Reef
Bwejuu Island
Mchungo
Rufiji River Delta
Nyuruandan
Bung
Kibit
B2
Ndundu
Rufiji
Mohoro
N
0 30 km
0 15 miles

Southern Mafia Island

Only the southern shores of Mafia Island have been explored to any extent. The waters off the rest of the island are still virginal as far as diving is concerned. This is mainly because of the recent proclamation of the marine park, but more because of the area's inaccessibility by air and the limited accommodation and diving facilities.

1 SEFO REEF

★★★★

Location: Approximately 15km (9.5 miles) from Ras Kisimani, to the northwest of southern Mafia. Not buoyed. See map.
Access: By boat from Ras Kisimani, which involves a long ride, or by live-aboard vessel.
Conditions: Best dived on slack tide during the diving season as strong currents may be encountered.
Average depth: 9–12m (30–40ft).
Maximum depth: 12m (40ft).
Average visibility: 10–30m (33–100ft).
Average water temperature: 25–29°C (77–84°F).
Sefo Reef lies in the Mafia Channel. It has a great variety of soft coral growing on it, as well as many varieties of hard coral, which are in pristine condition. As it is situated a considerable distance out to sea, the reef is the favourite haunt of large pelagic game fish. Huge schools of barracuda are often sighted, as are king mackerel and other hunters of the deep water. Sefo Reef is not often dived on due to the long distance from any facilities, but diving here may be well worth the trouble if you can make a day's outing of it.

2 BELAMI REEF

★★★

Location: Approximately 4km (2.5 miles) to the west of Ras Kisimani. Not buoyed. See map.
Access: By local boat from Ras Kisimani, or by live-aboard vessel.
Conditions: Best dived during the diving season from September through to the end of March.
Average depth: 12–15m (40–50ft).
Maximum depth: 17m (55ft) on the seaward side.
Average visibility: 10–30m (33–100ft).
Average water temperature: 25–29°C (77–84°F).
There is an exposed sandbank close to the reef which consists mainly of isolated coral bommies (heads) in and around which a great variety of small tropical fish occur. Fish life in general is abundant, and the soft and hard corals are in a pristine condition.

3 KAULE REEF

★★★

Location: Approximately 8km (5 miles) to the southwest of Ras Kisimani. Not buoyed. See map.
Access: By local boat from Ras Kisimani, or by live-aboard vessel.
Conditions: Best dived during the diving season from September through to the end of March.
Average depth: 12–15m (40–50ft).
Maximum depth: 18m (60ft) on the seaward side.
Average visibility: 10–30m (33–100ft).
Average water temperature: 25–29°C (77–84°F).
To the north of this submerged reef is a wall of coral of excellent variety and many lobsters may be seen here, especially during night dives.

Further out, the marine life is concentrated around the many coral bommies on the sandy bottom. Turtles are often seen here.

Chole Bay

At time of writing most diving activities centred in and around the protected Chole Bay area, as the Mafia Island Lodge, which at present offers the only comfortable tourist lodgings and diving facilities, is situated at Utende on the eastern tip of the bay. Chole Bay itself is named after the small Chole Island, which lies some 1.5km (1 mile) offshore of Utende Point. The waters inside the bay are calm and clear, but shallow, and are excellent for snorkelling excursions. The reefs further out through Kinasi Pass (a *mlango,* or natural opening through the reef) are more suitable for scuba diving and afford some excellent dives, which may count among the best in the East African area.

Black-spotted and barred sweetlips over hard coral.

4 CHOLE BAY REEF

★★★★★★

Location: Most of the reefs inside the bay are suitable for snorkelling. See map.
Access: By dive boat or local boat from Utende.
Conditions: Best dived during the incoming tide in the diving season (September through to the end of March).
Average depth: 2–8m (6–16ft).
Maximum depth: 8m (25ft).
Average visibility: 15m (50ft).
Average water temperature: 28–30°C (82–86°F).

The reefs inside Chole Bay occur mainly in the form of isolated coral outcrops in shallow water, which naturally attract a great number of colourful tropical marine life of outstanding variety. Due to the shallow depths the light penetration is excellent and this, coupled with clear waters, creates superb snorkelling conditions. It is less suited to scuba diving but will be diveable when conditions outside of the area do not allow. This entire area now falls within the borders of the newly proclaimed marine park, and the park rules and regulations apply.

5 KINASI PASS WALL

★★★★★

Location: Outside and to the south of the Kinasi Pass. See map.
Access: By dive boat from Utende or by live-aboard vessel from Kenya or Zanzibar.
Conditions: Best dived on slack within the diving season (from September through to the end of March), as strong currents are often encountered. When a strong current is present, it will be advisable to treat the dive as a drift dive.
Average depth: 15–20m (50–65ft).
Maximum depth: 22m (72ft).
Average visibility: 15–40m (50–130ft).
Average water temperature: 25–29°C (77–84°F).

The reef at this excellent dive site is formed of dense, unspoilt coral expanses, which have created walls and small drop-offs from about 6-8m (20–25ft) below the surface, down to the maximum depth of 22m (72ft). Marine life abounds, and an outstanding feature of this reef is the presence of the many large groupers which allow divers to approach really close.

There are also many stingrays in the area, and a number of moray eels have made their homes here. The reef is also a favourite venue for game fish, which come in from the deeper waters to the east. Some white-tipped reef sharks may be encountered during a dive, and small tiger sharks have been seen by divers. The entire section of the reef, which runs in a southeasterly direction for a considerable distance, is densely populated with tropical marine life of every description. This site is easily accessible during the diving season, but may become difficult or even impossible to reach during stormy conditions in the rainy season, as it squarely faces the southeast monsoon.

A diver surrounded by a multitude of tiny tropicals.

6 CHOLE WALL

★★★★

Location: Inside the Kinasi Pass to the northeast of Chole Island. See map.
Access: By dive boat or local boat from Utende.
Conditions: Best dived during an incoming tide during the diving season, when clear water is swept in.
Average depth: 15m (50ft).
Maximum depth: 18m (60ft).
Average visibility: 15–30m (50–100ft).
Average water temperature: 25–29°C (77–84°F).

This reef is a westward extension of Kinasi Pass Wall (No. 5) and similar conditions prevail, although it lies within the protection of the bay. The bigger varieties of pelagic fish are not often seen here, as they prefer to stay outside the natural opening in the reef.

The coral is in a pristine state and the only damage seems to have been caused by anchors. The variety is excellent and Chole Wall is richly inhabited by marine life along its entire length, which runs in an east-west direction for some distance. Be sure to approach really close: many sea turtles are encountered at close quarters.

Regional Directory: Mafia Island

How to Get There

By air:
Air Tanzania flies once a week to Mafia Island from Dar es Salaam. For all scheduled flight enquiries, contact **Air Tanzania,** P O Box 543, ATC House, Ohio Road, Dar es Salaam, tel. (051) 46643/44111. **Air Zanzibar** and **Sky Tours** fly regular charter flights to and from Das es Salaam. Bookings through **Coastal Travel Limited,** Upanga Road, Dar es Salaam, tel. (051) 37479/80, fax. 46045. A return trip costs around US$70 per person.

By sea:
The **FB *Canadian Spirit*** is a passenger vessel that completes the journey from Dar es Salaam to and from Mafia once a week. The boat stops at Mafia and carries on to Kilwa and Mtwara. It returns to Dar es Salaam via Mafia but will not stop if the ship is full or if there are no passengers who wish to disembark. Bookings can be made at the waterfront offices next to the port opposite the old post office and the Lutheran Church.

Dive Facilities

The only dive base on the island is operated from the **Mafia Island Lodge,** P O Box 2, Mafia, tel. Mafia 76, by Roberto Pisako. Full sets of good equipment are available, and rates vary for dives inside and outside Chole Bay.

Where to Stay

The **Mafia Island Lodge** offers comfortable but pricey accommodation. **Kinasi Camp** at Chole Bay is a luxury tented camp in the upper price bracket. There are cheap guest houses at Kilindoni: the **Lizu Hotel,** which offers Swahili fare for lunch and dinner; and the **Aswan Hotel** for rather basic accommodation.

Where to Eat

Apart from the **Mafia Island Lodge**, almost the only places to eat on the island are local *mkahawas* (cafes or restaurants) or *dukas* (shops) located in the main towns.

Regional Highlights:

There are a number of ruins, including a 13th-century mosque at **Ras Kismasi** and 14th-century ruins on **Juani Island.** The main attractions at time of writing are undoubtedly the **Mafia National Marine Park** and the superb diving, snorkelling and fishing conditions.

How to Get Around

Transport is available in wooden-sided trucks with bench seats, and in *matatus* (minibuses), but there are not many of these around.

Emergency Measures

The nearest **hospital** with adequate facilities is the Aga Khan Hospital in Dar es Salaam, tel. (051) 30081.

The nearest **recompression chamber** to all the islands is in Mombasa at the Kenya Navy's base, tel. (011) 451201 ext. 3308 (24-hour standby availability).

The international **emergency radio channel** is **#16.**

Sunset casts long shadows across the pleasant grounds of the Mafia Island Lodge.

DAR ES SALAAM

The sultry harbour city of Dar es Salaam sprawls around the curve of Kurusini Creek. The city is still relatively young in comparison with other East African cities, as can be determined by its architecture. Unlike other coastal towns, such as Lamu, Mombasa or Zanzibar, it is not the Arabian influence that predominates, but rather a mixture of German, British and Swahili building styles. Sultan Majid bin Said of Zanzibar planned to build his palace of coral stone in this 'haven of peace' in 1855, but this ambition was never realized.

Arab rule was replaced in 1877 by that of the Germans, and their presence is still strongly felt here today. German tourists account for the greatest number of visitors to Dar es Salaam, which was called German East Africa in colonial days. The Hotel New Africa was one of the first German hotels to be built here and was, during the days of German occupation, known as the Kaiserhof. In 1905 work began on the great Central Railway, which was planned to link Dar es Salaam with Kigoma on Lake Tanganyika. Completed seven years later, the railway vastly improved communications and encouraged business activity in the colony. Dar es Salaam's Bavarian-style railway station, the old post office, and the telegraph office are the best examples of architecture from this era.

After Germany's defeat in World War I, Tanganyika – as the country became known – was handed over to the British, who left their own stamp in the form of the many beautiful gardens and parks filled with frangipani, oleander, hibiscus and jacaranda trees, as well as the aptly-named flame trees that line the avenues.

A distinct Asian atmosphere reigns in parts of the city, such as India Street, where Indian merchants sell their varied wares. The strongly Muslim character of the city's inhabitants is mirrored in the many mosques throughout Dar es Salaam.

Today Dar es Salaam is back on the road to prosperity, but the long period of socialist administration that followed Tanzanian independence left a legacy of poverty and squalor, especially in the slumlike outskirts of the city. The shops are, however, once again well

Left: *Dawn reveals the outline of Dar es Salaam, with its busy harbour area.*
Above: *The beautiful royal angelfish feeds on algae and invertebrates.*

DAR ES SALAAM
INDIAN OCEAN
Bahari Beach
1 Fungu Yasin
2 Funguni Reef
3 Big-T Reef
Ras Kiromni
Fungu Mkadya
4
5 Mbudya North
Mbudya Island
Bahari Beach
Kunduchi
6 Coral Gardens (Mbudya West)
7 Mbudya East
8 Octopus Gardens
Silversands
Whitesands
Bongoyo Island
9 Buick Reef
Msasani Bay
Ras Kankadya
MSASANI PENINSULA
10 Wreck of the Schlammerstadt
Kibaha
A7
Oyster Bay
Oyster Bay
Outer Nyakatombe Island
Inner Nyakatombe Island
Palm Beach
Ubungo
DAR ES SALAAM
New Africa
Kendwa
Outer Sinda
Inner Sinda
Mjimwema
Ras Korongo
Mbwamaji
Ras Dege
DAR ES SALAAM INTERNATIONAL AIRPORT
Kisarawe
Ras Kimbiji
Vibura
B2
Mkuranga
Buyuni
N
Binga
0 5 10km
0 5 miles

stocked with local and imported goods, and restaurants in and around the city offer visitors Swahili, European and Asian cuisine. Nightlife may be found in Oyster Bay, to the north of the city, and at hotels to the north. To the south are a few luxury camps and resorts.

Diving Conditions

There are some very beautiful coral reefs and some diveable wrecks around the Dar es Salaam coastline. Organized diving is done on a relatively small scale, when compared to the Kenyan coast or even Pemba Island. Facilities for organized dive trips, equipment hire, and air fills may be found only at the Dar es Salaam Yacht Club (some club rules apply), at the Msasani Slipway and at the Bahari Beach Hotel to the north of the city. It is suggested that divers be as self-sufficient as possible when visiting this section of the Tanzanian coast, particularly with regard to equipment. Boats are available everywhere, although they are in varying states of seaworthiness. A most enjoyable experience is to hire a sailing dhow to reach a dive site, but one should have ample time in hand as a lot of tacking is usually involved. Be careful not to leave any valuables unattended on board, as these can be stolen while their owners are underwater.

The most popular dive sites around Dar es Salaam are mainly located to the north of the city. This is fortunately also where the best accommodation is to be found. If your are an experienced diver it will be well worth your while to visit some of the deeper reefs, where the coral is still in a pristine state. The small offshore islands, too, provide grand diving and snorkelling conditions.

The twobar clownfish will protect the anemone in which it shelters, and even attack divers who come too close.

The Bahari Beach Area

1 FUNGU YASIN

★★★★★★

Location: To the northeast of Bahari (Swahili for 'ocean') Beach. No buoys. See map.
Access: Approximately 20 minutes by local dive boat from Bahari Beach, or 45 minutes from the Msasani Slipway to the north of Oyster Bay (past the Dar es Salaam Yacht Club).
Conditions: Generally calm on the leeward (land) side of the sand bank and diveable in the rainy season.
Average depth: 3–18m (10–60ft).
Maximum depth: 30m (100ft).
Average visibility: 5–20m (16–65ft).
Average water temperature: 27–29°C (80–84°F).
Fungu Yasin (Swahili for 'sand island') is the top of an underwater formation that emerges from the depths and culminates in a lovely sand bank which almost disappears during high spring tides. The site is visited by thousands of terns, and interesting shells are often washed up.

The shallow section of the reef slopes gently down to a depth of about 8m (25ft) and then drops at a much sharper angle of about 45° to a depth of around 18m (60ft). The reef consists mainly of large isolated coral heads which offer shelter to many marine inhabitants. Because it is heavily fished, fish life is quite sparse and shy. Some large semicircle angelfish (*Pomacanthus semicirculatus*) have found refuge in the small caverns in the coral heads, and are often joined by vast numbers of sweetlips and fusiliers. Lionfish are often seen and small blue-spotted stingrays can be found hiding beneath coral plates. There are many sea cucumbers and a variety of starfish of different colours. Apart from the many small fish that have made Fungu Yasin their home, there are some large slatey sweetlips which are often joined by bluefin trevally (*Caranx melampygus*), on the hunt for small edibles.

Lucky divers may spot sea turtles, which are understandably quite wary as their shells are highly prized by beach vendors. Poaching of sea turtles is illegal, but there is no enforcement. The shallow sections of the reef are densely covered with short coral growths of good variety and are inhabited by numerous small reef fish.

An alarming number of the voracious and devastating crown-of-thorns starfish have been noted here, adding to the widespread damage caused by careless anchoring and dynamite fishing.

The shallows offer very good snorkelling opportunities, while the sandy sections among the coral heads provide excellent training sites for learner divers. To the northwest of the island at a depth of approximately 17–19m (55–62ft), an old anchor rests upright on the sandy bottom.

2 FUNGUNI REEF

★★★★★

Location: To the south of Fungu Yasin (No 1). No buoys. See map.
Access: Approximately 20 minutes by local dive boat from Bahari Beach, or 45 minutes from Msasani Slipway.
Conditions: Generally calm on the seaward side of the fringing reef, which has fortunately not been destroyed by dynamite. Can be dived during the rainy season as it is far enough out to sea to avoid the murky river waters.
Average depth: 5–18m (16–60ft).
Maximum depth: 20m (100ft).
Average visibility: 5–20m (16–65ft).
Average water temperature: 27–29°C (80–84°F).
Funguni (which means 'going to the sandbank' in Swahili), provides some of the best coral viewing in the Bahari Beach area. The seaward side of the reef is the most interesting, but the inner (leeward) side provides some beautiful isolated coral patches which are often inhabited by scorpion- and lionfish. Large coachwhip rays (*Himantura uarnak*) may be found hiding under huge coral plates, and there are often some pufferfish around. On the seaward side, the deeper sections of the reef have marvellous coral formations and these provide the much-needed shelter for moray eels and large schools of yellow snappers.

Camouflage helps the scorpionfish trap its prey.

Usually seen singly or in pairs, the exotic and arresting Indian lionfish is a member of the scorpionfish family.

A distinctive feature of this reef is the vast number of emperor and royal angelfish that dart around the coral formations. Large, solitary barracuda are often attracted by divers' silver bubbles, and they hover motionless, staring inquisitively.

The top of the reef is very shallow and barren, as it is exposed above the water during low spring tides. To reach the deeper sections, swim due east from a depth of around 6m (20ft). Take care when anchoring in the shallows; large swells may appear unexpectedly, and the anchor can damage the corals.

3 BIG–T REEF

★★★★

Location: A considerable distance out to sea, to the northwest of Bahari Beach, and situated close to the Dar es Salaam–Zanzibar ferry route. See map.
Access: Approximately 45 minutes by local boat from Bahari Beach or 15 minutes by speedboat. The reef is large, and during favourable conditions it can usually be seen from the surface, so land references should suffice to find it. It is marked on charts as Mbudya Patches. There are no buoys. See map
Conditions: As the reef lies far out to sea, it should only be attempted during calm weather, as the swells may otherwise be huge. The reef is best dived during the diving season, but should not be attempted alone or by inexperienced or very rusty divers.
Average depth: From 9–25m (30–80ft).
Maximum depth: Beyond maximum sport-diving levels.
Average visibility: 15–30m (50–100ft).
Average water temperature: 27–28°C (80–82°F).

A look at the sea chart of this area explains the name of this site, as the reef is in the shape of a large letter T. This is one of the most spectacular reefs in Tanzania and can be easily reached from the mainland. Experienced divers will find it well worth the effort to pay a visit.

As the reef lies out in the open ocean, strong currents may be present and this factor, together with the depth of the dive, precludes novice or inexperienced divers.

The shallow sections of the reef start at a depth of 9–12m (30–40ft) on the leeward side, sloping at a gentle angle to 15–18m (50–60ft) to the east. After this it starts to plunge at a steep angle and only levels out again on a sloping, sandy bottom at 50m (165ft). The average depth of Big-T has fortunately saved the reef from dynamite fishing damage, and on the top of the reef the coral is in an excellent, pristine condition. The top section is flattish and inhabited by a myriad of angelfish, butterflyfish, sweetlips and schools of fusiliers and yellow snappers. The tropicals all seem to be bigger here than they are on shallower reefs, and there are some exceptionally large emperor angelfish. Lobsters are found hiding beneath the large flat plate corals, and large solitary moray eels are often seen.

Before one reaches the drop-off, there are magnificent, tall vase sponges that harbour colonies of small cleaner shrimp and fish. These vases make magnificent photographic props, and the fish life is exceptionally abundant on this section of the reef.

On the deeper sections of Big-T Reef, large gorgonian fans adorn the sides, and Napoleon wrasse are sometimes spotted at depths of around 30m (100ft). Large game fish, such as kingfish, barracuda, tuna and jacks (caranx), often visit Big-T, and divers may suddenly find themselves surrounded by circling shoals of tuna that have come to investigate the peculiarity of these two-legged, bubble-blowing creatures.

The unexpected appearance of a large white-tipped reef shark gets the air consumption going, and solitary mako sharks *(Isurus oxyrinchus)* or bull sharks *(Carcharinus leucas)* have been seen on the deeper sections. Divers have on occasion been joined by groups of up to eight dolphins, who, after approaching warily, played around for about 15 minutes. The sight of any of these species is certain to turn a normally exhilarating dive into a never-to-be-forgotten five-star experience.

4 FUNGU MKADYA

★★★★

Location: Approximately 800m (0.5 miles) out, directly in front of the Bahari Beach Hotel. No buoys. See map.
Access: Approximately 10 minutes by local dive boat from Bahari Beach.
Conditions: Generally calm but will be murky during the rainy season.
Average depth: 3–11m (10–36ft).
Maximum depth: 12m (40ft) on the seaward side.
Average visibility: 5–15m (16–65ft).
Average water temperature: 27–29°C (80–84°F).

What was obviously once a spectacular reef has unfortunately been severely degraded by dynamite fishing. Here one can clearly see the devastating effects that dynamite fishing has on the environment: there are large craters and some huge brain coral heads which are split right through. This destructive practice still goes on, and the fish are shy and elusive. Fungu Mkadya itself is a small, round, underwater island, which reaches to within 3m (10ft) of the surface. On the top there are some wide sandy patches and these, together with the dive's proximity to shore, make it a very popular training reef for novice divers. Some good congregations of black-spotted sweetlips get very excited and start darting around frantically when divers approach. Cuttlefish are sometimes seen on the shallow sandy slopes, and small clusters of lionfish hide underneath the coral growths. Pufferfish are common, and there are some large spadefish on the top section of the reef. The seaward side of the reef has an interesting shallow bank which drops down to the sandy bottom at 12m (40ft), and lucky divers may see a few lobsters hiding in the dense pillar coral. A sizeable reef shark has been sighted nearby during a night dive: this is an experience that really gets the adrenaline rushing and the air consumption spiralling.

Mbudya Island

Known as 'Mini-Bar' to the crews of the Dutch airline KLM because of the small bar on the island, Mbudya offers fabulous snorkelling opportunities and is a favourite day outing for visitors to this section of the Tanzanian coast. To get to the island, one of many local motorized

The often-solitary Arabian angelfish inhabits fringing reefs that feature rich coral growth.

dhows and *ngalawas* can be hired. The hotels may be able to provide more modern transport. When opting for local transport, visitors should take care of their valuables. Be careful too about leaving personal items on a boat during a dive, as losses have been known to occur!

The island is situated about 3km (2 miles) offshore, within easy reach of the hotels on the north coast. There are lovely sandy beaches on the western and eastern sides. On the western side is the bar and a kitchen, and it is possible to have barbecued fish with chips, and drinks (not always cold). You can, of course, take your own picnic, as there is plenty of shade under the casuarina trees.

It is also possible to circumnavigate the island on foot, and there are lovely dead shells that may be collected. Do this in a group, or take along a trustworthy local, as the occasional mugging has occurred in the past.

The island is clothed with dense stands of palms and baobabs. The rare coconut or robber crab (*Birgus latro*) is found on the island: an entire family was recently seen nesting under the kitchen floor. (*See* box at right).

5 MBUDYA NORTH

★★★★★

Location: Off the northern tip of the island and about 100m (330ft) to the north. There are no buoys. See map.
Conditions: This reef is diveable even with a strong southeasterly wind, but is generally murky during the rainy season.
Average depth: 10m (33ft).
Maximum depth: 13m (43ft) on the sandy seaward side.
Average visibility: 5–15m (17ft–50ft).
Average water temperature: 27–29°C (80–84°F).

Normally dived when conditions prevent diving on other reefs in the area. There are some good heads of brain coral, but in general the reef is nondescript, consisting mainly of banks of brown pillar coral. The marine life is sparse, due to overfishing, and consists mainly of small tropicals. There are some resident lionfish, a few long trumpetfish, and some small moray eels. The top of the reef offers good snorkelling opportunities, with dense small coral growths inhabited by brightly coloured small fish. This is a good site for night dives – when large squid are often seen.

6 CORAL GARDENS (MBUDYA WEST)

★★★★★★★

Location: The best diving is done on the extreme left of the sandy beach, immediately before reaching the rocky outcrops (when facing the sea) and approximately 100m (330ft) out to the west. No buoys. See map.

THE COCONUT CRAB

Also known as the robber crab, this rare creature, which is still found on Mbudya Island, is the largest terrestrial arthropod (segmented-body animal) in the world. The coconut crab *(Birgus latro)* can reach up to 1m (38in) in length and weigh up to 3kg (7lbs).

Resembling a giant hermit crab, the coconut crab is almost totally terrestrial. However, the female is obliged to return to the sea, where she releases her eggs. Coconut crabs hide amongst the roots of palms or in rocky crevices during the day, and emerge at night to forage for coconuts and other fruit. These are stored in a burrow and the crab may feed on its hoard for several days.

The animal is confined to islands, and because it is regarded as a delicacy as well as an aphrodisiac, it has been hunted to the point of extinction. The coconut crab is listed as a 'rare' species in the Red Data Book. Rats, pigs, and monkeys, which are all introduced animals to islands, also hunt and eat the young crabs. The coconut crab is fully protected on the island of Aldabra, in the Seychelles, one of the few places where it is still found in abundance.

Access: Approximately 20 minutes by local boat from Bahari Beach.
Conditions: Normally calm and clear except during the rainy season when the sea will be rough and very murky.
Average visibility: 10–30m (33–100ft).
Average depth: 6–9m (20–30ft).
Maximum depth: 12m (40ft) on the sandy seaward side.
Average visibility: 5–15m (16–65ft).
Average water temperature: 27–30°C (80–86°F).

The coral reef is reached by swimming out in a direct line with Pangavini Island due west of the southern end of the beach. One first crosses a sandy area, after which a stretch of seagrass with sporadic coral heads occurs. After crossing this, one comes across the best feature of this dive – some of the most splendid coral formations in the entire area. Dense banks of staghorn and lettuce coral are found here. Unfortunately, they have been slightly damaged by dynamite fishing, anchoring, and dragnets. This is also a heavily fished area, and so the smaller fish are shy and the bigger ones are absent. The smaller tropicals that are protected by coral hideaways are, fortunately, still abundant and the reef makes an excellent site for macrophotography.

The isolated coral heads that occur further to the north also teem with marine inhabitants. The unusual and exquisite helmet gurnard (*Dactyloptena orientalis*) – a fish with beautifully coloured radial wings that give it the appearance of a giant sea moth – has been seen here, as have the elusive shovelnose lobster, the mantis prawn, squid and octopus. Sea turtles too, are often seen here, and the reef is richly upholstered with giant anemones, each with their cheeky resident clownfish.

Koran angelfish prefer to live in heavy coral growth.

The shallow depth affords ample natural sunlight to brighten up the colourful coral and fish life. This dive site is ideal for beginners, who may be introduced to the dive from shore. Because of this, it is also a superb snorkelling reef, and can be easily reached from shore either on snorkel or with scuba gear.

Coral Gardens is also a good night dive site, which may be done from shore. When diving from a boat, care should be taken with anchors as there are no buoys. There is sometimes a strong current present, which flows past the island from the south, and care should be taken when underwater not to be swept right past the island.

Surface marker buoys (SMB) should be carried, as boat traffic becomes quite hectic over weekends. Although this island was designated as a marine reserve as far back as 1975, lax control – blamed on a lack of finance – and the light penalties for offenders has meant that destructive fishing practices continue.

This is one area that meets all of the criteria for a successful marine park and tourist attraction, and if action is taken soon, it is almost sure to recover as a priceless asset to the country.

7 MBUDYA EAST

★★★★★

Location: On the eastern side of the island slightly to the north of the sandy beach. See map.
Conditions: Not to be attempted during the rainy season when the southeasterly winds create rough conditions on the seaward side of the island. During the diving season conditions here are calm with clear water.
Average depth: 5–15m (17–50ft).
Maximum depth: 16m (52ft).
Average visibility: 5–15m (17–50ft).
Average water temperature: 27–29°C (80–84°F).
The reef starts at a shallow depth of 4–6m (13–20ft) on the island side and breaks close to shore (care should be taken not to end up in the breaking water), dropping away gently to the seaward side. The coral growths on this reef are good and interspersed with sandy gullies at regular intervals. The fish life cannot be described as plentiful, but there are bigger species which come in from the open ocean to feed. Large barracuda and kingfish are often seen here, and schools of small tuna and bonito pass here on their way to deeper water. The coral formations are inhabited by numerous small tropicals, which include congregations of black-spotted sweetlips, and lionfish are often found hanging upside down under the coral heads. The sandy bottom to the seaward side is usually frequented by blue-spotted rays and flatfish.

8 OCTOPUS GARDENS

★★

Location: To the south of Mbudya Island and to the east of Pangavini Island. Ask a local diver or fisherman to indicate the site. See map.
Conditions: Generally calm conditions.
Average depth: 8–12m (25–40ft).
Maximum depth: 15m (50ft)
Average visibility: 10–20m (33–65ft).
A flat reef with small but mostly intact coral. Moray eels may be found poking their heads out of holes in the coral, and a variety of beautiful, colourful tropical fish abound. One expects to see many octopus on a reef named 'Octopus Gardens', but it appears that they have long ago joined the lobsters in the pot. This reef is popular with fishermen, which also accounts for the absence of big fish in the area.

9 BUICK REEF

★★★

Location: To the west, and on the seaward side, of Bongoyo Island. See map.
Conditions: Best dived during the months of October to March when a northwesterly wind prevails.
Average depth: 9–27m (30–90ft).
Average visibility: 10–20m (33–65ft).
Buick Reef falls away at a shallow incline towards the southwest, and the highest point of the reef is closest to the island. It is a flattish reef with colourful coral and sponges. Many lobsters can be seen hiding under the

coral crevices and there is an abundance of small tropical fish. Buick Reef is a popular venue for divers from the yacht club because of its close proximity, and because it is quite sheltered from the northwesterly monsoon during the diving season.

10 WRECK OF THE *SCHLAMMERSTADT*

★★★★★★

Location: Inside Oyster Bay, not far from the entrance to the harbour. The wreck is difficult to locate without the aid of Global Positioning System (GPS) equipment, and it may help to ask fishermen in the area. A crew member with a good knowledge of the wreck's location is a must. See map.
Access: The crew of the dhow from Msasani Slipway have a good knowledge of the wreck's location and the boat may be chartered at a reasonable price by a group of divers.
Conditions: Best dived outside of the rainy season when clear water should prevail.
Average depth: The top of the wreck lies at a depth of around 3m (10ft).
Maximum depth: 10m (33ft).
Average visibility: 10–20m (33–65ft).
This old German steam freighter was towed out and scuttled in its present position after it caught fire in the port of Dar es Salaam in 1908. The ship was carrying a cargo of cement, and the solidified bags – reminiscent of brick paving – can be seen clearly from the surface. The top of the hull reaches to only 3m (10ft) below the surface and it can easily be spotted. The hull is pretty much intact for a vessel of that age, and likely owes its good state of preservation to its protected position close to the harbour entrance.

The wreck rests upright on the reef, with the bow section pointing towards the east. As it is only approximately 30m (100ft) in length, the ship can be circumnavigated a few times during a single dive.

An outstanding feature of this dive is the number of large moray eels that have chosen to make their home here. As many as 15 morays have been counted during a single dive. They belong to various species, which include the large brown (*Gymnothorax flavimarginatus*) and honeycomb (*G. tesselata*) eels. Each of these reach lengths of well over 2m (6ft). They are often found in holes and tears in the hull, together with smaller lighter-coloured and spotted species such as *Siderea picta* and *Echidna nebulosa*. These moray eels are not tame, and the sight of a large fish being bitten cleanly in two by an eel should provide ample warning for divers not to approach these creatures too closely!

The hull is richly covered with soft and hard corals, which makes for a superb and colourful dive. Large moorish idols flit in and out of holes in the wreckage, and underneath the hull are some large groupers. To the south of the wreck, the ship's old anchor can be found lying approximately 50m (165ft) away. There is very little in the way of collectible souvenirs to be seen on the *Schlammerstadt*, but a few small ceramic tiles have been found. The reef extends from the wreck in a southwesterly direction, and makes for a colourful dive should one tire of visiting the wreck.

Black-spotted sweetlips tend to remain under coral ledges during the day, only becoming active at nightfall.

How to Get There

By air:
Dar es Salaam's international airport is well served by international and charter airlines from Europe, South Africa and neighbouring countries. Air Tanzania operates a flight between Dar es Salaam and Mombasa via Zanzibar, three times a week in either direction, but schedules and times may change on short notice. Contact **Air Tanzania,** Corporation ATC House, Ohio Street, Dar es Salaam, tel. (051) 46643/44111.

By road:
From Kenya: The main road from the Kenyan border passes through Tanga and turns to the east between Morogoro and Dar es Salaam. From Mombasa to Dar es Salaam is a total distance of 509km (305 miles) with the journey by car taking approximately 8hr. At time of writing, the route running between Lunga Lunga in Kenya, the border post and Tanga was a good compacted gravel road. This route should preferably be travelled during the daytime. The highway from Tanga to Dar es Salaam is a very good tarmac road. There are a number of buses that make the trip daily, and the journey may take 16–24hr. Buses depart from Mombasa on Kenyatta Avenue; and from Dar es Salaam on Msimbazi Street, close to the Kariakoo Market.

From Zambia: The main road from Zambia to Dar es Salaam turns to the east at Kapiri Mposhi, between Lusaka and Ndola in Zambia, and the first stretch of the road is in bad condition. Thereafter it improves greatly and crosses the border between Nakonde and Tunduma. Attitudes at the border post have recently relaxed and the crossing should present no problem. The distance from Lusaka is approximately 1 900km (1 187 miles). In Tanzania, the road passes through the Mkumi National Park, and astounding numbers of animals may be seen close to the road. Care should be taken when contemplating travel on this road by night. There are bus services, but these are not recommended. For safety, security and comfort, the train is a better option.

From Malawi: The main road from Malawi crosses the border between Karonga and Mbeya, and in Malawi it follows a spectacularly scenic route along the northern part of Lake Malawi. There are bus services, but a better way to get there by road will be to try and get a seat on one of the overland trucks that camp at the Silver Sands Hotel north of Dar es Salaam.

By train:
From Zambia: The TAZARA Express completes the journey between Kapiri Mposhi in Zambia and Dar es Salaam in a time of approximately 42–48hr. It departs Tuesdays and Thursdays from Kapiri Mposhi in the late afternoon and arrives in Dar es Salaam two nights later in the morning. From Dar es Salaam to Kapiri Mposhi, the train leaves around 10:00 in the morning on the same days of the week. The route passes through the scenic Rift Valley and the Selous Game Reserve in Tanzania. Numerous animals (including elephants) graze close to the railway line, oblivious of the passing train. Food and drinks are served, but it is advisable to take one's own water and perhaps even a good supply of food. Insist on a first-class ticket, as the rest of the train is absolute chaos. Beware of snatch-and-run thieves at the stations, as well as customs officials looking for a bribe when checking visas. If common sense prevails, this journey is an experience not to be forgotten.

From Kenya: After an interval of 18 years, Kenya and Tanzania have restored rail links. A passenger train departs once a week from Voi in Kenya at 05:00 in the morning on Saturdays, and arrives across the border in Moshi at 11:00 the same morning.

By sea:
From Mombasa: There are weekly ferry services between Dar es Salaam and Mombasa via Zanzibar. Enquire at the **Africa Shipping Corporation** offices, tel. (051) 33114/35337, fax. 30560. Passage may also be obtained on a dhow, but sailings are irregular. Enquiries may be made at the dhow harbour in Dar es Salaam or the Old Port in Mombasa.

Dive Facilities

The best facilities are available at:

Bahari Beach Hotel, tel. (051) 47101, approximately 25km (15 miles) north of Dar es Salaam on the Bagamoyo Road, where **Indian Ocean Divers** have set up a fully equipped diving centre and school with good equipment and PADI tuition.

Dar es Salaam Yacht Club in Msasani Bay is restricted to members only, though visiting divers may be able to join them over a weekend for a dive.

Mike Sismey, an affable Englishman, has a diving facility at the **Silver Sands Hotel,** tel. (051) 47231, on the north coast. He is well acquainted with the dive sites in the area and offers BSAC tuition, as well as courses for beginners.

It may also be worthwhile to enquire at the **Msasani Slipway** (located next to the yacht club; no telephone). There was at time of writing a well-stocked dive shop here.

Getting Around

There are a number of car hire firms in Dar es Salaam and taxis are plentiful, but it is wise to negotiate a fare before getting in. There is shuttle bus service, operated by the State Transport Corporation, that runs between the city centre and the hotels on the north coast. Buses depart from the New Africa Hotel a few times throughout the day.

Where to Stay

Dar es Salaam
The brand-new and very much top-of the-range **Sheraton Hotel,** tel. (051) 44830, on Ohio Street in Dar es Salaam is a better alternative to the much overrated and -priced **Kilimanjaro Hotel,** tel. (051) 21281, on Sokoine Drive.

The **New Africa Hotel,** tel. (051) 29611, in Maktaba Street, was under renovation at time of writing, and should be a good bet when work is completed.

Other popular top-bracket hotels in the city are the **Motel Agip** in Pamba Road, tel. (051) 23511/3, and the **Hotel Embassy** in Garden Avenue, tel. (051) 30006.

Oyster Bay

To the north of Dar es Salaam, in Oyster Bay, are the recommendable but very expensive beachfront **Oyster Bay Hotel,** Toure Drive, tel. (051) 68062; and the somewhat less pricey **Karibu Hotel,** one street back. On the way there, at the intersection of Upanga Road and Ocean Road, is the medium-priced **Palm Beach Hotel,** tel. (051) 28892, which has a very popular beer garden and restaurant.

North Coast

On the coast north of the city (a distance of approximately 20km (12 miles) along the Bagamoyo Road is the highly recommended **Bahari Beach Hotel,** P O Box 9312, Dar es Salaam, tel. (051) 47101 or 31957, now managed by the Protea Hotels chain of South Africa. (Airline crews from KLM and Swissair were staying at the hotel at time of writing). There is now a modern diving centre set up at the hotel.

There is also the new **Whitesands Hotel,** P O Box 3030, Dar es Salaam, tel. (051) 44484, to the south of the Bahari Beach Hotel.

The greatly overrated, government-run **Kunduchi Beach Hotel,** P O Box 9331, Dar es Salaam, tel. (051) 47621, is housed in a beautiful Arabian-style structure but was, at time of writing, only suited to visitors who do not care about indifferent service.

The **Silver Sands Hotel,** tel. (051) 47231 (close to the Bahari Beach Hotel), is in somewhat rundown condition, but offers good-value-for-money accommodation. There is a campsite with basic ablution facilities right on the beach; this is also where most of the overland trucks stay. At time of writing, the Silversands Hotel was almost the only facility on this section of the Tanzanian coast where diving gear could be rented and dives organized.

There is also a campsite at the **Rungwe Hotel,** tel. (051) 47021, but this seems to be sinking fast due to indifferent management.

To the south of Dar es Salaam is the **Ras Kutani Beach Resort.** Bookings may be made through the **Selous Safari Company,** P O Box 1192, Dar es Salaam, tel. (051) 28485.

Where to Eat

Apart from hotel restaurants, there is the pricey but highly recommended **Smokey's Restaurant** (no telephone) in Msasani Bay; the **Rendezvous** (no telephone), **Cassanovas** in Oyster Bay and the **Alcove,** tel. (051) 37444, on Samora Machel Avenue in the city centre. There is a good bookshop and hairdresser at Cassanovas in Oyster Bay.

The **Summit Restaurant,** on the roof terrace of the Kilimanjaro Hotel, tel. (051) 21281, offers splendid views of the port.

The Coffee Shop, tel. (051) 23511/3, below the Motel Agip in Pamba Road, has excellent snacks and a good lunchtime menu.

The **Cafe Espresso** on Samora Machel Avenue, after Bridge Street, has a good selection of coffees and snacks.

The most popular discotheque in the city is **Club Bilicanas,** on the corner of Bridge and Kaluta streets.

For fast foods, try **Jamaa Fast Foods,** Samora Machel Avenue, tel. (051) 38347, or **Chick King,** at Jamhuri Avenue and Mwisho Street.

The **Bahari Beach Hotel,** tel. (051) 47101 or (051) 31957, has a band for most evenings of the week, as well as a traditional floorshow on Wednesday nights and an outdoor barbecue on Friday nights.

In Kawe, north of the city, on the way to the beaches, is the pleasant **Euro Pub** (no telephone), which opens at 17:00 during the week and 10:00 on Sundays. Excellent meals are served at a reasonable price.

TJ's take away (no telephone) in Namanga, to the north of the city, has great burgers and light snacks.

Regional Highlights

Dar es Salaam's attractions include the **Kariakoo Market** between Mkunguni and Tandamuti Streets; Mwenge, 3km (1.8 miles) north on the Bagamoyo Road, for *makonde* carvings; the **art centre** and the **Village Museum**. There is a new casino in Ali Hassan Mwinyi Avenue and one at Whitesands Hotel on the north coast. The **fish market** on the beachfront is a great place to shop for fresh prawns, lobsters, crabs and a fantastic array of fish of all sizes. A little negotiation may secure a bargain, but beware of tricksters, pickpockets and bag-snatchers. Do not attempt to take photographs of the state buildings across the road as this is strictly against the law.

A visit to either **Bangoyo Island** or **Mbudya Island** is worth the effort. Trips to Bangoyo Island can be arranged from the Msasani Slipway; and to Mbudya Island at the Bahari Beach Hotel. (*See* page 134 for more details on Mbudya Island). To get to Mbudya Island, there are many motorized dhows and *ngalawas* in varying states of repair that can be hired; more modern transport may be available from the hotels. When opting for local transport take care of valuables. This holds true for leaving personal possessions on a boat during a dive! The island offers fabulous snorkelling. A kitchen and bar serves beer, soft drinks and barbecued fish.

Unfortunately even the islands are not safe from crime, and muggings of solitary tourists have taken place. If you are going for a long walk, take along a trustworthy local, as the muggers are normally known to them.

To the south of Dar es Salaam (accessible via the ferry from the fish market) are many popular venues for day trips and weekend outings. More information on these may be obtained from the Msasani Slipway or the Selous Safari Company, tel. (051) 28485.

The **Tanzanian Tourist Board** (TTB), P O Box 2485, Dar es Salaam, tel. (051) 37479/80, in Maktaba Street, can supply further information. **Coastal Travel Limited,** Upanga Road, tel. (051) 37479/80, fax. 46045, has more information on getting to the main islands.

Emergency Measures

The best **hospital** in Dar es Salaam is the Aga Khan Hospital, tel. (051) 30081, on Upanga Road.

Recompression facilities are available at the Kenya Navy's base in Mombasa, tel: (011) 451201 ext. 3308 (24–hour standby availability).

The international **emergency radio channel** is **#16.**

THE MARINE ENVIRONMENT

East African Reefs and Reef Life

The coral reefs off the coast of East Africa are as diverse, and in some cases even more so, than those found in many other world-class dive sites, and host some of the richest and most varied marine inhabitants of the world's oceans. This section of the Indian Ocean carries as many as 162 families of marine fauna, and the different species of fish found here number perhaps as many as 3 000. The main reason for this incredible variety of life may be found in the prevailing South Equatorial Current, which reaches the East African coast from as far away as Australia and Indonesia, with the outer reaches of this current also varying according to the reigning monsoon or trade winds.

Along the Kenyan and Tanzanian sections of the East African coast, the continental shelf, which generally extends offshore to depths of approximately 180m (600ft), is remarkably narrow, and does not, on average, exceed a distance of between 3 and 8km (1.8–4.8 miles) from the shore. The maximum depths to which reef-building corals will flourish along this shelf is approximately 55m (180ft). As the waters in this region retain an average temperature of between 25°C and 29°C (77–84°F) to depths of as much as 110m (370ft), it means that the reef-building corals always receive the warm tropical waters that encourage the formation of reefs. This also has a significant effect on the formation of fringing reefs along this coast and around the islands, as the much colder waters of the deep sections below 110m (370ft) never reach the shallower depths where the reef-builders thrive.

The Nature of Corals and Reefs

Tropical reefs are built mainly from corals, which are primitive animals closely related to sea anemones. Most of the coral types that contribute to reef construction are colonial, which means that numerous individuals – called polyps – come together to create what is essentially a single compound organism. The polyps produce calcareous skeletons; when thousands of millions of them are present in a single colony, they form large, stony (in fact, limestone) structures which build up as reefs.

What happens is that, when corals die, at least some of the skeleton remains intact, thus adding to the reef. Cracks and holes then fill with sand and the calcareous remains of other reef plants and animals, and gradually the whole becomes consolidated, with new corals growing on the surface of the mass. Thus only the outermost layer of the growing reef is alive.

Corals grow slowly, adding about 1–10cm (0.4–4in) growth in a year. Once over a certain age they are able to reproduce, releasing tiny forms that float freely among the plankton for a few weeks until settling to continue their growth on the reef.

The forms that corals create as they grow vary enormously according to the species and to the place on the reef where that species is growing. Coral colonies range in size from a few centimetres in diameter to giants that measure several metres across and are many hundreds of years old. Some formations are branched or bushy, others tree-like; some take the the form of plates, tables or delicate leafy fronds; and yet others are encrusted, lobed, rounded or simply massive.

Microscopic plants called zooxanthellae are of great importance to the growth and health of corals. These are packed in their millions into the living tissues of most reef-building corals (and of various other reef animals, such as giant clams [*Tridacna* spp.]). Although reef corals capture planktonic organisms from the water, a significant amount of their food comes directly from the zooxanthellae. It is for this reason that the most prolific coral growths are in the shallow, well-lit waters that the zooxanthellae prefer.

Types of Reef

In most regions with large coral communities, the calcareous skeletons have built up to form a variety of different types of reef:

- fringing reefs
- patch reefs, banks and shoals
- barrier reefs
- atolls

Left: *Shoaling fish over hard and soft coral formations off Pemba Island.*

Fringing Reefs

Occurring typically in shallow water near to land, fringing reefs extend to depths of 15–45m (49–148ft), depending on factors such as the profile and depth of the seabed, and the clarity of the water.

Corals do not occur where rivers flow into the sea because the influx of fresh water reduces the salinity levels of the seawater that the corals require to be able to grow and flourish. Instead the river estuaries support stands of mangroves – another significant marine ecosystem of enormous importance. Mangroves are a heterogeneous group of plants which have independently (since there is no systematic or taxonomic relationship linking them) evolved mechanisms which enable them to adapt to a normally hostile habitat. The outstanding feature of this habitat is that, being part of the intertidal zone, it is inundated with seawater at high tide. In order to cope with constant tidal flooding and the high salinity levels in the water, mangrove trees have developed special branching root systems, as well as the ability to exclude much of the salt content in the seawater that they absorb. Those salts that are absorbed are exuded in concentrated form through glands situated on the underside of the leaves.

Mangroves occur along many stretches of the East African coastline and on the shores of the islands. Mangroves play an important part in the local economy, and are used as building material for the construction of roofs, dwellings and furniture. Dense mangrove-rich shores occur notably along the southern coast of Kenya and the northern coast of Tanzania. These stands of mangroves are the home of the mangrove crab, which is also an important source of food.

There are no classical barrier reefs or atolls along the East African coastline. Two forms of fringing reefs occur, namely those which fringe the mainland and the main islands and are separated from land by a lagoon; and those which grow on the submerged slope of the smaller islands. The uppermost sections of the reefs around the small islands are often exposed during low spring tides. Soft corals predominate, with the deeper sections of the slope covered in a luxuriant growth of a great variety of hard and soft coral, which in turn attracts a large and diverse number of marine life.

Patch Reefs, Banks and Shoals

In theory, reefs can develop anywhere where the underlying rock has at some time been close enough to the surface for corals to become established and grow. Sea levels may have risen considerably since then, or other geological changes may have occurred to lower the depth of the bed beneath the surface; either way, there are many places where reefs exist as isolated mounds or hillocks on the seabed.

Patch reefs are found in relatively shallow waters off the East African coastline. They vary in size, from a couple of metres in length to many hundreds of metres. In some parts of the world patch reefs stretching for a number of kilometres occur, often lying in deep waters with their tops rising to within 20m (66ft) of the surface. These are usually referred to as banks or shoals.

Reef Life

Along the coral reefs and within the lagoons that line the shores of the East African mainland and the islands, there is a world of immense fascination. Staghorn corals (*Acropora* spp.), a spiky coral with many branches that resemble the antlers of a stag, is a fast growing coral and an early colonizer of disturbed areas. Plate coral (*Leptoseris* sp.) is very common and is made up of flat, plate-like sheets, some up to 1m (3ft) in diameter, which spread out in layers across the reef. Other typical corals include mushroom (*Fungia scutaria*), knob-horned (*Pocillopora verrucosa*), honeycomb (*Favites* spp.), brain (*Platygyra daedalea*), turbinate (*Turbinaria mesenterina*) and turret (*Denrophyllia aurea*) corals.

Fish life on coral reefs is another area of great interest to divers. There are herbivores (marine plant feeders), carnivores (those that feed on animals), and omnivores (those that eat both plants and animals).

Sea urchins are relatively common; the slate pencil urchin (*Heterocentrotus mammillatus*), which has large, smooth and attractively banded spines is found in the deeper waters off-shore, while its cousin (*Diadema setosum*), which has long, needle-like spines, is found mainly in the lagoons and shallower waters.

Reef Zones and Habitats

Reefs can be divided into a number of zones reflecting differences in such features as depth, profile, distance from the shore, amount of wave action, and type of seabed. Associated with each zone are characteristic types of marine life.

The Lagoon

A lagoon fills the area between the shore and the seaward reef. Lagoons are more sheltered than those on the seaward reef, and are also more affected by sedimentation. Here there are many attractive seaweeds. Most of the corals are delicate, branching types. Large sand-dwelling anemones are often found in lagoons and, in places, soft corals and 'false corals' are likely to form mats over the seabed. Especially where there is a current you may find beds of seagrasses, the only flowering plants to occur in the sea. Among the many animals that make these pastures their home are sea cucumbers.

Although some typical reef fishes are absent from the lagoon environment, there is no shortage of interesting species such as the roving predators – snappers, wrasses, triggerfish, emperors and others – on the lookout for worms, crustaceans, gastropods, sea urchins and small fish. Then there are the bottom-dwelling fishes that burrow into the sand, emerging only to feed.

Most entertaining to watch – if you spot them – are the small gobies that live in association with pistol shrimps. In this partnership the shrimp is the digger and

A moray eel opens its mouth to facilitate breathing.

the goby, stationed at the entrance to the burrow, is the sentry. The small fish remains ever on the alert, ready to retreat hurriedly into the burrow at the first sign of disturbance. The shrimp has very poor eyesight; it keeps its antennae in close touch with the goby so that it can pick up the danger signal and, likewise, retire swiftly to the safety of the burrow.

The Seaward Reef Front

In East Africa most scuba diving takes place on the reef front, because this is where the deeper waters lie and where spectacular features and impressive displays of marine life are found. Brightly lit, clean, plankton-rich water provides ideal growing conditions for corals, and the colonies they form help to create habitats of considerable complexity.

There is infinite variety, from shallow gardens of delicate branching corals to walls festooned with soft corals and sea fans.

The top 5m (18ft) or so of the seaward reef is especially full of life. Here small, brilliantly coloured damselfish and anthias swarm around the coral, darting into open water to feed on plankton.

Butterflyfish show their dazzling arrays of spots, stripes and intricate patterns as they probe into crevices or pick at coral polyps. Many have elongated snouts especially adapted for this delicate task, such as the Moorish idol (*Zanclus canescens*) which scans the reefs, usually in pairs, but occasionally in threesomes.

By contrast, you can see parrotfish biting and scraping at the coral, over time leaving their characteristic white scars. Open-water species like fusiliers and snappers cover quite large areas when feeding, and wrasses often forage far and wide over the reef. But many species are more localized and can be highly territorial, on occasion even being prepared to take on a trespassing diver.

Clownfishes (*Amphiprion* spp.), or anemonefish, are among the boldest of the little fish, dashing out from the safety of anemone tentacles to give chase to those who venture too close.

Fish-watching can provide a diver with endless pleasure, but there is much else to see. Any bare spaces created on the reef are soon colonized, and in some places the surface is covered with large organisms that may be tens or even hundreds of years old. These sedentary reef-dwellers rely on, aside from the omnipresent algae, water-borne food. Corals and their close relatives – anemones, sea fans and black corals – capture planktonic organisms using their tiny stinging cells.

Sea squirts and sponges strain the plankton as seawater passes through special canals in their body walls. Other organisms have different techniques: the Christmastree worm, for example, filters out food with the aid of its beautiful feathery 'crown' of tentacles.

Apart from the fishes and the sedentary organisms there is a huge array of other life forms to observe on the reef. Tiny crabs live among the coral branches and larger ones wedge themselves into appropriate nooks and crannies, often emerging to feed at night. Spiny lobsters hide in caverns, coming out to hunt under cover of darkness. Gastropod molluscs are another type of marine creature seldom seen during the day, but they are in fact present in very large numbers, especially on the shallower parts of the reef; many of them are small, but on occasion you might come across one of the larger species, like the giant triton (*Charonia tritonis*).

Some of the most easily spotted of the mobile invertebrates are the echinoderms. Most primitive of these are the feather stars, sporting long delicate arms in all colours from bright yellow to green, red and black. The best known of their relatives, the sea urchin, is the black, spiny variety that lives in shallow reef areas and is a potential hazard to anyone walking onto the reef. Many of the small, brightly coloured starfish that wander over the reef face feed on the surface film of detritus and micro-organisms. Others are carnivorous, browsing on sponges and sea mats, and a few feed on living coral polyps. The damage they cause depends on their size, their appetite and, collectively, their population density. Potentially the most damaging of all is the large predator, the crown-of-thorns starfish *(Acanthaster planci)* (see feature on page 72 for further details).

Whether brilliantly attractive or frankly plain, whether swift or sessile (attached), all the life forms on the reef are part of its finely balanced ecosystem. Divers are intruders: make it your obligation to cause as little disturbance and destruction as possible in this wonderland.

Marine Conservation in East Africa

In a world hastening to its own suicidal doom with overcrowding and with noisome technology, coral reefs are tranquil, wild places where man can restore at least part of his battered soul.

Ken Bock, *A Guide to Common Reef Fishes of the Western Indian Ocean & Kenya Coast.*

The coral reefs of East Africa host some of the richest and most varied marine inhabitants in the world. As with many developing countries, Kenya and Tanzania's reefs are under severe threat, both from natural causes and from over-exploitation by humans. If these processes remain unchecked, they will result in the calamitous destruction of some of the world's most precious natural resources. Most East African reefs are of the fringing type, and form a barrier as close as 500m (1 650ft) to the shore. The reefs come right up to the surface in many cases, and this accessibility and shallow depth facilitate over-exploitation.

Threats to the coral reefs of East Africa

Coral reefs rank among the most stable, biologically productive, and most diverse ecosystems on earth. They are, as a rule, restricted to shallow tropical waters of temperatures ranging between 25 and 29°C (77 and 84°F) and between latitudes of 30° North and 30° South, generally up to depths of 30m (100ft), where they flourish. They provide habitat to enormous numbers of other marine organisms, and their solid mass also serves as a barrier to protect beaches from wave erosion.

Unfortunately coral reefs are fragile (though maybe not as fragile as was at one time believed) but are highly exploitable. To flourish, reefs require very specific seawater parameters regarding temperature, water clarity and light, salinity, pH contents and oxygen.

Natural threats

Run-off and sedimentation: Slash-and-burn agriculture and the decimation of forests for firewood and charcoal contribute to soil erosion, which in turn leads to soil run-off and sedimentation. Soil particles carried by rivers may settle on and destroy large parts of the fringing reefs. Severe floods will distribute run-off much further out to sea, as demonstrated by the astonishing arrival of an adult hippopotamus on Pemba Island (50km [30 miles] offshore) during the floods of 1961. The inflow of raw sewage is a widespread cause of reef pollution, especially in Third World countries where few proper facilities exist to cope with human waste.

Coral predators: The gluttonous crown-of-thorns starfish (*Acanthaster planci*) preys on coral reefs and has devoured an extensive part of Australia's Great Barrier Reef. It has been sighted on several occasions on reefs off Kenya and Tanzania, and though it may not pose a problem at present, a careful watch should be kept. The natural predator of the crown-of-thorns is the giant triton or triton's trumpet (*Charonia tritonis*). The mollusc is prized for its size and attractive appearance, and unfortunately is being removed for sale as souvenirs by curio vendors. Large colonies of sea urchins may cause surface erosion of reefs, and in many cases overfishing has led to an eruption of these. It is also suspected that large sea turtles may cause considerable damage to delicate coral growths when they land on them.

Human threats

Dynamite fishing: This destructive form of indiscriminate fish harvesting has devastated large sections of the East African coast, especially in Tanzanian waters. Fishermen practising this method usually dispatch one of the crew into the water with a dive mask to look for large congregations of schooling fish. When the fish are located, a length of fuse that corresponds roughly with the depth is attached to a stick of dynamite and thrown overboard. The resulting explosion not only kills most fish within proximity of the blast, but also smashes the coral to smithereens. This of course destroys the natural habitat of a myriad of marine organisms. The fish may eventually move away from the reef altogether as a result of this upheaval in the food chain.

The protection afforded by the fringing reefs is also disrupted when large sections of the reef are destroyed. The results of this shortsighted method of fishing are evident on the beaches to the north of Dar es Salaam, where hotels are being flooded while the beaches are eroding into the sea. The futile attempts to stop the erosion by building rocky breakwaters at right angles to the beaches have not only spoilt their natural beauty, but have not solved the problem.

Dynamite is obtained from large quarries or smuggled into the country. In some cases, a volatile homemade explosive is prepared in backyard laboratories. The unpredictable results can sometimes be seen among the crippled beggars on the streets of Dar es Salaam, who blame sharks for their misfortune.

Dynamite fishing carries a heavy fine, but the sad truth at time of writing is that there are no funds available for proper patrol boats and law enforcement facilities. The voluntary efforts of local divers to assist in the eradication of this practice have met with indifference from the authorities in Dar es Salaam. At present the practice is still common in Tanzanian waters, and every effort should be made to halt dynamite fishing before it is too late.

Exploitation of coral reefs: In both Kenya and Tanzania the more accessible reefs close to shore and in shallow waters are being destroyed by plunderers for curio vendors. Large, delicate pieces of staghorn and tube coral are broken off the reef to be sold to gullible tourists. In some cases, the specimens are dyed in unnaturally gaudy orange and lilac colours, which seem to be the final insult to both coral and buyer.

The indiscriminate collecting of live shells is also seriously depleting the reef habitat. Even the collecting of dead shells may be frowned upon, as these often provide a home to hermit crabs and other small crustacea. The only positive way to stop this will be for tourists to stop buying coral and shells. Some attempts are being made in Kenya to educate the public. Fortunately the customs authorities of some European countries are now confiscating coral and shells brought in without a permit, and in some cases fines are being imposed.

Coral mining: After dynamite fishing, coral mining is probably the greatest threat to reefs. A large quantity of coral reef is used in the production of lime for construction, while compacted coral is used to produce building aggregate. When living coral is cut, the resulting mess in the water also kills off some remaining coral, together with other reef inhabitants. Where the livelihood of a great number of people depend entirely on these local industries, careful planning is needed to introduce bans. In many cases compensation must be implemented.

The impact of divers: Careless diving methods inevitably damage coral reefs. In high-density diving regions, careless diving has a serious impact on the wellbeing of the reefs. Training dives should always be carried out in sandy areas. Diving habits should ideally be closely monitored by dive masters and dive guides. The dive briefing should emphasize the delicate nature of reefs, as education is really the only way to prevent damage.

Marine aquarium collecting: When the resource is well managed and selective catching is done, collecting should not have a detrimental impact on reefs. Marine aquariums do have the beneficial effect of helping people develop an appreciation for reef environments. Destructive collecting techniques, however, will seriously damage and destroy reef ecology.

Kenya's Marine National Parks

To protect the country's rich marine wildlife, the Kenyan authorities had the laudable foresight to establish marine national parks and reserves as far back as 1968. These have proved a huge success, as the number of visiting divers on the Kenyan coast attests. Most of the coral reefs in the parks are in pristine condition. In some cases where previous damage was done, the recovery can be clearly seen. The abundance and tameness of the marine fauna is also proof of the magnificent success of these protected areas. Kenya has managed to create a working symbiosis between the authorities and the local fisherfolk who are dependent on harvesting the sea for their livelihood, by allowing them still to fish selectively in some of the areas. The Kenyan marine parks and reserves should serve as an example and model for other countries, where coral reefs are being depleted and destroyed at an alarming rate. The following areas of the Kenyan coast have been proclaimed as marine parks and reserves:

1968	Malindi Marine National Park 6km^2 (2 sq miles)
1968	Malindi Marine National Reserve 213km^2 (82 sq miles)
1968	Watamu Marine National Park 10km^2 (4 sq miles)
1968	Watamu Marine National Reserve 32km^2 (12 sq miles)
1978	Kisite Marine National Park 28km^2 (11 sq miles)
1978	Mpunguti Marine National Reserve 11km^2 (4 sq miles)
1979	Kiunga Marine National Reserve 250km^2 (97 sq miles)
1986	Mombasa Marine National Park 10km^2 (4 sq miles)
1986	Mombasa Marine National Reserve 200km^2 (77 sq miles)

General rules and regulations can be obtained from the Kenya Wildlife Service; *see* below (offices in Nairobi, Mombasa and Shimoni).

Tanzania's National Marine Parks

As far back as 1975, the Tanzanian government designated a number of areas, which include Mbudya Island, Fungu Yasin and Pangani, for proclamation as marine parks and reserves. Unfortunately no further progress was made. Dynamite fishing increased to such an extent that one small island, the breeding ground of sea turtles, disappeared completely! Fortunately it seems that the authorities have woken up to the importance of the country's coral reefs. In December 1994, Mafia National Marine Park was officially proclaimed. It can only be hoped that proper enforcement of the rules will ensure that this marine park will receive adequate protection.

Marine Groups and Conservation Organizations

Kenya:

Kenya Wildlife Service
Langata Road, P O Box 40241, Nairobi.

The Provincial Wildlife Officer (Marine National Parks)
P O Box 82144, Mombasa.

The East African Wildlife Society,
2nd Floor, Museum Hill Centre
P O Box 20110, Nairobi
tel. (02) 748 170/1/2/3; fax. 746 868.

Tanzania:

Tanzania National Parks Board
P O Box 3134, Arusha.

Some Tips on Responsible Diving

Here are just some of the ways in which you, as a diver, can help preserve the reefs that have given you so much.

• Try not to touch living marine organisms with either your body or your diving equipment. Be careful to control your fins, as their size and force of kicking can damage the reef. Don't use deep fin-strokes near the reef because the surge of water can disturb delicate organisms. it may not look elegant but, when you are close to the reef, especially in a gully, it is best to keep your feet still and propel yourself along by making small swimming strokes with your hands until you are clear of the reef.

• Look behind you to see if your console is dragging across the reef and, if it is, hold it in your hand or tuck it into your BC or weight belt.

• Learn the skills of good buoyancy control – divers ascending too rapidly or crashing into the living reef while trying to adjust their buoyancy may cause irreparable harm. Make sure you are properly weighted and learn to achieve neutral buoyancy.

• If you haven't dived for a while, practise your skills, especially buoyancy control, in a pool or a relatively barren area which is devoid of marine organisms, such as a sandy spot near the reefs.

• Avoid kicking up sand. Clouds of sand settling on the reef can smother corals and other invertebrates. Snorkellers should be careful not to kick up sand when treading water in shallow reef areas.

• Never stand on corals, however robust they may seem. Living polyps are easily injured by even the slightest touch. Never pose for pictures by standing inside giant basket sponges or barrel sponges. Even the apparently robust local orange 'wall' sponges can be harmed by careless contact.

• If you are out of control and about to collide with the reef, steady yourself with your fingertips on exposed rock, a part of the reef which is already dead, or on one of the more robust algaes, such as kelp.

• Unless you are sufficiently experienced to ensure that you don't injure the reef inhabitants, don't dive when there is a strong surge.

• If you need to adjust your mask or any other part of your diving equipment, try to do so in a sandy area well away from the reef.

• Don't collect or buy shells, corals or any other marine souvenirs, and be very particular about where, when and from whom you buy seafood or any marine products.

• On any excursion, whether it is with an operator or privately organized, make sure you take your garbage back for proper disposal on land, and please remember to pick up any litter that you may find.

• Take great care in underwater caverns and caves. Avoid crowding into the cave and don't stay there too long; your air bubbles collect in pockets on the roof of the cave, and delicate creatures living there could possibly 'drown in air'.

• Don't feed fish. It may seem harmless but it can upset their normal feeding patterns, provoke aggressive behaviour and be unhealthy for them if you give them food that is not part of their normal diet.

• Don't move marine organisms around to photograph or play with them. In particular, don't hitch rides on turtles: it causes them considerable stress. When observing marine animals, take into account that they may be resting, feeding or breeding, and that your presence may disturb them; this is particularly important in the case of larger animals such as sharks.

• When booking a live-aboard dive trip or a stay at a resort, ask about the company's environmental policy regarding waste management, relationship with the local community (particularly in rural areas), anchoring, and usage of energy and fresh water. Boycott dive boats that cause unnecessary anchor damage, have bad oil leaks, or discharge untreated sewage near reefs, and do not support operators who exploit the local environment and community without returning any benefit. (Yes, you are entitled to ask them if they repatriate profits to a foreign country, who they employ, what they pay them and how the local community benefits form their operation.)

• Try to be conservative in your use of water and power.

• If you spearfish or hunt any seafood, make sure you are familiar with all local fish and game regulations and obtain any necessary licensing. Prove your expertise in spearfishing by killing exactly the right size, number and species of fish for the next meal. Any more is wasteful, destructive and counter-productive.

• Most important, enjoy your dive and, yes, take only photographs and leave only bubbles!

UNDERWATER PHOTOGRAPHY AND VIDEO

Photography has become one of the most popular underwater pastimes. Being able to capture on film some of the amazing creatures we see underwater is highly rewarding, but can also prove incredibly frustrating, as the real difficulties of underwater photography – backscatter, fish that refuse to stay still, flooded camera housings and so on – become apparent. You need a lot of perseverance – and luck – to get really good results, but if you're prepared to persist you'll find you've developed a passion that will last for a lifetime of diving.

Shallow-Water Cameras

There are several cameras on the market that are suitable for snorkelling. Kodak and Fuji both offer cheap, single-use cameras that are waterproof down to about 2m (6.6ft) and work well enough in clear, sunlit waters. If you object to disposables, Minolta and Canon make slightly more expensive cameras that can be used down to depths of about 5m (16ft).

Submersible Cameras and Housings

You have essentially two main options for serious underwater photography. The first is to splash out on a purpose-built waterproof camera; the second is to buy a waterproof housing for your normal SLR or land camera. Each system has its pros and cons.

The submersible camera used by most professionals is the Nikonos, a 35mm non-reflex camera with TTL (through-the-lens) automatic exposure system and dedicated flashguns. (A popular alternative is the Sea & Sea Motor Marine II.) The specially designed Nikonos lenses give sharper results underwater than any of the housed lenses, but the lack of reflex focusing makes it difficult to compose pictures, and you can easily cut off part of a subject. They range from 15mm to 80mm in focal length, but must be changed above water. Underwater, the 35mm lens is of much use only with extension tubes or close-up outfits, though it can be used on land. The 28mm lens should be considered the standard.

Other companies supply accessories for the Nikonos: lenses, lens converters, extension tubes and housings to accommodate fish-eye and superwide land-camera lenses. Lens converters are convenient: they can be changed underwater. The Motor Marine II makes good use of these, with converters for wide-angle and macro. The Nikonos close-up kit can be changed underwater. Nikonos has recently introduced the RS-AF, a fully waterproof reflex camera with autofocus and dedicated lenses and flashgun, but it is extremely heavy and expensive. It is a poor buy in comparison with land cameras like Nikon's 801, F90 and F4 in housings; these are more versatile, weigh less, and can also be used on land.

Land cameras can be used underwater in specialist metal or plexiglass housings. Housings without controls, as used for fully automatic cameras, require fast films to obtain reasonable shutter speeds and lens apertures in the low ambient light underwater. Housings are available for all top-grade reflex cameras, but there are advantages and disadvantages to each system:

• Metal housings are strong, reliable, work well at depth and last a long time if properly maintained; they are heavier to carry, but are buoyant in water. Their higher cost is justified if your camera is expensive and deserves the extra protection.

• Plexiglass housings are fragile and need careful handling both in and out of the water; they are available for a wide range of cameras. They are lightweight, which is convenient on land, but in water are often too buoyant, so that you have to attach extra weights to them.

• Some models compress at depth, so the control rods miss the camera controls ... but, if you adjust the rods to work at depths, they do not function properly near the surface! However, as most underwater photographs are taken near the surface, in practice this drawback is not usually serious.

'O' Rings

Underwater cameras, housings, flashguns and cables have 'O' ring seals. These and their mating surfaces or grooves must be kept scrupulously clean. 'O' rings should be lightly greased with silicone grease to prevent flooding; too much grease will attract grit and hairs. Silicone spray should not be used, as the cooling can crack the 'O' ring. Removable 'O' rings should be stored off the unit to stop them becoming flat, and the unit itself should be sealed in a plastic bag to keep out moisture. User-removable 'O' rings on Nikonos cameras and flash-synchronization cables are best replaced every 12 months, and nonremovable ones every 12–18 months. 'O' rings usually last the life of the housing.

A diver uses a video camera and lights to record large sponges off the coast of Zanzibar.

Lighting

Sunlight can produce spectacular effects underwater, especially in silhouette shots. When the sun is at a low angle, or in choppy seas, much of the light fails to penetrate the surface. To get the best of it, photograph two hours either side of the sun's highest point. Generally you should have the sun behind you and on your subject.

Water acts as a cyan (blue-green) filter, cutting back red, so photographs taken with colour film have a blue-green cast. Different filters can correct this in either cold or tropical waters, but they reduce the already limited amount of light available. The answer is flash, which will put back the colour and increase apparent sharpness.

Modern flashguns have TTL automatic-exposure systems. Underwater, large flashguns give good wide-angle performance up to 1.5m (5ft). Smaller flashguns have a narrower angle and work up to only 1m (3ft); diffusers widen the angle of cover, but you lose at least one f-stop in output. Some land flashguns can be housed for underwater use.

Flashguns used on or near the camera make suspended particles in the water light up like white stars in a black sky (backscatter); the closer these are to the camera, the larger they appear. The solution is to keep the flash as far as possible above and to one side of the camera. Two narrow-angle flashguns, one each side of the camera, often produce a better result than a single wide-angle flashgun. In a multiple-flash set-up the prime flashgun will meter by TTL (if available); any other flashgun connected will give its pre-programmed output, so should be set low to achieve modelling light.

When photographing divers, remember the eyes within the mask must be lit. Flashguns with a colour temperature of 4 500K usually give more accurate skin tones and colour.

Fish scales reflect light in different ways depending on the angle of the fish to the camera. Silver fish reflect more light than coloured, and black fish almost none at all, so to make sure you get a good result you should bracket exposures. If using an automatic flashgun, do this by altering the film-speed setting. At distances under 1m (3ft) most automatic flashguns tend to overexpose, so allow for this.

The easiest way to balance flash with available light is to use TTL flash with a camera set on aperture-priority metering. Take a reading of the mid-water background that agrees with your chosen flash-synchronization speed, and set the aperture one number higher to give a deeper blue. Set your flash to TTL and it will correctly light your subject.

Film

Once you have learnt the correct exposures for different situations you can begin experimenting aesthetically with manual exposure. For b/w photography, fast 400 ISO film is best. For beginners wishing to use colour, negative print film is best as it has plenty of exposure latitude. (Reversal film is better for reproduction, but requires very accurate exposure.) Kodachrome films are ideal for close work but can give mid-water shots a blue-green water background; although this is in fact accurate, people are conditioned to a 'blue' sea. Ektachrome and Fujichrome produce blue water backgrounds; 50-100 ISO films present the best compromise between exposure and grain, and pale yellow filters can be used to cut down the blue.

Subjects

Subject depends on personal interest. Macrophotography, with extension tubes and fixed frames, is easiest to get right: the lens-to-subject and flash-to-subject distances are fixed, and the effects of silting in the water are minimized. Expose a test film at a variety of exposures with a fixed set-up; the best result tells you the exposure to use in future for a particular setting and film.

Some fish are strongly territorial. Surgeonfish, triggerfish and sharks may make mock attacks; you can get strong pictures if you are brave enough to stand your ground. Manta rays are curious and will keep coming back if you react quietly and do not chase them. Angelfish and butterflyfish swim off when you first enter their territory, but if you remain quiet they will usually return and allow you to photograph them.

Diver and wreck photography are the most difficult. Even with apparently clear water and wide-angle lenses there will be backscatter, and you need to use flash if you are going to get a diver's mask to show.

Underwater night photography introduces you to another world. Many creatures appear only at night, and some fish are more approachable because they are half-asleep. However, focusing quickly in dim light is difficult, and many subjects disappear as soon as they are lit up, so you need to preset the controls.

On the Shoot – Tips

• Underwater photography starts before you enter the water. If you have a clear idea of your subject, you are likely to get better results. And, remember, you can't change films or prime lenses underwater!

• Autofocus systems that work on contrast (not infrared) are good underwater only for high-contrast subjects.

• When you are balancing flash with daylight, cameras with faster flash-synchronization speeds – 1/125sec or 1/250sec – give sharper results with fast-moving fish. The lens aperture will be larger, so focus must be accurate.

• Masks keep your eyes distant from the viewfinder. Buy the smallest-volume mask you can wear.

• Cameras fitted with optical action finders or eyepiece magnifiers are useful in housings but not so important with autofocus systems.

• Coloured filters can give surrealistic results, as do starburst filters when photographing divers with shiny equipment, lit torches or flashguns set to slave.

• Entering the water overweight makes it easier to steady yourself. Wearing an adjustable buoyancy lifejacket enables you to maintain neutral buoyancy.

• Remember not to touch coral and do not wear fins over sandy bottoms – they stir up the sand.

• Photographers do not swim around much, so wear a wetsuit for warmth.

• Refraction through your mask and the camera lens makes objects appear one-third closer and larger than in air. Reflex focusing and visual estimates of distances are unaffected but, if you measure a distance, compensate by reducing the resultant figure by one-third when setting the lens focus.

• When there is a flat port (window) in front of the lens, the focal length is increased and the image sharpness decreased due to differential refraction. Most pronounced with wide-angle lenses, this should be compensated for by using a convex dome port.

Dome ports need lenses that can focus on a virtual image at about 30cm (12in), so you may have to fit supplementary +1 or +2 dioptre lenses.

Video

Underwater video photography is easier. Macro subjects require extra lighting but other shots can be taken using available light with, if necessary, electronic improvement afterwards. Backscatter is much less of a problem. You can play the results back on site and, if unhappy, have another try – or, at the very least, use the tape again somewhere else.

A major problem for travelling photographers and videographers is battery charging. AA or D cell batteries are available in East Africa, particularly in Nairobi and Mombasa, but they may be old or have been badly stored – if the weight does not preclude this, it is best to carry your own spares.

Despite their memory problems, rechargeable nickel-cadmium batteries have advantages in cold weather, recharge flashguns much more quickly and, even if flooded, can usually be used again. Make sure you carry spares and that your chargers are of the appropriate voltage for your destination. Quick chargers are useful as long as the electric current available is strong enough. Most video cameras and many flashguns have dedicated battery packs, so remember to carry at least one spare and to keep it charged.

HEALTH AND SAFETY FOR DIVERS

The information in this section is intended as a guide only and is no substitute for thorough training or professional medical advice, nor is it intended to imitate a comprehensive manual on the subject.

The information is based on currently accepted health and safety advice. It is strongly advised that the reader obtain a recognized manual on diving safety and medicine before embarking on a trip.

Please note that:

• Divers who have suffered any diving-related injury or symptom of an injury, no matter how minor, should consult a doctor, preferably a specialist in diving medicine, as soon as possible after the symptom or injury occurs.

• If you are the victim of a diving injury, do not hesitate to reveal your symptoms no matter how minor they may seem to be. Mild symptoms can develop into a major illness with life-threatening consequences. It is better to be honest with yourself and live to dive another day.

• No matter how confident you are in formulating your own diagnosis, remember that unless you are a trained medical practitioner, *you are not a doctor.*

• Always err on the conservative side when considering your ailment: if you discover that your illness is only minor, the worst that can happen is that both you and your doctor will be relieved.

General Principles of First Aid

The basic principles of first aid include:

• DOING NO HARM
• SUSTAINING LIFE
• PREVENTING DETERIORATION
• PROMOTING RECOVERY

Safety

In the event of any illness or injury, a simple sequence of patient assessment and management can be followed. The sequence first involves assessment and definition of any life-threatening conditions followed by management of the problems found. The first things to check are commonly known as the ABCs, i.e.:

A. AIRWAY (with care of the neck)
B. BREATHING
C. CIRCULATION
D. DECREASED level of consciousness
E. EXPOSURE

Ensure both the patient's and your own safety by removing yourselves from the threatening environment (usually the water). Make sure that whatever your actions, they in no way further endanger the patient or yourself.

NEVER ASSUME THAT THE PATIENT IS DEAD.

Check the ABCs, as follows:

A. AIRWAY
1. With attention to the neck, is there a neck injury?
2. Is the mouth and the nose free of obstruction? Any noisy breathing is a sign of airway obstruction.

B. BREATHING
1. Look at the chest to see if it is rising and falling.
2. Listen for air movement at the nose and mouth.
3. Feel for the movement of air against your cheek.

C. CIRCULATION
1. Feel for a pulse next to the windpipe (carotid artery).

D. DECREASED LEVEL OF CONSCIOUSNESS
1. Does the patient respond to any of the following procedures (AVPU)?

A. Is he *awake*, aware, spontaneously speaking?
V. Does he respond to *verbal stimuli*, i.e. to a loud call to 'Wake up!'?
P. Does he respond to *painful stimuli*, i.e. to a sharp pinch or slap?
U. Is he totally *unresponsive*?

E. EXPOSURE
The patient must be adequately exposed in order to examine him properly, so remove clothes as necessary.

NOW, SEND FOR HELP.

If you think the patient's condition is serious following your assessment, you need to send or call for help from the emergency medical services (ambulance, paramedics). Whoever you send to get help should return to confirm that help is indeed on its way.

Recovery Position

If the patient is unconscious but breathing normally, there is a risk of vomiting and subsequent choking. It is therefore critical that the patient be turned onto his side in the recovery position.

1. Place the patient's right hand under his head with the palm forwards (facing up).

2. Cross the left leg over the right ankle.

3. Fold the left arm over the chest.

4. Grasp the left hip and pull the patient over onto his side with your right hand, supporting the patient's right cheek with the left hand.

5. Now flex the patient's left knee to 90°.

6. Flex the patient's left arm to 90° and place the forearm flat on the ground.

7. The patient is now in a stable recovery position.

If you suspect a spinal or neck injury be sure to immobilize the patient in a straight line before you turn him on his side.

Cardiopulmonary Resuscitation (CPR)

Cardiopulmonary resuscitation is required when a patient is found to have no pulse. It consists of techniques to:

- VENTILATE THE PATIENT'S LUNGS
  (EXPIRED AIR RESUSCITATION)
- PUMP THE PATIENT'S HEART
  (EXTERNAL CARDIAC COMPRESSION)

Once you have checked the ABCs (*see* Safety) you need to do the following:

A. AIRWAY
1. Gently extend the head (head tilt) and lift the chin with two fingers (chin lift). This will lift the tongue away from the back of the throat and open the airway.
2. If you suspect a foreign body in the airway sweep your finger across the back of the tongue from one side to the other. If an obstruction is found, remove it.

Do not attempt this on a conscious or semiconscious patient as they will either bite your finger off or vomit.

B. BREATHING
If the patient is not breathing you need to give expired air resuscitation, in other words, you need to breathe into the patient's lungs:

1. Pinch the patient's nose closed.
2. Place your mouth, open, fully over the patient's mouth, making as good a seal as possible.
3. Exhale into the patient's mouth hard enough to cause the patient's chest to rise.
4. If the patient's chest fails to rise, you need to adjust the position of the airway. The 16% of oxygen in your expired air is adequate to sustain life.
5. Initially you need to give two full, slow breaths.
6. If the patient is found to have a pulse at this stage, continue breathing for the patient once every five seconds, checking for a pulse after every 10 breaths.
7. If the patient begins breathing on his own you can turn him into the recovery position.

C. CIRCULATION
After giving the two breaths as above you now need to give external cardiac compression.

1. Kneel next to the patient's chest.
2. Measure two finger breadths above the notch where the ribs meet the lower end of the breast bone.
3. Place the heel of your left hand just above your two fingers in the centre of the breast bone.
4. Place the heel of your right hand on your left hand.
5. Straighten your elbows.
6. Place your shoulders perpendicularly above the patient's breast bone.
7. Compress the breast bone 4-5cm to a rhythm of 'one, two, three...'.
8. Give 15 compressions.

Continue giving cycles of two breaths and 15 compressions, checking for a pulse after every five cycles.

The aim of CPR is to keep the patient alive until more sophisticated help arrives in the form of paramedics or a doctor with the necessary equipment. Make sure that you and your buddy are trained in CPR – it could mean the difference between life and death.

Diving Diseases and Illnesses

ACUTE DECOMPRESSION ILLNESS

Acute decompression illness means any illness arising out of the decompression of a diver, in other words, by the diver moving from an area of high ambient pressure to an area of lower pressure. It is divided into two groups:

- DECOMPRESSION SICKNESS
- BAROTRAUMA WITH ARTERIAL GAS EMBOLISM

It is not important for either the diver or first-aider to differentiate between these two conditions because both are serious and both require the same emergency treatment. The important thing is to recognize acute decompression illness and to initiate emergency treatment.

The differences between decompression sickness and barotrauma are described below:

• DECOMPRESSION SICKNESS

Decompression sickness, or 'the bends', arises following inadequate decompression by the diver. Exposure to higher ambient pressure under water causes nitrogen to dissolve in increasing amounts in the body tissues. If this pressure is released gradually during correct and adequate decompression procedures the nitrogen escapes naturally into the blood and is exhaled through the lungs. If this release of pressure is too rapid the nitrogen cannot escape quickly enough and physical nitrogen bubbles form in the tissues.

The symptoms and signs of the disease are related to the tissues in which these bubbles form and the disease is described by the tissue affected, e.g. joint bend. Symptoms of decompression sickness include:

- Nausea and vomiting.
- Dizziness.
- Malaise and loss of appetite.
- Weakness.
- Joint pains or aches.
- Paralysis.
- Numbness.
- Itching of skin or skin rashes.
- Incontinence.
- Shortness of breath.

• BAROTRAUMA WITH ARTERIAL GAS EMBOLISM

Barotrauma refers to the damage that occurs when the tissue surrounding a gaseous space is injured following a change in the volume of air in that space.

An arterial gas embolism refers to a gas bubble that moves in a blood vessel usually leading to obstruction of that blood vessel or a vessel further downstream.

Barotrauma can therefore occur to any tissue that surrounds a gas-filled space, most commonly the:

• ears	middle ear squeeze	burst ear drum
• sinuses	sinus squeeze	sinus pain, nose bleeds
• lungs	lung squeeze	burst lung
• face	mask squeeze	swollen, bloodshot eyes
• teeth	tooth squeeze	toothache

A burst lung is the most serious of these and can result in arterial gas embolism. It occurs following a rapid ascent during which the diver does not exhale adequately. The rising pressure of expanding air in the lungs bursts the delicate alveoli, or lung sacs, and forces air into the blood vessels that carry blood back to the heart and ultimately the brain. In the brain these bubbles of air block blood vessels and obstruct the supply of blood and oxygen to the brain, resulting in brain damage.

The symptoms of lung barotrauma and arterial gas embolism include:

- Shortness of breath.
- Chest pain.
- Unconsciousness or altered level of consciousness.
- Weakness, incoordination and paralysis.
- Blurred vision, loss of balance.

Treatment

1. ABCs (*see* Safety) and CPR (page 151) as necessary.
2. Put the patient in the recovery position with no tilt or raising of the legs.
3. Administer 100% oxygen by mask (or demand valve).
4. Keep the patient warm.
5. Remove to the nearest hospital as soon as possible. The hospital or emergency services will arrange the recompression treatment required.

CARBON DIOXIDE OR CARBON MONOXIDE POISONING

Carbon dioxide poisoning can occur as a result of:

- skip breathing – diver holds his breath on SCUBA
- heavy exercise on SCUBA
- malfunctioning rebreather systems

Carbon monoxide poisoning occurs as a result of:

- exhaust gases being pumped into cylinders
- hookah systems air intake too close to exhaust fumes

Symptoms would be:

- Headache.
- Blue colour of the skin.
- Shortness of breath.
- Decreased level of consciousness or loss of consciousness.

Treatment

1. ABCs (*see* Safety) as necessary.
2. CPR if required.
3. 100% oxygen through a mask or demand valve.
4. Remove to nearest hospital.

HEAD INJURY

All head injuries should at all times be regarded as potentially serious.

Treatment

The diver should surface and any wound should be disinfected. There should be no more diving until a doctor has been consulted.

If the diver is unconscious, the emergency services should be contacted. If breathing and/or pulse has stopped, CPR should be administered.

If the diver is breathing and has a pulse, check for bleeding and other injuries and treat for shock; if wounds permit, put the sufferer into recovery position with no elevation of the legs and administer 100% oxygen. Keep him warm and comfortable, and monitor pulse and respiration constantly.

DO NOT administer fluids under any circumstances to an unconscious or semiconscious diver.

HYPERTHERMIA (INCREASED BODY TEMPERATURE)

A rise in body temperature results from a combination of overheating, normally due to exercise, and inadequate fluid intake. The diver will progress through heat exhaustion to heat stroke with eventual collapse. Heat stroke is a serious illness and if the diver is not cooled and rehydrated immediately he can die.

Treatment

Remove the diver from the hot environment and remove all clothes. Sponge with a damp cloth and fan either manually or with an electric fan. If the patient is conscious, he can be given fluids orally.

If unconscious place him in the recovery position (*see* page 127) and monitor the ABCs. Always seek advanced medical help thereafter.

HYPOTHERMIA

Normal internal body temperature is just under 37°C (98.4°F). If for any reason it is pushed much below this – usually, in diving, through wearing inadequate protective clothing – progressively more serious symptoms may occur, with death as the ultimate endpoint.

- A drop of 1°C (2°F) leads to shivering and discomfort.
- A 2°C (3°F) drop induces the body's self-heating mechanisms to react; blood flow to the peripheries is reduced and shivering becomes extreme.
- A 3°C (5°F) drop leads to amnesia, confusion, disorientation, heartbeat and breathing irregularities, and possibly rigor.

Treatment

- Move the patient to a sheltered, warm area or prevent further heat loss by wrapping him in a space blanket, surrounding the diver with your and your buddies' bodies, and covering his head and neck with a woolly hat, warm towels or anything suitable.
- In sheltered warmth, re-dress the diver in warm, dry clothing and then put him in a space blanket.
- If the diver is conscious and coherent, a warm shower or bath and a warm, sweet drink should be adequate treatment. If it isn't, call the emergency services and treat for shock while deploying the other warming measures noted.

NEAR DROWNING

Near drowning refers to a situation where the diver has inhaled some water. He may be conscious or unconscious. Water in the lungs interferes with the normal transport of oxygen from the lungs into the blood and near drowning victims are therefore often hypoxic.

Treatment

Remove the diver from the water and check the ABCs. Depending on your findings commence EAR (*see* Breathing under CPR page 151) or CPR where appropriate, beginning with EAR in the water if necessary. If possible, administer oxygen by mask or demand valve.

All near drowning victims can develop secondary drowning at a later stage; this is a condition where fluid oozes into the lungs causing the diver to drown in his own secretions. All near drowning victims should, therefore, be observed for 24 hours in a hospital.

NITROGEN NARCOSIS

The air we breathe is about 80% nitrogen. Breathing the standard mixture under compression, as divers do, can lead to symptoms very much like those of drunkenness – giving rise to the popular term 'rapture of the deep'.

Some divers experience nitrogen narcosis at depths of 30–40m (100–130ft). Up to a depth of about 60m (200ft) – that is, beyond the legal maximum depth for sport diving in the UK, East Africa and USA – the symptoms need not (but may) be serious; beyond about 80m (260ft) the diver may become unconscious. The onset of symptoms can be sudden and unheralded. The condition itself is not harmful; dangers arise through secondary effects, notably the diver doing something foolish.

Treatment

The only effective treatment is to return immediately to a shallower depth.

OXYGEN TOXICITY (POISONING)

Oxygen, if breathed at a partial pressure of greater than 1.5 atmospheres, can be poisonous to the lung and brain tissues.

- Lung toxicity is a more chronic event and is not commonly seen in sports divers.
- Brain toxicity is common and manifests when breathing pure (100%) oxygen at depths greater than 7msw (metres of sea water) or air deeper than 90msw.

The advent of Nitrox diving (increased oxygen percentage in the breathing mixture) will inevitably increase the incidence of brain oxygen toxicity. The clinical presentation of oxygen toxicity is sudden and unpredictable with unconsciousness and seizures which can be catastrophic under water.

Treatment

In the case of oxygen toxicity, prevention is definitely better than cure:

• Don't dive on 100% oxygen.
• Don't dive deeper than recommended for a particular Nitrox mix.
• Don't dive deeper than 70m (250ft) on air.

SHOCK

Shock refers not to the emotional trauma of a frightening experience but to a physiological state in the body resulting from poor blood and oxygen delivery to the tissues. As a result of oxygen and blood deprivation the tissues cannot perform their functions.

There are many causes of shock, but the most common are loss of blood or hypovolaemic shock.

Treatment

Treatment is directed at restoring blood and oxygen delivery to the tissues. Therefore maintain the ABCs and administer 100% oxygen. Control all external bleeding by direct pressure, pressure on pressure points and elevation of the affected limb. A tourniquet should only be used as a last resort, and only then on the arms and legs.

Unconscious, shocked victims should be placed on their side with the legs elevated.

GENERAL MARINE-RELATED AILMENTS

Apart from the specific diving-related illnesses the most common ailments divers are inflicted with include cuts and abrasions, coral cuts and stings, swimmer's ear, sea sickness, jellyfish stings and sunburn.

BITES FROM FEEDING FISH

Although fish-feeding is practised by some of the dive centre operators in East Africa, it is done under controlled conditions and it can be dangerous as some fish can become aggressive. For example, sharks' feeding frenzies are uncontrollable, and sharks often bite light-coloured fins. Triggerfish can come at you very fast, and groupers and moray eels have nasty teeth. Napoleon wrasses have strong mouth suction and can bite. Even little sergeant-majors can give your fingers a nasty nip.

Treatment

Be wary of feeding fish and of sticking your fingers into places into which you can't see. Wear gloves when diving.

CUTS AND ABRASIONS

Divers should wear appropriate abrasive protection for the environment. Prominent areas – hands, knees, elbows and feet – are most likely to be affected.

Treatment

The danger with abrasions is that they become infected, so all wounds should be thoroughly rinsed with water and an antiseptic such as hibitane in alcohol as soon as possible after the injury has occurred. Infection may progress to a stage where antibiotics are necessary. Spreading inflamed areas should receive medical attention.

SWIMMER'S EAR

Swimmer's ear is an infection of the external ear canal resulting from constantly wet ears. The infection is often a combination of a fungal and bacterial virus.

Treatment

Swimmer's ear can be prevented by always thoroughly drying the ears after diving and, if you are susceptible to the condition, by inserting alcohol or acetic acid drops after diving.

Never stick anything into your ear (including ear buds) as this will damage the normal lining and predispose the ear towards infection.

Once infected the best possible treatment is by halting diving or swimming activities for a few days and seeking medical advice.

If you are prone to swimmer's ear and are likely to be in a remote area, carry antibiotic drops with you as recommended by your diving physician.

SEA OR MOTION SICKNESS

Motion sickness can be an annoying complication on a diving holiday involving boat dives. If you are susceptible to motion sickness, seek medical advice prior to diving.

Treatment

To prevent sea sickness only eat light meals before going to sea and avoid alcohol the night before.

Normally a combination of metaclopamide (maxolon) and an antihistaminic (Valoid) or similar drugs can offer a simple preventative solution.

A cautionary note must be made that the antihistamine can make you drowsy, which may impair your ability to think and act while diving, so divers on antihistamines should limit their diving depth to less than 30m (100ft). Chewing root ginger is considered to be the best antidote.

A seasick diver should not attempt to dive.

SUNBURN

The sun on the East African coast is particularly harsh.

Treatment

Divers are advised to wear appropriate wide-brimmed hats and protective clothing. High-protection-factor sun creams are recommended at all times.

TROPICAL DISEASES

Yellow fever and malaria.

Treatment

Officially Kenya and Tanzania require a yellow fever vaccination certificate for all travellers.

Kenya, Tanzania and Zanzibar are all malarial areas year-round, with many strains of the disease resistant to certain prophylactics. Specialist advice on the correct anti-malarial prophylaxis can be obtained from your pharmacy or doctor.

MARINE ANIMALS THAT BITE

SHARKS

Sharks rarely attack divers but should always be treated with respect. Attacks are usually associated with the spearing of fish and the resultant vibrations and blood released into the water.

The great white shark, uncommon as it is in East African waters, is an exception to the rule. It has an unpredictable nature and should be avoided. Leave the water if a great white makes an appearance. Seals are their normal prey but theories that divers are often mistaken as such fodder have not been disproved. Grey reef sharks can be very territorial. If a shark displays any agitated behaviour involving arching of the back and ventral pointing of the pectoral fins, this may be a sign of impending attack and the diver should leave the water.

Treatment

Injuries are normally severe and involve severe blood loss resulting in shock. Blood loss control is the main objective. Control bleeding by applying direct pressure to wounds, pressure on pressure points and by elevating the affected limb. Tourniquets (preferably a wide rubber bandage) may be used on limbs above an amputation.

The diver should be stabilized as far as possible with the available medical help before being transported as soon as possible to a hospital.

BARRACUDAS

Barracudas are usually seen in large safe shoals of several hundred fish, each up to 80cm (30in) long. Lone individuals about twice this size have been known to attack divers in tropical waters, usually in turbid or murky shallow water, where sunlight flashing off a knife blade, camera or jewellery has confused fish into thinking that they are attacking prey such as sardines. Serious incidents involving barracudas in East Africa are unknown.

Treatment

Clean the wounds thoroughly and use antiseptic or antibiotic cream. Bad bites will need antibiotic and antitetanus treatment.

MORAY EELS

Probably more divers are bitten by morays than by all other sea creatures added together – usually through divers putting their hands into holes to collect shells or lobsters, removing anchors or hiding baitfish. Often a moray eel, once it has a hold on you, refuses to let go. You can worsen the wound immensely by tearing your flesh as you try to pull the fish off, so rather attempt to persuade it to release its hold by using your knife.

Treatment

Thorough cleaning and, more often than not, stitches. The bites nearly always go septic, so have antibiotics and antitetanus available as a precautionary measure.

TRIGGERFISH

Large triggerfish – usually males guarding eggs in 'nests' – are particularly aggressive, and will attack divers who get too close. Their teeth are very strong, and can go through rubber fins and draw blood through a 4mm (⅙in) wetsuit.

Treatment

Clean the wound and treat it with mercurichrome.

MARINE ANIMALS THAT STING

Scorpionfish (*Scorpaenopsis gibbosa*), firefish (*Pterois miles*), Anglerfish (*Antennarius* sp.) and stonefish (*Synancea verrucosa*) are the most common venomous fish. Many envenomed creatures are bottom-dwellers, hiding among coral or resting on or burrowing into sand. If you must move along the sea bottom, do so in a shuffle, so that you push such creatures out of the way and minimize your risk of stepping directly onto their sharp, venomous spines, many of which can pierce rubber fins.

Antivenins require specialist medical supervision, do not work for all species and need refrigerated storage, so they are rarely available when required.

Most of the venoms are high-molecular-weight proteins that break down under heat. Immerse the limb in hot water (e.g. the cooling water from an outboard motor, if no other supply is available) at 50°C (120°F) for two hours, or until the pain stops or eases. Several injections of local anaesthetic (e.g. procain hydrochloride) around the wound will ease the pain.

Remember that venoms may still be active in fish that have been dead for 48 hours.

Younger or weaker victims may need CPR.

CONE SHELLS

A live cone shell (*Conidae* family) should never be handled. The animal has a mobile tube-like organ that shoots a poison dart. The result is initial numbness followed by local muscular paralysis, which may extend to respiratory paralysis and heart failure.

Treatment

Apply a broad ligature between the wound and the body. CPR and supportive care may be necessary.

CROWN-OF-THORNS STARFISH

The crown-of-thorns starfish (*Acanthaster planci*), has sharp spines that can even pierce gloves and break off under the skin, causing pain and sometimes nausea lasting several days.

Treatment

Apply the hot-water treatment (e.g. the cooling water from an outboard motor, if no other supply is available) at 50°C (120°F) for 30min, until the pain stops. Clean and treat with disinfectants and anti-allergic preparations. Septic wounds require antibiotics.

FIRE CORAL

Fire corals (*Millepora* spp.) are more closely related to the stinging hydroids. Some people react violently to the slightest brush with them, and the resulting blisters may be 15cm (6in) across.

Treatment

Apply vinegar/acetic acid or allergic preparations locally. Carry a few lemons or limes on board for this purpose

JELLYFISH

Most jellyfishes sting, but few are dangerous. As a general rule, those with the longest tentacles tend to have the most painful stings. The box jellyfish or sea wasp and the blue bottle are the most common stingers encountered. Blue bottle and sea wasp stings can be treated with vinegar or alcohol, which should be applied locally. Urine is also a good neutralizing agent.

Divers commonly develop allergies to jellyfish and blue bottle stings and those sensitized should always carry a supply of antihistamines and, if necessary, their injection of adrenaline.

LIONFISH / TURKEYFISH / FIREFISH

These are slow-moving except when swallowing prey. They hang around on reefs and wrecks and pack a powerful sting in their beautiful spines.

Treatment

Use the hot water treatment, i.e. immerse the limb in hot water (e.g. the cooling water from an outboard motor, if no other supply is available) at 50°C (120°F) for two hours, until the pain stops.

Several injections of local anaesthetic (e.g. procain hydrochloride) around the wound will ease the pain.

Younger or weaker victims may need CPR.

SCORPIONFISH

Other scorpionfish are less camouflaged and less dangerous than the stonefish but are more common and quite dangerous enough.

Treatment

There is usually intense pain and swelling. Clean the wound, give the hot water treatment (immerse the limb in hot water, e.g. the cooling water from an outboard motor, if no other supply is available) at 50°C (120°F) for two hours, until the pain eases; follow up with antibiotic and antitetanus.

SEA URCHIN

The spines of sea urchins can be poisonous. Even if they aren't, they can puncture the skin, even through gloves, and break off, leaving painful wounds that can go septic.

Treatment

For bad cases of poisoning by a sea urchin's spine, give the hot water treatment (immerse the limb in hot water, e.g. the cooling water from an outboard motor, if no other supply is available) at 50°C (120°F) for two hours, until the pain stops. This also serves to soften the spines, helping the body reject them. Several injections of local anaesthetic (e.g. procain hydrochloride) around the wound will ease the pain. Younger or weaker victims may need CPR; *see* page 151).

Soothing creams or a magnesium-sulphate compress help reduce the pain, as will the application of the flesh of the papaya (paw-paw). Alcohol applied after the heat might also be useful. Septic wounds require antibiotics.

STINGING PLANKTON

You cannot see stinging plankton, and so cannot take evasive measures. If there are reports of any in the area, keep as much of your body covered as possible.

Treatment

Apply vinegar/acetic acid locally.

STINGRAYS

Stingrays vary from a few centimetres (in some parts of the world), to several metres across. The sting consists of one or more spines on top of the tail; though these point backwards they can sting in any direction. The rays thrash out and sting when trodden on or caught. Wounds may be large and severely lacerated.

Treatment

Syringe with warm seawater; remove debris and spines when bleeding stops. Apply the hot water treatment (immerse the limb in hot water, e.g. the cooling water from an outboard motor, if no other supply is available) at 50°C (120°F) for two hours, until the pain stops; apply local anaesthetic if available. A tourniquet might be necessary. Follow up with antibiotics and antitetanus.

STONEFISH

Stonefish are the most feared, best camouflaged and most dangerous of the scorpionfish family. The venom is contained in the 13 spines of the dorsal fin, which is raised when the fish is agitated.

Treatment

There is usually intense pain and swelling resulting from an encounter with a stonefish.

Give the hot water treatment immediately (immerse the limb in hot water, e.g. the cooling water from an outboard motor, if no other supply is available) at 50°C (120°F); when pain subsides, inject emetics into the puncture marks. Follow up with antibiotics and antitetanus.

MARINE ANIMALS THAT SHOCK

The one-fin electric ray is common around islands in the Indian Ocean, and is normally found on sandy bottoms. Contact will result in a powerful shock which could unsettle the diver sufficiently to cause an accident.

MARINE ANIMALS THAT ARE POISONOUS TO EAT

Eating shellfish can result in gastroenteritis, allergic reactions or paralytic shellfish poisoning. Avoid eating anything but fresh shellfish. If considering eating mussels, first find out from the local inhabitants if it is safe or if there has been a recent red tide.

Ciguatera poisoning can result from eating reef and game fish contaminated by a dinoflagellate. Obtain local advice on which fish are safe to eat. Avoid all but the freshest fish. Pufferfish and sunfish are not edible and ingestion of their flesh can result in death. Scromboid poisoning results from eating mackerel and tuna that have been allowed to lie in the sun.

DIVING RESCUE

One of the most common questions asked by divers is, 'What must I do if I find a buddy or another diver unconscious in the water?' Fortunately this is a rare occurrence as statistically most diving incidents and accidents happen on the surface.

The short answer to the question is that incidents and accidents should be avoided as far as possible, as a result of the following measures:

- Thorough training both initially and continuously in personal diving, rescue and emergency care skills.

- Maintaining good physical and mental fitness for diving and avoiding substances like alcohol and drugs which compromise that fitness.

- Equipment maintenance with regular servicing and checks to ensure reliable function.

- Familiarizing yourself with new equipment in the pool before using it in the sea.

- Diving with equipment appropriate to the complexity of the dive.

- Wearing appropriate thermal protection.

- Thorough pre-dive checks of equipment.

- Attention to buoyancy ensuring that you are not over- or underweight and that buoyancy control mechanisms are functioning normally.

- Detailed attention to thorough dive planning no matter how apparently routine the dive. Dive planning is an exercise in accident prevention.

If you find yourself in a situation where a diver requires active rescue, the situation can be managed in the following sequence:

1. DIVER RECOVERY
2. DIVER RESUSCITATION
3. DIVER EVACUATION

Diver recovery involves freeing the diver from any entrapment underwater and then providing buoyancy and lift to get him to the surface without further injury. The emphasis in getting the diver to the surface is on control of the ascent. The diver must be brought up from the dive in a controlled manner to avoid the possibility of barotrauma and air embolism.

To provide positive buoyancy it may be necessary to release the weight belt, inflate the victim's buoyancy compressor or inflate your own buoyancy compensator. A position behind the diver should be taken up with your right hand under the chin, keeping the airway open, and the other hand on the victim's BC inflator / deflator hose. Swim upward at a controlled moderate pace, being conscious of your own exhalation and a need not to become exhausted.

Once on the surface, resuscitation should begin in the water with expired air resuscitation while the diver is towed to the nearest boat or land where CPR can be initiated. Resuscitation is continued while preparations are made to evacuate the injured diver.

Treatment would include:

- EAR or CPR (see page 151) as necessary with or without the assistance of medical equipment.

- 100% oxygen by mask through a bag/valve/mask or demand valve.

- Keeping the diver warm.

- Maintaining hydration by intravenous therapy if skills and equipment are available.

Evacuation of the diver is by the quickest available means to the nearest resuscitation facility (or hospital trauma unit), the options being by sea, land or air, or a combination of all three.

The recompression treatment that may be required is arranged from the resuscitation facility once the diver has been adequately assessed.

Ignorance is your greatest enemy in a rescue situation and time and money spent on dive rescue training is an investment in life.

Approach your nearest agency for this type of training and before going for a dive find out what rescue facilities are available in the area of the dive and how they are contactable in an emergency.

RECOMPRESSION (HYPERBARIC) CHAMBER

There is only one facility in East Africa, situated at the Kenya Navy's base in Mombasa. Make a note of the emergency number before diving.

Bibliography

ALLEN & STEENE. 1987. *Reef Fishes of the Indian Ocean.* T.F.H. Publications.
AMIN, M., WILLETS, D. & TETLEY, B. 1982. *Journey Through Kenya.* Bodley Head, London.
1989. *Journey Through Tanzania.* Camerapix Publishers International, Nairobi.
1987. *The Last of the Maasai.* Bodley Head, London.
BLIXEN, K. (Isak Dinesen). 1984. *Out of Africa.* Penguin Books, London.
BOCK, K. 1978. *A Guide to Common Reef Fishes of the Western Indian Ocean & Kenya Coast.* Macmillan.
BOYD, W. 1983. *An Ice Cream War.* Penguin, London.
CROWTHER, G. & HUGH FINLAY. 1991. *Kenya: A Travel Survival Kit.* Lonely Planet Publications, Hawthorne, Australia.
1987. *East Africa.* Lonely Planet Publications, Hawthorne, Australia.
DEBELIUS, H. 1993. *Indian Ocean Tropical Fish Guide.* Aquaprint, Germany.
ENDEAN, R. 1982. *Australia's Great Barrier Reef.* University of Queensland Press, St Lucia.
FOX, J. 1984. *White Mischief.* Random House, New York.
HALTENORTH, T. & DILLER H. 1977. *A Field Guide to the Mammals of Africa.* Collins, London.
HATT J. 1982. *The Tropical Traveller.* Penguin, London.
HOWARTH, D. 1977. *Dhows.* Quartet Books, London.
JEWELL, J. H.A. 1969. *Dhows at Mombasa.* East African Publishing House, Nairobi.
JOUBERT, J-D. *Zanzibar.* Tanganyika Wildlife Safari.
LIESKE, E. AND MYERS, R. 1994. *Collins Pocket Guide to Coral Reef Fishes.* HarperCollins Publishers, London.
MATTHIESON, P. 1972. *The Tree Where Man Was Born.* E.P. Dutton, New York.
MERCER, G. 1996. *Globetrotter Travel Guide: Tanzania.* New Holland, London.
MILLER, C. 1971. *The Lunatic Express.* Westland Sundries, Nairobi.
MOLLISON, S. 1971. *Kenya's Coast.* East African Publishing House, Nairobi.
RICCIARDI, L. 1980. *The Voyage of the Mir-El-Lah.* Collins, London.
RUARK, R. 1962. *Uhuru.* Hamish Hamilton, London.
1955. *Something of Value.* Hamish Hamilton, London.
SIMON, N. 1993. *The Guinness Guide to Nature in Danger.* Guinness Publishing Ltd. Middlesex.
Spectrum Guide to Kenya. 1989. Camerapix Publishers International, Nairobi.
Spectrum Guide to Tanzania. 1992. Camerapix Publishers International, Nairobi.
TRILLO, R. 1991. *The Rough Guide to Kenya.* Penguin Books, London.

Index

Individual dive sites are represented in **bold**